For all those
enlightened folks
who use The
Ocean Shores Library
— My Best to y'all
for more good Reading.

Shelly Scott

Seattle, 11 Sept. '01

WAR AND POLITICS
BY OTHER MEANS

WAR AND POLITICS BY OTHER MEANS

A Journalist's Memoir

SHELBY SCATES

UNIVERSITY OF WASHINGTON PRESS

SEATTLE & LONDON

To publishers, editors, colleagues, and competitors

who made this adventure possible, and to Lady Luck,

who kept it moving despite the odds

This publication was supported in part by the

DONALD R. ELLEGOOD INTERNATIONAL

PUBLICATIONS ENDOWMENT

Library of Congress Cataloging-in-Publication Data can be found at the end
of the book.

The paper used in this publication is acid-free and recycled from 10 percent
post-consumer and at least 50 percent pre-consumer waste. It meets the minimum requirements of American National Standard for Information Sciences—
Permanence of Paper for Printed Library Materials, ANSI Z39.48–1984.

War *is not merely a political act,*

but also a political instrument,

a continuation of political relations,

a carrying out of the same by other means.

—KARL VON CLAUSEWITZ, ON WAR (1832)

CONTENTS

WAR AND POLITICS BY OTHER MEANS

OBION COUNTY

MY BEST FRIENDS in those hard times in the 1930s in West Tennessee were John Lee, Jerry, Wolf (pronounced Wuff), Hunter Byrd, and Charles. We played football, baseball, and imaginary war games and fought each other. On Saturdays we went together to the cowboy picture show at the Capitol Theatre, cheering Buck Jones, the Lone Ranger, Ken Maynard, Hopalong Cassidy, and even Gene Autry, although the singer looked kind of sissy.

I shared my allowance with John Lee, Jerry, and Wuff. Times were harder for them, or so it seemed from their ragged clothes and perpetual search for green apples. At the theater entrance on Main Street, Union City, the Obion County seat, we parted. They went to a side door and then up to the colored section in the balcony. They paid the same price for the ticket, 10 cents, and cheered as loudly as Hunter Byrd, Charles, and I when Buck and Ken routed the black hats and Indians. It was especially good when, occasionally, Randolph Scott was the star. He had a noticeable Southern accent, like us.

My allowance, 15 cents a week, came from chores. In winter these were strenuous for a lad. It turns cold in the damp of West Tennessee near the Mississippi, Obion, and Forked Deer Rivers, an alluvial plain patched with hardwood thickets where creeks come down and run to the rivers. My task was to make fires in the fireplaces that heated the room of my mother, Stella, recently widowed, and the dining room. I was a firemaker, but that was the easy part. The hard part was busting large chunks of coal into small pieces, then hauling the fuel in metal scuttles to the yawning fireplaces. We were a large Southern family—ten siblings—but by that time in 1940 all had left Obion County except myself and a younger brother and sister. They were of little help with heavy chores.

We lived in the old Waddell place, a fiercely ugly piece of post–Civil War architecture with 15-foot ceilings, and windows that ran the same length. The windows were shuttered with cedar venetian blinds that moved up and down in grooves along the frames, a bit of Victorian luxury. The house was made of brick but smelled of decaying wood. The lovely part was its great, sloping lawn and fixed rows of old oak, elm, and walnut. This is where we played games and climbed trees. I attained a close bond with one of the young maples, odd as this may sound. The tree became a refuge, then a friend; a refuge because when Addie Ross, the family serf, a field hand never fully broken to the work of wash and kitchen, would give me chase for some improper act. I'd run from the old house, down the lawn to a small branch of the young maple. One leap and I'd be free, scrambling up the branches to its limber summit, leaving Addie barefoot and frustrated on the earth below.

"You ain't fitten to be a white boy," she would announce with terminal disgust and turn away. Safe from her fury and a serious beating, I'd hold to the maple and gently sway, grateful to the tree for deliverance. Much later when the mountaineer-philosopher Willie Unsoeld wrote, "I am son of the rock, brother to the ice," I understood.

But once I failed to break free of the dreadful house. I was alone with my Grandmother Victoria when Addie launched a search and destroy mission against me for some outrage. We ran in circles in the big, cold dining room. I was fast and nimble. Addie was huge and clumsy. Grandmother was an island of calm. She knelt by one of the dining room windows—this I saw as I raced ahead of the black woman—fixed in a pool of sunlight coming through a venetian blind. She prayed while Addie pursued: "Dear Jesus protect this precious lad from the wrath of Addie Ross. He is a good child, despite his mischief. And, sweet Jesus, bless this good woman Addie, a child of God and duty." All this was said in Grandmother's clear, declarative English sentences. It mixed with Addie's litany of reproach: "I'm fixing to skin you alive, boy. You ain't fitten to be white."

I don't know whether it was by the grace of the Lord or my fresh legs, but that day I was spared a whipping.

Addie Ross loved me as much as I loved her and when, some years later, I went off to a military school in Middle Tennessee, where rowdy behavior was even less tolerated, she sent me a package and a note, crudely lettered, which said, "U wont get no thin this fit to eat so I cooked specal." The package contained a dozen of her biscuits. How all of this love, rage, and biscuits went down with our Savior is a matter I leave to theologians.

The old Waddell place is gone now, probably torn down for its bricks. We came to it from a modern home, built by my father on our farm east of the county seat. There we had electricity from a Delco generator, a rarity in our country at that time, and a radio which brought in dance band music from the Peabody Hotel in Memphis and the live broadcast of the trial of Bruno Richard Hauptmann for the kidnapping of Charles Lindbergh's baby. He was sentenced to death and electrocuted. We had a show horse named Gold Dust and a tenant farmer, Manlis, who would come to the living room of our home when mother and father were away and play blues on the baby grand piano. Like almost every other tenant farmer in the county—white or black—Manlis and his family lived in a wooden shack lit by coal-oil lamps. Until the coming of the Tennessee Valley Authority, a New Deal revolution denounced by my father as "communism," only the privileged had electric lights. We lost the farm, my father lost his life, to the great economic Depression, and then moved to the Waddell place at the edge of town. A literate in-law promptly renamed the place Bankrupt Manor. It was an abrupt fall from prosperity.

THERE WERE ALWAYS TALES of "the war," the nation's tragic struggle when our Southern forebears rolled the dice, all or nothing, in the bloody attempt to separate from the rest of the nation, and, as our elders put it, "preserve our way of life." These tales, however, became increasingly bitter once we domiciled in Bankrupt Manor; the glories of our grandfathers and great-grandfathers all the more splendid, Yankees all the more perfidious when magnified by near poverty. The fact of the war was seven decades past, yet it lingered like a banked fire. Memories kept fanning it. Once in 1937 we drove down to the Shiloh battlefield where, 75 years earlier, soldiers of the Union and the South slaughtered each other in the bloodiest battle in Western history. (It was soon surpassed, alas.) There were monuments to the Yankee dead all over green fields of this patch of Southwest Tennessee. My mother stood atop a common grave for the Confederate victims, tears coming from inflamed eyes, cursing the stately obelisks of stone placed on behalf of soldiers from Illinois, Iowa, Michigan, Minnesota, and Indiana. It is easy to win, hell to lose.

Such bitterness did not seize Grandmother, a devout believer in the Gospels yet just as much the creature of English rationalists Hume and Locke. She was a child in Hickman, Kentucky, when General U.S. Grant launched his guns and men at Columbus, only a few miles away up the Mississippi, and at Belmont, just across the great river. This began Grant's war to sever the Confederacy at Vicksburg. In contrast with others, Grandmother's tales of the sound of battle and the subsequent Yankee occupation were benign—some Yankees were gentlemen, not predators. At the request of small fry, she told these war tales repeatedly: the loss of her favorite mare, Buttercup, to Yankee cavalry, who returned the animal, wind-broken, after the war; the coming of the murderous guerrilla Tom Hook (not as famous as Jesse James but more dangerous); and the murder of a Union veteran by his brother, a Confederate, on the Hickman dock. She gave no signal of good or evil in these narratives. Perhaps she assigned them to God's will. But for us young ones, the stories dramatized to the point of reality the struggle that rent our nation, the residue of which now shaped our consciences.

Like the war, racial segregation was a fact of life, unexamined beyond the bald premise that blacks were inferior to whites, thus subject to our natural dominance. My friends, John Lee, Jerry, and Wuff, lived in colored town, a ghetto that, I realized years later, looked remarkably like Soweto in South Africa. Streets were un-paved, water was drawn in buckets from infrequent hydrants. Come election times, votes were solicited with free barbecue and prepaid poll taxes. There were outhouses for sanitation and a ramshackle school named for Mayor Miles, a banker and politician who always dressed finely and smiled like a man with a card up his sleeve. Schoolbooks, hand-me-downs from our white schools, were as tat-tered and woebegone as Miles School itself. There were many among us whites who believed education for blacks was a wasteful, if not dangerous, social policy. Credit Mayor Miles for allowing a measure of education. In fact, blacks and whites were separate and unequal and this was plain for an eight year old to see.

Yet these racial barriers were not so rigid for small fry, a para-dox of the South where social fraternization between adult blacks and whites on the basis of equality could literally be fatal. Since they lived not far away, John Lee, Jerry, Wuff, and I spent our summers in games, sometimes slipping off to swim in a creek running through a thicket about a mile away. John Lee, two years older, was our nat-ural leader. One day he staged a fight between Wuff and me, the ring an army blanket laid out in the cow pasture. We fought until blood-ied, no winner either declared or in fact. Hunter Byrd Whitesell lived about ten miles away in the antebellum home of his farmer an-cestors. His cousin Charles lived in the country near Bankrupt Manor on a farm that turned emerald green in summer from long rows of corn. They came frequently to visit and play.

"Hunter Byrd and Charles are coming today," I told John Lee one summer afternoon while we lay at the foot of an elm tree seek-ing refuge from the heat and talking about what to do.

"I reckon that means we play Silver War," he sighed. Indeed, that was always the game played with Hunter Byrd, who outranked John Lee in our social order, not because of his age or physical prowess, about which they were equals. But Hunter Byrd knew of the war. He could talk with authority on how the South could not endure attachment to the barbarian society that started north of the Ohio River. Slavery was Lincoln's excuse for making war on us. What he really wanted was our cotton for the mills in Massachusetts and Pennsylvania. The names of those remote states sounded ugly when Hunter Byrd spoke them. And he had been to Stones River, which ran red with blood from the fallen as the Yankees pressed toward Chattanooga, and also to Shiloh. He would tell of Pickett's charge at Gettysburg, and Nathan Bedford Forrest's raid and capture of the entire Yankee garrison at Union City, thus thwarting Grant's main supply line from the north. This was the railroad junction which connected to Hickman and Columbus where steamboats bearing war material from northern factories came to dock. He learned all of this from his father and grand-fathers, and related it to us and our black friends, sons of slav-ery. They listened without display of passion, eager to get on with the game.

Hunter Byrd assigned ranks. He would be General Robert E. Lee (a hero for whom one of my older brothers was named), I would be Stonewall Jackson, Charles was J.E.B. Stuart. The Yankee lineup featured John Lee as Grant, Jerry as William T. Sherman, and Wuff as General Phil Sheridan. Weapons were fallen walnuts and long, slender canes used for beanstalks in Addie's garden. Had she been near, Addie would thrash the lot of us. The Yankees held one side of a sunken road behind Bankrupt Manor, one that carried the over-whelming fragrance of honeysuckle. We Confederates attacked from the other side, hurling cannonballs of canes, minié balls of wal-nuts. We warred furiously, our dogs howling and yapping at the spectacle. Only once did anyone cry from pain. Jeb Stuart caught the point of a cane hurled by William T. Sherman. He cried for a minute, then ceased before his mother came to take him home. He would return for another war, the name of which John Lee must have confused with the name of the Lone Ranger's horse.

After the fourth grade, John Lee, Jerry, Wuff, and I went sepa-rate ways to our worlds of black and white. The rigor mortis of our social system set in. School, games, Christian worship, which we all shared, and parlor conversation had to be done separately.

I knew of only one exception to those strict rules of apartheid, although there was talk of a "communist," a cotton planter across the river in Charleston, Missouri, who was a "nigger lover." But we never saw him. Grandmother, however, was conspicuous to all of the town. She lived with a widowed daughter on a shaded street near the border separating white houses and black shanties. Very quietly, she reconciled the conflict between Jesus' teachings and Southern racial mores by ignoring the latter. The moral force of the old woman—by then she was in her 90s—shielded her from the rage, potentially fatal, that otherwise attended any breach in the racial code. Her conduct was ignored by the town. Most conspicuous was her treatment of Uncle Simon, a stump of an old black man with gray hair and a philosopher's pessimism. Uncle Simon walked about town wearing a worn-out dress coat and pulling a small wagon. He was not feebleminded like one of the Gibbs boys, whose father came home from the battle at Antietam missing a leg, to farm 500 acres. The Gibbs boy, in his 50s, made bicycle deliveries for the Evans Drug Co., always talking to himself in what most people thought was gibberish. Uncle Simon was dour but coherent.

"Dear Simon," Grandmother would hail the old man as he shuffled past her kitchen porch. "How are you today?"

"Just tolable, Miz Vickie. I got the miseries in my legs and hips and it looks like it's gwine to spread up."

"Then you must come in for tea before you return home," Grandmother would reply.

The black man would enter the old woman's home, seat himself at the dining room table and drink a sweet mixture of tea, sugar, and milk served from a white porcelain pitcher.

"The weather is coming up, Miz Vickie. It's shore ugly. It will make my miseries worser."

"You must take care of yourself, Simon. Perhaps you would feel better if you did not pull your wagon on your walks."

I'd watch this calm exchange, the destruction of the racial barrier, in awe. Grandmother's manner with Uncle Simon did not differ from her treatment of Mayor Miles, who called sometimes to discuss town matters with the Christian lady. He had attended Princeton. She would sit upright, drinking tea, bowing slightly to address the visitor. The linen tablecloth was always fresh. The fact of formal rapport between a white and black fixed a contradiction

between social practice and the Christian example of my Grandmother. I did not resent this, but it was a worrisome thing.

Grandmother died in the summer of 1946. I went off to school
in Middle Tennessee. For all of her English rationalism, she had believed in Heaven, so death for her meant deliverance. John Lee, Jerry,
and Wuff were long gone from my life. I would never again see Jerry
or Wuff. At Christmas I came home to Obion County on vacation.
There were dinners, dances, and young romance. I shared a bottle
with Hunter Byrd and other young lions of the West Tennessee social set; a fine vacation. One morning someone knocked at the back-
door. I answered. A tall black man, cap in hands, an expression of
his traditional status, bowed and spoke: "Mister Shelby." I then
knew his identity.

"John Lee, don't ever call me mister. I am your friend." His
eyes shifted, feet shuffled in acute discomfort. I remembered Grandmother's tale of her young mare, Buttercup, wind-broken.

"I been living in Chicago, but I come down on the Illinois
Central so I could see you, Mister Shelby, and my grandaddy. You
looks good."

"John Lee, please don't ever call me mister."

"Yessir," he said, and then there wasn't much else to talk
about.

Not long after, I decided the only way to resolve the contradiction between conscience and social practice, and be liberated
from a culture that had become uncomfortable, was to leave. There
was no longer sufficient reason to remain in Obion County—it
weighed and hurt too much. So I headed West to a new life. From
that time, neither my empathy for the less powerful nor my disdain
for the powerful who would exploit their advantage has waned.
This mindset fueled a career as a journalist as powerfully as an in-
nate curiosity.

THE MAKING
OF A JOURNALIST
BLUE SKY,
BLUE WATER

LIFE ON MERCHANT SHIPS in blue water is like a marriage without love. The seaman is intimate with all the sounds, smells, and details of his partner—the vessel, crew, and water—and wed for the length stated in documents signed before the voyage. But the union loses its passion and becomes monotonous. The sea itself is a giver and a taker. One comes to accept it, more with resignation than joy. The romantic embracing such an experience journeys toward disillusionment.

My first ship, a rust-bucket Liberty, from the fleet of homely vessels that carried our war against Hitler and Tojo to Europe and the South Pacific, was reclaimed from a graveyard for surplus vessels on Budd Inlet near Olympia, Washington. Boarding it fulfilled an ambition that began years earlier on the rolling alluvial plain of West Tennessee. Having hunted and explored the Obion and Forked Deer river bottoms of that country, I aimed to see for myself the world beyond. As a lad I fantasized about being kidnapped and pressed into work as a cabin boy on a steamboat on the nearby Mississippi. That I would come to see the world through the narrow focus of a porthole, instead of from the vantage of a leisurely traveler or a working journalist, was an insight I had yet to gain. I was 18 years old, naive, and romantic.

I made a furtive stab at remaining in that native place, a tryout with a Class D farm club of the beloved St. Louis Cardinals. Baseball was an alternative for boys of un-landed gentry as well as uneducated country boys. I failed, unable to hit the breaking curve balls—at that time we called this pitch a "drop"—hurled by my teenaged peers, all white boys like myself, some no doubt destined for careers on the diamond. "Good field, no (! ! !) hit" might have been the report to St. Louis, if a scout bothered to note my inadequate performance. So much for the Cards. I hit the road west to fulfill my dream of discovery by working as a merchant seaman.

The road was roundabout. I hitchhiked across middle America. Wherewithal came from farm jobs, usually driving a truck or tractor in the wheat harvest as it flowed from Oklahoma through the Texas Panhandle, and up through Kansas, Colorado, and Nebraska. The work was strenuous, sunup to sundown, the pay $8 a day, three meals a day, and an army cot on which to sleep at night. I moved westward over the great tapestry of our central plains, sometimes sleeping at night under the stars and a Rand McNally road map—beautiful but chilly—or, more comfortably, riding a Greyhound bus. The freedom rivaled the landscape in beauty. The auto drivers were a cross section of lower-brow American culture, captives of whiskey, or hard-shell religion and the classic—as yet unrivaled—American songs of Ernest Tubb, Hank Williams, and Bob Wills, the Gershwin, Kern, and Cole Porter of our lonely, agrarian interior. I loved the music, but remained impervious to the religious messages.

The road stopped in Bridgeport, Nebraska, ranch country in the Sand Hills where the Oregon Trail, indelibly marked by ruts, once traversed. A traveling salesman dropped me with good wishes and apologies. He was going back to Denver. I was stranded for lack of traffic. For 40 cents I got a cot in the backroom of the town tavern and slept, despite the racket of drinkers and a jukebox playing the great Ernest Tubb's lament for vagabonds, "The Freight Train

Blues." ("All around the water tank, waiting for a train, a thousand miles away from home just-a sleeping in the rain.") Before sleep I had thoughts of quitting my ambition and going back to Tennessee.

A church bell, not a jukebox, awoke me shortly after dawn. "Fire at the implement dealer's!" a young man shouted as I stumbled out of the tavern, half dressed, half asleep. He was standing on the running board of a volunteer fire truck. "Get on," he commanded. I joined other townsmen and roared off to find a blaze in the implement dealer's shop a garden hose could have extinguished. It had sent off a lot of smoke.

The young man introduced himself—Ben Schuenemeyer—and wondered what this stranger was about. I told him I was stuck in Bridgeport and about to get a bus going east, back to Tennessee.

"We have work on the ranch for two weeks, if you are able. Can't afford a slacker—$8 a day, room and board. Enough for bus fare." I said yes and for six weeks became a member of the Schuenemeyer family, German homesteaders who lived 20 miles from town in a stone ranch house that came up out of the Sand Hills like an Edward Hopper painting.

The winter had been hard. They lost cattle to its severity and still had strays loose to the north where the Platte River wound down from the Rockies under the shadow of Chimney Rock, the wagon train landmark. It was hard to sit after a day on a horse in search of cattle. We shocked rye and stacked wheat, and every day at noon I went down to a copse along a creekbank with a .22 rifle to kill two or three pheasants for our midday meal. On Saturday nights Ben and I drove to town to drink beer and dance at the tavern with local belles. I'd guess he soon married one of these eager ranch girls.

September came and the weather changed. "Blue northers" moved down on us, turning the sky from deep blue to black, sending temperatures from hot to freezing, usually bearing rain or hail. With my purse fattened and courage restored, I decided to push on west. Ben got the implement dealer to line me up with a used car salesman in Cheyenne who needed a driver to ferry a '49 Cadillac to the Northwest. I bid Ben, his family, blue skies, and wide open plains farewell and drove west to the mountains, the Pacific, and to sunsets. I have never looked back.

My first sense of Seattle was not its rain or low cloud cover, gifts of the warming Japanese current, but its sea-smell, a strong metallic odor composed of seaweed, anemones, and—probably— effluent. It rose up from the waterfront almost to First Avenue, a long street of cheap hotels, vintage Alaska gold rush, cheaper women, seamen's taverns, and pawnshops where one could trade his pants or birthright for one of the Avenue's pleasures. First Avenue ended in Skid Road, literally the end of the road for those with little left to pawn—drunks, lunatics, forgotten men, and a few women.

I got a night-shift job at a warehouse adjacent to Skid Road unloading boxcars and loading trucks. This allowed me to enter the University of Washington and maintain grades good enough to stay. My friends at the university were, in the main, first or second generation Scandinavians or expatriate Southerners—the latter being less comfortable about their place than the former. The city was beautiful, but socially cold to migrants from the South. Local natives minded their business without much backslapping and storytelling. There was a lot of hard drinking to complement the hard working people of the city in the early 1950s. Otherwise it was a living cathedral of Calvinism.

I had arrived about one hundred years after the first white men landed at Alki Beach on the peninsula now called West Seattle. This vanguard, and many more to follow, were welcomed by aboriginal Americans they would soon corrupt and displace. The year was 1851. The date is etched into my mind because it is etched into an upstairs window at Oaks Place, home of my great-great-grandfather in Huntsville, Alabama. George Steele was an architect as well as a cotton farmer, and the house was an artistic ode to himself. Its dining room once hosted a banquet for President-elect James K. Polk of Murfreesboro, Tennessee. They dined on a roasted ox named "Van Buren" after Polk's political rival, Martin. George had two sons, Matthew, my great-grandfather, and John, who left his visible imprint on the window in his room: "John Steele, Oaks Place, 1851." Glory that was. Both sons went to war for the Confederacy, and

Oaks Place became headquarters for a Yankee general named Wheeler of whom I know no other distinction. The place still stands, the cotton fields once around it displaced by tract housing for workers at a nearby rocket factory whose products have carried men to the moon.

A bastion of nineteenth-century liberalism, the University of Washington was easy to enter but academically demanding. The student kept at least a C-plus grade average or was dismissed. By the end of my first year, 1951, unloading boxcars by night and struggling with studies by day turned the romantic urge to go to sea into an enormously attractive economic alternative, one to which I could retreat in the summer gaps between university classes.

Thus I joined the *Mary E. Kinney*, the namesake of an Oregon state legislator and early suffragette, now a rust-bucket ship with a rum crew. College would have to wait.

I signed on as an engine room wiper, the maritime equivalent of an auto mechanic's grease monkey. So did Cece Hohenbaum, a onetime university student from Gig Harbor, Washington, who had spent the previous year in Hollywood trying to crack the movies as a "Mickey Rooney type." He was 26 years old, I was 19. Our job was to help the oilers, firemen-watertenders, and engineers and clean the low-tech machinery in the bowels of the vessel. The engine, a triple expansion steam combustion model, consisted of two boilers and three exposed pistons, each 9 inches in diameter, turning an exposed crankshaft. It moved the loaded 10,000-ton vessel 12 knots an hour.

Sandell, the Second Engineer, greeted Cece and me on our first day aboard, unwilling (or unable) to conceal a snarl at our college credentials. The *Kinney* was tied up in Tacoma in preparation for the voyage across the Pacific to Yokohama. The city reeked of the smell of pulp mills, an aroma most folks regard as offensive. To this day, I salivate at the smell, associating it with the acute hunger I relieved in the ship's mess that first day.

Like all second engineers, whose primary duty is to tend the ship boilers, Sandell was a mite crazy from overexposure to steam. He had the wild eyes of a tent preacher, and muscles that came up in knots around his neck when he got aroused. He limped from an injury received in a ship torpedoed by Germans on the run to Murmansk, Russia, during the recent war. It provided a built-in source of permanent anger. He put us straight to work, lifting, scraping, and wrenching—preparation for going to sea. We pleased Sandell with our willingness, important since he kept the engine room day watch where we would work for the next three months.

A few days later the rest of the crew boarded. Several were veterans of the 1934 West Coast maritime strike, a watershed on the waterfront, a line of demarcation in the society of the ship's crew as certain as the Plimsoll line on the vessel's hull. Those seamen who had participated in the strike were the equivalent of maritime royalty. Those who had not were their social lessers. The *Kinney*'s strike veterans included Able Seamen Linstad, Bergin, and Schieler; Oilers Althouse and Sepanich; and Fireman-Watertender Maki, a Finn, and a 50-year survivor of the Pacific and, no doubt, other seas. The skipper was Carl Jones, a member of the Sailors' Union of the Pacific goon squad in the 1934 strike, a magnificent man—self-educated and self-assured.

Had these seamen been forewarned in the maritime union halls that the bosun would be Eddie Schieler, or that the black gang (engine room) union steward would be Gill, a rapacious homosexual? Probably not. No matter to Cece or me. We were hungry and this ship was manna, food and relief from unloading railroad boxcars.

Schieler was notorious as a knife artist, mean and possibly brain-damaged from his years as a prizefighter who boasted that he once fought ten rounds against Benny Leonard, the lightweight champion. The bosun had long, sloping shoulders, and arms that dropped abnormally below his waist into fists gnarled by breakage. His ears were like cauliflower, his nose flat and bent. Whatever his other claims to celebrity, the bosun had been a fighter. His face alone bore the proof.

Linstad, a giant, had played professional football with Don Hutson and the Green Bay Packers. Sepanich, a burly Greek of impressive intellect, was said to be on the fly from Seattle police who wanted to question him about an illegal gambling hall a few feet north of the city limits. "The trouble with Gill," Sepanich told me of the alcoholic and predatory oiler who lusted for boys, "is that he had no part in the '34 strike."

Five of us were less than 27 years old, thus somewhat at risk to the union steward. Buck, the third cook, was a black man whose color dissolved once we got to sea and confronted matters of greater consequence than race. Cokie drove race cars on Northwest tracks, ultimately graduating to a start in the Indianapolis "500." Salazar, an Ordinary Seaman, was a ranked lightweight fighter in California whose manager, Maxie Weisbarth, was the Seattle boss of the Sailors Union of the Pacific. Maxie took care of his fighters, to the displeasure of Schieler, the knife artist.

"Free to be at sea with thou, white gull wing," I exulted (privately, on paper) when Cape Flattery vanished behind the *Kinney's* stern under a sky as blue as all of outdoors Nebraska. A few days later, when a 90-knot wind blew out of it, teasing the 10,000-ton vessel like a kite in a whirlwind, I realized that it was a conditional freedom with a price. The sea boiled. So did my insides, heaving as I tried to avoid being thrown against the bulkheads, or worse, the machinery. "One hand for the company, one hand for yourself," Gill commanded. I was seasick for two days, the butt of insults from Osborne, the second cook, a lantern-jawed seafarer with a slightly hunched back.

"We got slumgullion today, Scates, but you got to be a man to eat it and you don't look like no man, puking up like you do." I hung to the iron rail around my bunk when not heaving.

When this North Pacific blow abated, the bosun, Schieler, proposed a kangaroo court, consisting of the vessel's able seamen. Officers and "black gang"—the engine crew—were excluded. The issue was Salazar. He was Mexican-Italian, and thus, according to Schieler, unfit for this ship's crew. The real reason, I suspect, was not the seaman's ancestry, but his connection with Maxie Weisbarth, the bosun's enemy.

Violence at sea was much discussed in the union halls of the sailors and black gang up above the Seattle waterfront. There were tales of "finks" burned alive in the coal fires beneath the ships' boilers, punishment for defying the union and snitching for the shipping company. Whether true or not, I cannot say. But such tales made a vivid impression. Schieler's call for Salazar's consignment to the North Pacific was not a union hall tale. And into the sea he would have gone, but for the interposition of Louis Linstad. "Salazar goes over my body," Linstad told the sailors, and Schieler relented. The incident solidified a social order in the crew: Salazar became a boon companion with Buck, Cokie, Cece, the Able Seaman Roberts, and myself for the balance of a nine-month voyage around the world—from Japan, to Malaya, India, the Suez Canal, the United Kingdom and home to the United States. It was crude collective security, but effective; an attempted rape or threat to one would be regarded as an offense to all and would be retaliated. My guess is that the same bonding takes place in prisons and for the same reasons.

ASHORE IN SINGAPORE in September 1951, at the peak of a Communist-led revolution against British colonials, we drank at the New World cabaret alongside Scottish soldiers on leave from jungle combat. Their tales of this warfare made seafaring seem like the romantic dream that it had been—no prisoners, no Geneva convention. I left them, accompanied by a beautiful whore from Bali, when the Malay barmaid warned me—but not the soldiers—there would soon be shooting.

There was such, but I was oblivious, asleep with my love of the evening in a large room in the White House Hotel, a pale but clean imitation of Raffles, a pride of the Empire celebrated by Somerset Maugham. Awakening at dawn to realize my watch commenced in one hour, I raced through the dead calm streets of Singapore, so dehydrated from liquor that I sucked water from an open hydrant at dockside careless of its impurities. At the end of the engine room watch Sparks, the radio operator (what else could he be called), spread word that on the previous evening the British High Commissioner for Malaya and the Straits Colonies had been shot down just north of the city. Sir Henry Gurney was bushwhacked and slain by guerrillas—a first for the Empire: never before had one of the Majesty's High Commissioners been assassinated.

The sun was setting, the Empire near its close. Three years earlier Britain had struck its colors from India, the world's newest and largest ex-colony.

Steaming up the windless Hooghly River to Calcutta, engine room heat became fatal outside a four-foot circle of air coming down from topside shafts. A thermometer at the engineer's desk showed 125 degrees Fahrenheit. Firemen and oilers moved from the circle only to perform essential duties and then only for a few minutes. Yet it was too much for the ancient fireman, Maki. He began to wobble. Sandell ordered him topside. The old man pulled himself up steel ladders almost too hot to touch to reach the sweaty air of India. There he dropped like a man who had quit on his 275-pound weight.

"He's done. Heat got him," Schieler announced to Linstad and Bergin. They walked away. Cece and I refused to acknowledge this fate and began, taking turns, giving the old Finn artificial respiration. We worked until dark came down and a full moon, colored golden by a million open-air fires, came over Kidderpore, the Calcutta slum where we docked. This misbegotten light illuminated dozens of small brown bodies, longshoremen about to relieve our holds of the cargo of wheat. They shied from the body. Maki was dead, already turning blue. Cece and I were exhausted from the struggle to restore his life.

"I'm putting in four hours of overtime for each of you guys for working on the old man," said Gill. "That's what we got [union mandated] conditions for." He was otherwise unmoved by the death of his shipmate.

Calcutta's poverty was stunning. Thousands of people, many refugees from Muslim Pakistan, lived and died on its streets. They were human debris from the partition of the subcontinent three years earlier into its Muslim and Hindu halves. Above them vultures waited, a sight fatal to any religious notion that man could be perfected. A human ant line unloaded cargo, bearing on their short, skinny legs 100-pound sacks of wheat, their wages one handful of wheat and one handful of rice per day. Salazar tried to muscle one of these sacks to the top of his head and wobbled. Thomas Hobbes, I recalled, described man's life as "nasty, brutish, and short," but he had not visited the Kidderpore docks where it was not that nice.

At night, while the ant line worked, we escaped to the Princess cabaret in the Grand Hotel on Chowringhee Road, mingling with ex-RAF fighter pilots who had saved Britain in World War II, and a few Eurasian women who were saving the morale of several American seamen. From the balcony of the Grand we drank beer and watched trained monkeys perform a pantomime, a soap opera with a heroine, the rancher's daughter, and a villain, the foreclosing banker, scant relief from the overwhelming reality of the city. Calcutta's staggering gap between the rich few and suffering masses wrought havoc with a Christian's sense of justice, if not his sanity. Never mind his notion of salvation.

Once en route to the Grand Hotel we drove through Kidderpore past a column of marchers, two abreast, bearing torches and banners, but utterly silent except for a shuffle of feet on pavement. They were protesting "conditions," not the least being the abject poverty of Calcutta's hungry people. They were led that night by Communists, just as Communists had organized and led the 1934 maritime strike in Seattle. But they were driven by want of food, not the inspiration of ideology. The column stretched for several miles. Its portent sent a shiver down my back: The oppressed didn't aim to stay that way. Our world was changing.

Once I went with shipmates to the Welcome Number 7, Kidderpore's full-service sailor's refuge, offering food, whores, dope, and horrible but potent bootleg whiskey. Schieler and Bergin were there, greeting old comrades from East Coast vessels. Everybody knew Eddie. I returned with a painful urinary tract disease bestowed by one of Number 7's 10-rupee, 20-minute dates. The *Kinney*'s carpenter, an ersatz medic, cured it with a massive shot of penicillin to my rump. It hurt to sit for days.

For two months the ant line unloaded grain and then another group loaded coal into the *Mary E. Kinney*'s holds. Like most of its crew, the *Kinney* was a tramp without a predestined route. It carried cargo where consigned. This coal consignment was for the United Kingdom, perhaps Newcastle itself. The Brits were selling their quality coal to Europe and substituting this cheaper fuel from their former colony for their own hearths.

Before sailing, I advanced up the engine room ranks, replacing Cece Hohenbaum as a fireman-watertender. Cece had replaced the dead Maki, then fell ill unto death with typhoid fever and was flown back to Seattle. The job required little skill and less intellect, the marvelous Liberty ships having been designed with apprentices such as myself in mind.

Down the coast during a stop in Madras all hands got drunk. Without warning Schieler and Bergin began to argue. The angry bosun erupted from his chair in the Marine Club and pressed the switch on his seven-inch blade. I'd watched him use this knife, slicing a quarter-inch heaving line as though it was whipped cream. Now, arm slung low, he advanced across a table to Bergin. Bergin arose, showing neither fear nor defense. He was drunk. He would have been sliced lifeless, save for Roberts and Buck, the cook and able seaman. They leaped from our table and raised two heavy wooden chairs above their heads. Schieler observed and stopped his forward motion. He was crazy, but not mindless of a superior force. In a flash I had witnessed man's depravity and his bravery. The incident was never mentioned in any formal report, and Schieler and Bergin thereafter, as before, remained the best of friends.

The *Kinney* thrashed down the Bay of Bengal, past Ceylon across the Arabian Sea to the tip of the great Arab desert, Aden. The sun was broiling. We lived to the methodical whump-whump of propeller against water and the routine of watches and waits. The older crew played poker and cribbage. I read Scott Fitzgerald's novels for pleasure, and every political tract I could gather from Singapore, Calcutta, and Madras for education. There were a lot of these. Western imperialism, two centuries old, was in its twilight. The Brits were already out of India and, like the French in Indochina, were being tossed out of Singapore, Malaya, Aden, and Egypt. I wanted to understand why and what might come next. The idea that Americans should try to arrest this change, in the defense of colonialism, seemed mindless at that time and even more so much later. From what I had observed and now read, history was on the side of these native people. So were our American ideals.

We got a preview of coming Mideast attractions, steaming in a strictly controlled convoy past Suez and up the canal to Port Said: skirmishing between British Tommies and Egyptian Nationalists in revolt against their masters. The crew was ordered to remain below deck for this passage. My curiosity was too great for constraint. I slipped a guard and went up to the base of the ship's stack to watch Tommies, armed with automatic rifles, storm a nationalist position on the canal's western shore about 75 yards from the *Mary E. Kinney*. A snapshot of things to come.

Under these circumstances, there was no shore leave to enjoy the fleshpots of Suez, Ismailia, or Port Said—bad news for a crew already three weeks at sea. There was word we were destined for Glasgow with our load of cheap coal, and there was hope of a day ashore at Ceuta, Spanish Morocco, where we would stop for fuel. Once we were docked in this port opposite Gibraltar at the western entrance to the Mediterranean, the captain's orders of no pay draws, no going ashore, nearly triggered mutiny.

The crew calmed only when, after a fashion, the shore came to us. A schoolbus loaded with whores and whiskey came alongside on the dock. Captain Jones and two trusty mates thwarted the women, but not the booze. In the absence of money there was barter. It's likely there are Stillson wrenches turning pipes and heaving lines belaying craft in use to this day on the Ceuta dock. What they purchased was a mass drunk, all hands staggering, some falling down.

The alcoholic orgy ceased when the captain, a .45 automatic in his hand, and a mate stormed the locked door to the bosun's forecastle and tossed every liquor bottle into the water. He then commanded the vessel to sail. Two able seamen, one engineer, and myself were sober enough to answer the command. I was merely seeing things, such as the boilers' burners, double. Nevertheless, I managed the fires and we passed from what might have been a night in paradise into the restless Atlantic. This was early January 1952.

The storm struck abruptly off the northern coast of Spain, heaving the Atlantic above the vessel's flying bridge to the base of the stack. The soon to be famous steamship, *Flying Enterprise*, was breaking up in the tempest. Its skipper, Captain Kurt Carlsen, requested help. Captain Jones radioed his answer: "No. I have 40 men of my own to save."

Carlsen refused to leave his ship and quickly became the center of a media storm—radio, newspapers, and newsreels flying out to record a maritime epic and celebrate its hero, Carlsen. In Europe, at least, it was the news story of the year.

Unaware of the epic sea struggle to the north, the *Mary E. Kinney* was nearly helpless in this natural fury of a hurricane. We were, thank God, able to keep the bow of the ship into the sea, but not to make headway. For four days and nights we were shoved backwards. But we did not broach, which would have allowed waves to strike the ship broadside with a fatal result. Nor did the old rust bucket's hull crack under the stress. Neither did the crew.

Off watch, we strapped ourselves to our bunks. We ate only bread, water, and crackers. Osborne was most ill. "Eating your slumgullion?" I asked the second cook. Maintaining the balance of fire and water needed to produce steam, my job meant timing the ship's pitch and roll and then moving at the null point. Thus we adjusted our work in this womb of steel and fire to the rhythm of the storm. Fortunately, it was not erratic. It was severe. Once we rolled to one side by 30 degrees, just short of the angle that would have allowed cold seawater to pour down the stack and into the boilers. We knew that if this occurred, the explosion would be fatal. Those on engine room watch would die at once in a steam bath; the hull would be rent by the explosion. No survivors.

In the control of such overwhelming force, there is nothing to do about the possibility of catastrophe. Fear is set aside, perhaps to be reckoned with later in nightmares. Work becomes a matter of intense concentration. Nothing is more vital than producing steam for the engine in order to keep the ship's bow into the storm. Thus we endured until the morning of the fifth day when we began to see the tops of waves from a porthole. The storm abating, we resumed our

12-knot-an-hour journey past Lands' End and on up the River Clyde past the mighty John Brown shipyards to the coal dock in Glasgow.

THE SIGHTS AND LIGHTS of Glasgow, Scotland's industrial capital, the foundry and think tank of our iron and steam age, gave question as to which side won World War II. Lights were dim, bomb damage unrepaired, food scarce and rationed, one egg per person per week in February 1952. The crew had a few minutes of fame for having survived the great Atlantic storm that took down the *Flying Enterprise*—but not its skipper, Carlsen, who leaped to safety shortly before his vessel quit the struggle and sank.

"I'm a bird," the oiler Gill shouted from the mezzanine of a dance hall on Glasgow's main street where Buck, Salazar, Cokie, Roberts, and I with our new Scottish girlfriends were celebrating our survival after 52 days at sea. We looked up at Gill, a slight figure always twitching from a body that stuttered, his eyes gone wild and crazy. The orchestra began to play "My Beautiful Alice Blue Gown" in the style of Guy Lombardo. When my new love Mary and I got up to dance, I shouted back, "One hand for the company. One hand for yourself."

"I'm a bird," the oiler repeated. So saying, he flapped his arms and fell forward over the balcony onto the floor 12 feet below. There was only a brief stir. The orchestra did not quit its music. Ushers lifted and carried the booze-soaked seaman out of sight. Gill was alive but injured, they reported. We would cross the Atlantic to Newport News, short one oiler. No one regretted the loss. It made for more overtime pay.

Buck said goodbye to his shipmates in the unaccustomed calm of the Newport News dock. We could no longer be shore companions. This was America, 1952. Regardless of their kinship, blacks and whites could not safely congregate much of anyplace, least of all Mathews County, Virginia. Buck knew the rules better than the rest of us. I never saw him again.

Salazar came to Seattle to fight a preliminary in the Civic Auditorium. Cokie would race his midget car at a track near Seattle. I went back to the university, shipping out during summer breaks as

Family portrait, Easter Sunday, 1939. Back row (l-r): Busy Bee, her husband, Manlis, and A. D. (Addie) Ross; below them: Jerry and John Lee. The rest, all in white, are cousin Kay, brother George, sister Martha, and (the palest) me. Addie, as usual, shows an attitude.

Grandmother Victoria Tamms Scates (right), honored on her eighty-fifth birthday by the Leonidas K. Polk Chapter of the United Daughters of the Confederacy, at a formal tea. Union City, Tennessee, ca. 1939.

These Israeli troops are about to enter mortal combat to capture the West Bank of the Jordan River from the Hashemite Kingdom of Jordan, June 1, 1967. Much talk, but little change in territory since then. Photo: UPI

Oval Office, Air Force One, March 4, 1968. The press pool: (l-r) Sam Donaldson, ABC; Syd Davis, Group W; Robert Pierpont, CBS; Barbara Furlong, US News; *Henry Hubbard,* Newsweek; *Dick Dudman,* St. Louis Post Dispatch; *John Pierson,* Wall Street Journal; *George Packard,* Philadelphia Bulletin; *Al Sullivan, USIA; Carroll Kilpatrick,* Washington Post; *Shelby Scates, Hearst News. Three weeks later President Johnson (addressing Packard) threw in the towel.*

◄ *Ambassador Richard Parker, one of our best, and me in the garden of my home-away-from-home in Jerusalem, the American Colony Hotel.*

◄ *Coming up for air from a steel-reinforced bunker along the Suez Canal, part of the Bar Lev line, the front in the War of Attrition between Israel and Egypt. The air outside is about 115 degrees and fraught with steel. Inside it's cool and safe.*

The straight scoop from Representatives Dave (Checkers) Cecceralli, King Lysen, and Bob Perry (back to camera), Washington State Legislature, 1971. Perry would vanish, then come back alive a few years later to tell his tale of a Capitol fix.

▶ *Jimmy Carter's last hurrah. Seattle campaign rally in a Boeing hangar the night before the 1980 general election. Senator Henry Jackson, meeting the press, has privately informed two of us that it's all over: Carter will lose the White House to Ronald Reagan. That explains the expression on my face. (Photo: Seattle Post-Intelligencer)*

▶ *On top of Mount Rainier, a memorial to the assassinated Bobby Kennedy, July 1968.: (l-r) Jim Whittaker, Kennedy's 1968 state campaign chairman; Joan Hansen, Seattle attorney; and me.*

Windy Gap, 22,000 feet, at the China-Pakistan border, August 1978, with K2, the top of the Karakoram, in the background. Below to the right: China's Sinkiang Province. Photo: Craig Anderson

▶ *Camp One, K2 at 19,000 feet, the world's highest wire service to Hearst News, New York, via VHF transmission to Skardu, telegraph to Islamabad, UPI wires to New York. I filed daily. Sometimes the report even got there.*

▶ *Exhausted at 17,000 feet, Mount McKinley, after a 3,000-foot struggle. "I feel old, tired, and cold," said Stim Bullitt (right). So did I. Photo: Bill Sumner*

Be it ever so humble, Camp One, K2. Bill Sumner designed the twin-peaked tent nestled beneath the mountain. Photo: Bill Sumner

◄ *Stim Bullitt follows me on the road to Mount McKinley, sans Sherpas. Packs and sleds hold 125 pounds per man, needed to reach the top. Photo: Bill Sumner*

◄ *The oldest team to have climbed Mount McKinley (background) as of June 1981: (l-r) Stimson Bullitt, Shelby Scates, and Bill Sumner.*

The end of the trail. Motor transport to Skardu, Pakistan, after eight weeks of walking and climbing to the top of K2. Photo: Bill Sumner

The road to K2, rickety, almost as dangerous as the mountain itself.
I'm less self-assured than this photograph indicates.

Main temple, Angkor Wat, a house of worship to rival the chief pyramid at Giza or the Milan Cathedral and one of the world's most impressive treasures, isolated for too long by jungle and warfare.

After the battle for Talei. Fatigue. Photo: Bill Sumner

Plotting the skirmish at Talei, Cambodia; one squad attacks from the right, one from the left. May the Buddha be with you. Photo: Bill Sumner

I found a shady spot in a hot jungle war. Ampil, Cambodia, March 1984.
Photo: Bill Sumner

an oiler on *The Aleutian* or *The Baranof*, Alaska Steamship vessels plying the inside passage between Seattle and Seward, Alaska.

In the summer of 1953 I signed on a coastwise tanker of World War I vintage, a triple expansion steam combustion engine so dangerous to oil only two of us would take the job. It required the oiler to place his head within six inches of the steel coupling at the top of the engine's three pistons. One slip and the oiler would fall, headless. We worked six hours on, six hours off, sailing between Seattle, Portland, San Pedro, Hilo and Honolulu, and our homeport, a refinery up the river from San Francisco.

The weather was pleasant, the crew decent, and shore time sufficient for girls and games. At a bar in Hilo I talked with a carnival operator who exulted about prospects for his freak show coming out of Hiroshima as the result of mutations from our atomic bomb.

Whatever was left of my life as a merchant seaman would end that summer when the tanker took on a new first engineer in Portland. He had "strange" written into his looks and body language, a Chinese American with the social habits of a recluse. He would stand watch, never speaking except to issue orders, eat quietly, then retreat to his cabin. We never saw him ashore and speculated that, like Gill, his sex life might run to young boys.

I became close friends with Siegel (pronounced, naturally, Seagull), a Trotskyite college student who liked to discuss economics and Russian history, and Ardahl, a quiet able seaman with a crooked arm. Ardahl played tavern shuffleboard with the intensity of chess. As a 15-year-old messenger for the Norwegian underground, he had been nabbed by the Gestapo and tortured by having his arm fixed into a blacksmith's vise and crushed. We never asked if he betrayed secrets. We respected his silence.

One night at dock in San Pedro, I stood the midnight to 8 A.M. watch in the fireroom, maintaining enough steam to run the ship's generators and water system. I spent most of the watch reading, but alert, so I saw the first engineer when he loomed, unwanted and unexpected, at 3 A.M. on the far side of the fireroom. He said nothing, but stood wide-eyed as if possessed, looking at me and yet beyond me. At port arms across his chest he carried a 10-inch Stillson wrench, a heavy weapon for a fireroom brawl. He advanced, holding the wrench in his small hands. Suddenly I was very alert, sensing that he aimed to use the wrench on my skull even as I used the skull to wonder why.

In response to this bizarre encounter, I picked up a 12-inch pipe wrench and raised it to serve notice of my defense. He jerked to a stop and snapped his wide eyes as if aware of a disadvantage. Then he turned about and left the fireroom. When day came he resigned his office and left the vessel. The same morning, when my adrenaline subsided, I vowed never again to sail past Cape Flattery unless I was master of a ship bound into the Pacific.

I've kept that vow, watching the point at the northwestern tip of the continental United States drop beneath the horizon, sailing to sea as skipper of a 35-foot sloop I own with my companion for the past 29 years, Joan Hansen. I go with no regrets for my life as a seaman, but no illusions either. The lessons learned from observing the world and the character of my shipmates became the foundation of formal observations I would make as a journalist.

POLITICS

ALL POLITICS, to paraphrase former House Speaker Tip O'Neill, was personal when I grew up in the rural South. It was also (Big D) Democratic, the result of Republican-imposed Reconstruction after the Civil War. There was one Republican family in Obion County, Tennessee, where I spent most of my early years, none at all in Leflore County, Mississippi, where I spent the rest.

In Tennessee I learned by the age of eight years about politics. The knowledge came along with the grammar school reader and the Presbyterian catechism (Q: "What is God?" A: "God is all things"), and it was even more simplistic. There was good and evil. There was the Crump machine in Memphis, the Mayor Miles machine in Obion County, both bad and thus enemies of the family. There were the Carmacks of Murfreesboro, and their ally, J. Ridley Mitchell, all good and friends of the family. Everybody loved Robert A. "Fats" Everett, clerk at the Obion County Courthouse, where there now stands a statue in his honor. The slimmer, bronze figure of Senator Edward Carmack graces the front of the state Capitol in Nashville, a massive structure in the mode of a Greek temple, still bearing scars from Yankee cannonballs.

In Mississippi, I learned of but one significant political figure, Walter Silers, speaker of the state House of Representatives, as in my uncle's instructions to the local representative from the Delta: "Go down there to Jackson and vote whatever Walter tells you to vote. We'll provide a hotel room and send a regular case of whiskey." To paraphrase Vince Lombardi, Walter Silers wasn't everything in the Jackson statehouse—he was the only thing.

Above these local political personalities was the incarnation of political evil, Abraham Lincoln, who had visited the hated Yankee armies on our land when our forebears, as they perceived their constitutional right, tried to separate from the Union. An older brother, Thomas, made a sight of himself with a speech to the high school assembly denouncing Lincoln on the Republican preservationist's mandated birthday celebration in February 1935. It was a reflection of our family sentiment, and most likely those of a majority of the Confederate heirs.

Simply put, Southern politics of this era was racial politics, as in "who can do most to keep the nigger in his place." His "place" was subject to economic exploitation as well as social inferiority. Campaigns were segregated and then, as now, essentially entertainment. The candidate would draw a crowd to the Union City park near the junction of the Nashville, Chattanooga, and St. Louis (NC&St.L) and the Gulf Mobile and Ohio (GM&O) railroads—a critical intersection in 1861 when General Grant began his campaign to split the South. General N. B. Forrest raided and seized the junction and town, killing or seizing hundreds of Yankee troops and looting Grant's supply larder. Forrest's Union City raid became a factor in Grant's decision to feed his army off the Southern land, instead of bringing supplies from the North.

The park had a covered bandstand in its center where the candidates, all vying for the Democratic nomination, would set up their loudspeakers and hillbilly band. The band played and the white crowds flocked, most of them, in the 1930s, commuting from the county's hinters by mule or horse-drawn wagon. The men usually wore clean overalls and always chewed tobacco. The women wore clean, bright-colored dresses made of flour sacks. Horses hitched, the men sat on their haunches listening and whittling on pieces of hickory. When the twanging, hill-drenched music stopped, the candidate would tell how he—as opposed to his opponent—would keep the nigger in his place.

Not far away, on the other side of the GM&O tracks, the

small island of nigger-town had a few stores, a broken-down hotel for the infrequent black travelers, a "jook-house" (meaning a house with a juke box) selling whiskey, playing race-music (a.k.a. "the blues"), and sheltering a dice game. Candidates would come on Saturday nights with a free barbecue and a dollar or two for loyal blacks. The dollar was to compensate payment for the state's poll tax, another device for keeping blacks, along with poor whites, in their places. I cannot explain how the candidate made certain the black men "voted right," if in fact they did, instead of using the money in a dice game.

Such were our political ways. Given our family values we could not conceive of our political friends being corruptible or corruptive; only the others, politicians of the "machines."

This mind-set created some emotional conflicts in 1948 when Estes Kefauver, of Chattanooga, defied Boss Crump by running against Senator Tom Stewart, one of the Boss's main men in Washington, D.C. Kefauver was suspected (rightly, as it turned out) of having "Yankee attitudes" toward our way of life, which was, of course, racial segregation. Some even called him a "nigger lover." Yet he opposed the corrupt and evil Crump machine. The Boss himself called Kefauver a "pet coon" of the anti-Crump Nashville Tennessean, a slander the contender turned to his advantage by campaigning in a coonskin hat such as worn by Tennessee pioneers. The hat trick helped Kefauver win the Senate seat, from where he would oppose an unequivocal stand in favor of segregation and even move close to a campaign for the White House. It was a near miss that would cause Teddy White, the great reporter of presidential campaigns, to lament that "Estes Kefauver was the greatest President we never had."

The conflict within our family was resolved by Ned Carmack, son of the late senator, a frequent guest at Bankrupt Manor, a handsome man who walked with a limp as the result of a physical beating by political opponents. Ned came out in favor of Kefauver. There was a lesson learned from the race between Stewart and Kefauver: politics, more often than not, is a choice between bad and less bad instead of good and evil, the beginning of knowledge that politics is the art of the possible, not the art of perfection. From this understanding, "personal" politics was giving way to common sense and personal interest. Four years later in 1952 as a student at the University of Washington and a spear-carrier for local Democrats, I helped arrange a speech for Kefauver, candidate for the Democratic presidential nomination, at Eagleson Hall just off the campus. It was a signal disappointment for me, if not my college colleagues.

To put this kindly, Kefauver, a man with a strong taste for liquor and women, came on the stage looking road-weary. A few days earlier, campus Democrats heard Senator Hugh B. Mitchell, candidate for governor, and Representative Henry M. "Scoop" Jackson, candidate for the U.S. Senate, both of them untarnished, unmitigated heroes to our young crowd. On the same day as Kefauver's visit, the platform at Eagleson Hall was held by Stimson Bullitt, a brilliant, handsome, Purple Heart veteran of World War II turned candidate for Congress from Washington State's First District. These were acts too tough for the road-weary to follow. The tall Tennessean would have finished last to Mitchell, Jackson, and Bullitt in a vote among our college group for the Democratic presidential nomination, which, in fact, he would lose to Governor Adlai Stevenson of Illinois.

Politics was now intensely ideological. An anti-Communist fervor swept the nation like nothing since the "Great Awakening" of religion on the early nineteenth-century frontier. Nowhere up to 1949 had it created more havoc than in Washington State. No matter that communism had ceased to exist as an influence in the state after Stalin signed a pact with Hitler in 1939. The state legislature, backed by Hearst's *Seattle Post-Intelligencer*, unleashed state Representative Albert Canwell and his investigative committee on the University of Washington. They were to root out Commies from the college campus.

With no regard for and perhaps not even familiarity with Anglo-Saxon rules of law, proper legal procedure, or common respect for their fellow man, Canwell and his "Commie hunters" frightened a timid university president into firing three professors. Canwell, a precursor of Senator Joe McCarthy, was to civil rights what Joe

Stalin was to fair trials. Professors, ordinary citizens, any person who had taken part in the 1930s in organizations to fight fascism or racism, cowered under the threat of social ostracism or loss of jobs. Even the normally imperturbable Senator Warren Magnuson, perhaps the toughest and most astute liberal of his era, bowed a tad to the hysteria. After all, he had sought and won endorsement by the Communist Party in his first campaign for Congress. To be designated "soft on Communism"—never mind being a party member—was tantamount to political death in 1952. Mitchell and Bullitt lost their elections for, respectively, proposing a Columbia Valley Authority ("Communism on the Columbia," said its private utility critics) and opposing "loyalty" oaths for public employees. Jackson barely defeated the Republican incumbent, Harry P. Cain, an irascible reactionary already written off by Luce's *Time* magazine as an embarrassment to the party.

A domestic liberal of probity, Jackson went on to become a leading Cold Warrior, unyielding friend of the Pentagon. He appeared to adopt the state of Israel as a second constituency. Twice he ran for the Democratic presidential nomination, never overcoming an underwhelming personality, the inspiration for Mark Russell's jibe: "Jackson gave a fireside speech last night. The fire went to sleep." But he would never again be accused of being "soft on Communism," the phoney, hysterical rap laid on him in the campaigns of 1950 and 1952.

DESPITE THIS EXTRACURRICULAR campus activity, in June 1954, following graduation from the university, where I had studied history and philosophy, I suspended political judgments—personal, ideological, practical—to serve as a line officer in the 60th Infantry Regiment, charged with protecting a piece of the line along the Czech-German border from Warsaw Pact invaders. I had taken a soldier's oath on commission as a reserve officer and that was it. The rights and wrongs of the Cold War were beside the point for two and a half years, and I knew their contemplation might be a drag on the performance of duties. I drew a mental curtain down on politics, and this included a semicurtain around the presence of a semi-truck trailer hauling a 280 mm cannon alongside our battalion as we moved, every month or so, from our barracks to our fighting positions along the border. The cannon, we all knew, fired shells with atomic warheads of about the same potency as those bombs dropped on Hiroshima, Japan. The lesson of their presence could not be blocked from thought: if the Soviets invaded, we'd be on the front lines of a tactical nuclear exchange. In that case, it was good-night to all, the 2nd Battalion of the 60th Infantry, my men of the machine gun platoon, me. I chose not to think of it nor of the political decisions that would set such terminal events into motion. Nor did we speak of it among ourselves, the captains, lieutenants, and sergeants of the battalion.

Looking back now, near the close of the twentieth century, armed with greater detachment and far greater knowledge of the events of 1954–56, I cast a shaky vote in favor of President Eisenhower's judgment. Men smarter and less addled than Albert Canwell and Joe McCarthy truly feared a Soviet invasion of Western Europe. One upshot of this judgment was Eisenhower's decision to avoid U.S. troop commitment in Indochina where the French were being tossed out by their colonial subjects, the Vietnamese. So doing, Eisenhower saved men and ammunition, including the scant supply of those primitive atomic warheads, for defense of European civilization against the Communist hordes.

Not even the approximate number of atomic warheads supplied our forces is public knowledge today. What is known is a terrible irony: that in order to save Western Europe we would destroy it and make it radioactive should the Warsaw Pact armies invade. And we know the anticipation of a conflict was great. So, against good and practical argument, we rearmed West Germany in 1955 and rushed with every available troopship, all of them overloaded, to fortify NATO with our soldiers. By the end of 1955, the 60th Infantry had at least one extra second lieutenant (platoon leader rank) for each two platoons. This was spare commissioned officer cannon fodder, since they had no official duties other than to observe and wait. Thank God, their wait was never fulfilled.

Did the militarization of West Germany and the buildup of

NATO thwart a Soviet invasion, as some of our later generals have stated? Yes, indeed. I've been told by officers of the Bundeswehr and officials of the German Foreign Office. Not so, others have argued. The threat was never real. Perhaps we'll never know the answer. At that time—too busy in preparation for the conflict—I turned away and never considered the question, and now leave it to scholars working through the archives of Washington, Bonn, and Moscow.

EVEN WITH THE TWO-YEAR HIATUS from critical thought, it was an easy jump from matters along the German-Czech border to the trenches of American politics where I labored for 35 years. I carried a legacy of interest in politics and its practioners in the Congress, the legislatures of Louisiana, Oklahoma, and Washington, and, for a short time, the White House under President Lyndon Johnson. These venues and the campaigns waged by those seeking public office were my workplace. One had to love it, or leave it. The tough transitions would come later, shifting from deadly political conflicts in the Mideast to the civil processes of American democracy.

JOURNALIST

I CAME TO JOURNALISM by happenstance, a string of accidents, the most significant being shrapnel from a .30-caliber bullet taken in the face at the end of live ammunition field maneuvers at Hohenfelds, Germany, in October 1955. I survived, although minus one eye, and thus unfit for further duty as an infantry line officer. Such casualties were not exceptional. The idea behind these maneuvers was to accustom the infantryman, as near as possible, to combat without killing him. The course was run for one mile over a pair of 500-foot ridge lines by platoon-sized units, each soldier firing his rifle while the company's mortars and machine guns fired over and just ahead of the platoon's advance. The casualties usually happened when rounds fell short. My wound came after I had given orders to cease fire and clear weapons on the final ridge line. My radio operator failed to clear a round from his gun chamber and pulled the trigger. The .30-caliber round hit a rock at my feet and, instead of ricocheting, it splattered and came back up into my face.

I spent the next two months in U.S. Army hospitals, two weeks of this in the critical ward of the hospital in Nuremberg, Germany, a medical halfway house between a recovery and a grave. Eventually I was shipped to New York for discharge. There the Army, in its peculiar way, assigned me to the U.S. Naval Hospital in St. Albans, Long Island, an easy subway commute to Broadway.

Lucky to be alive and curious about what to do with the rest of my life, I took to Manhattan's wire-service and newspaper offices looking for a job. The inspiration for this search came from an evening in the Munich officers' club, drinking and talking with the United Press and Associated Press correspondents stationed in that Bavarian capital. Neither the city nor the reporters were much reconstructed from the recent war. Ruddy veterans, the newsmen told stirring tales and had easy manners. It seemed to me theirs was an excellent, if not exemplary, way of life, not particularly harried, socially mobile, and certainly not routine. I was unable to conceive either of these gentlemen of the press behind a corporate desk, commuting to a suburban home and wife or relaxing over golf at a restrictive country club. They were unbound—men of the world and action. Journalism might be suspect as a respectable profession, but it was still a step above my previous occupation as a seaman on blue-water tramps and Alaska steamships out of Seattle. Two years of blue water and erratic shipmates were enough.

Another piece of fortune at this critical juncture: the major in charge of the Army detachment at St. Albans was working, on the side, toward a master's degree in government at a nearby Long Island college. What he lacked in academic zeal he compensated with Army know-how. He made a deal with me. In exchange for papers I'd write on the Soviet Union and China, subjects I had studied as a student at the University of Washington, he would cover my leave from the hospital where I was supposed to remain bedded. I had to show up, pro forma, once a week. Otherwise I was footloose in New York. This lasted two months until discharge from the hospital and retirement as a first lieutenant of the Infantry.

Manhattan, in those days, had eight daily newspapers and headquarters for three wire services. Armed with a college degree and a letter of commendation from the commanding general of the 9th Infantry Division, I knocked on all of their doors. The letter was a help and a mild embarrassment. I got it not for troop leadership but for an editorial written for the Division newspaper.

International News Service, the Hearst wire, had a Manhattan office that could have been a stage set for *The Front Page*—editors in shirtsleeves and green eyeshades, a bare floor softened only by cigarette butts, the clatter of teletypes mixed with high decibel conversation. It smelled of unlaundered shirts. Tom Breslin, the editor in charge of personnel, had a small office with a door that could be closed. I entered, by chance, about one hour after an INS staffer in Dallas, Texas, got fired—for lack of speed, I later learned. "Get it first, but first get it right," was the code of the wire services. He apparently couldn't get it first.

Breslin read my meager credentials and the letter of commendation. He was harried and jerky in his movements but decisive in action: "Sixty-five dollars a week in the Dallas bureau, starting with sports," he said. I damned nearly jumped out of my skin. A job! However, I remained under sufficient control to manage a bluff: "I've already got an offer for $92." (True, but the job was public relations, which he didn't need to know.) "Okay," Beslin countered. "Seventy-two a week. You pay expenses to Dallas." We shook hands and I departed with the telephone number and name of the Dallas Bureau Chief, Ray Baumgardner. The transaction that set my career for the next 35 years lasted less than ten minutes.

Baumgardner was 73 years old, a cheerful, round-shaped man who could have doubled for a movie grandfather. He wore a belt and suspenders to hold up his pants and had covered every president from William McKinley to the incumbent Dwight Eisenhower. It was hard to reconcile his genial manner with his abrupt discharge of my predecessor. This, I surmised, was serious business. Baumgardner was not to be taken lightly.

"If you can write sports, you can write anything," according to the Hearst wire service Bible. Unsaid was another commandment, laid down not only by Baumgardner, but by every veteran newsman I would encounter: "If it isn't right, or if it isn't fair, it doesn't move." A violation of these strictures at that time was unthinkable. I recall this stringent indoctrination and subsequent practice in light of recent journalistic notoriety where news is not only wrong, it's sometimes made up; where a reporter's personal bias may stick out and besmirch his news story like a mixed metaphor.

There were about 200 members of the Southwest Chapter of the Wire Service Guild, all veterans, the only members of the journalists' union in Texas, Oklahoma, and New Mexico. All had been economically conditioned by the great Depression and had served in the U.S. military. Some were newspaper tramps, moving from city to city and jobs from beat reporter to copy desk editor—a restless, hard-drinking breed. I was the only college graduate in this group. There came a newsroom sea change in the 1960s when newspapers, under the press of television, began to fold or, perhaps worse, sell out to chains. A new breed, reared in the postwar American suburbs, well-fed, and above all college graduates, replaced the tramps and up-from-the-ranks reporters.

As new man in Dallas, I opened the bureau every morning at 6 A.M., rewrote Texas news from the *Dallas Morning News* and *Fort Worth Star-Telegram*, punched it into teletype tape, and moved it via wires leased from Western Union to newspaper clients around the Southwest. The wire-service writing style, sawed-off sentences and active verbs, was a design of bookkeepers wary of Western Union wire rates, not poets thinking of music—"Save Words, Save Money!" The early rewrite work was done by 8 A.M. when the balance of the staff, all veterans, arrived. The rest for me was sports. The wire services were no place for a prose stylist. Marcel Proust would have been on welfare five days after his first rewrite trick under the iron mandate of a "deadline every minute." They were places to learn, under extreme duress, speed, and accuracy, the blocking and tackling of good journalism.

Texas had two religions: Baptist and football. They complemented each other rather than conflicted, as refined theologians might have wished. There was also baseball and golf—Byron Nelson and Ben Hogan, Lone Star idols of a rank akin to Slinging Sammy Baugh and Bobby Layne, lived nearby—as well as Presbyterians and Methodists. I loved football and baseball in high school and played both games with some skill and much enthusiasm. Golf was a mystery. I couldn't make sense of an athlete striking the end of a stick against a small white ball, much less the attraction of this act for an audience ("gallery" in golfese). But sports was my immediate fate until I could work free.

High Church was Southwest Conference football, rites every fall, four or five games each Saturday—all of which I was responsible for covering, writing, and filing on the INS wire. The service being four decades dead, I can tell you how this was done without threat of legal action. The INS office, a low-rent space in the Texas Bank Building, had concrete floors and swivel chairs which could be wheeled about from desks to teletypes. On Saturdays, I stocked it with three radios tuned to three of the conference games and one primitive television set dialed to the "game of the day," say Texas vs. Oklahoma. Thus equipped, I wheeled and swiveled from broadcast to broadcast, scribbling notes, glimpsing TV action and contemplating metaphors and similes. If the game was one-sided, I could whip out four or five paragraphs in advance, adding the final score at the whistle. If they were close, the process was frantic. Once they were finished I'd pop from typewriter to teletype, dispatching compact, clichéd ("Tip-toeing down the sideline for 90 yards, brushing aside tacklers like flies," etc.) stories over the INS wire. By some miracle I kept the games separated, making sure Baylor–Rice didn't get confused with Texas–Baylor, Texas Christian–Southern Methodist. Speed kills, but in this case the victim was the competition, AP and UP. INS was always first, if not definitive, with its football stories. The experience, however, left me with the self-image of Charlie Chaplin stuck in the gears of *Modern Times*. Being "first" was pleasing to my competitive instincts, even better for the wire service: "First" meant INS stories would be displayed in the client newspapers instead of UP or AP.

Despite the flow of quotes and clichés, all I can recall of my Texas sports reportage is that Dandy Don Meredith, originally of Mount Vernon, Texas, later of Manhattan and Hollywood, ran 65 yards for a touchdown against Texas on his first play as quarterback for Southern Methodist and that country clubs where they played golf tournaments were places where men in casual suits sold cars, insurance, and stocks to each other while the athletes, intense as brain surgeons knifing a tumor, stalked a small white ball. The memory of Meredith may be suspect, but I'm sure of the country clubs. That's where Algie Choate, originally of Kenton, Tennessee, sold me ten shares of American Express which doubled in value in less than a year.

Given youth, strong legs, and a mite of in-house fame for having followed a tornado through its path of death and destruction in Dallas into national headlines—I beat the cops and ambulances into the dead and wreckage of a trailer court—I got a break from the sports beat in September 1957. It also helped to have a Southern accent when INS assigned me to cover the racial integration of Little Rock's Central High School. The Arkansas clash of federal and state governments ranked with the Soviet Union's Sputnik, man's first orbiting satellite, as the story of the decade. It came three years after the U.S. Supreme Court (*Brown v. Board of Education*) ruled against segregated common schools. It provoked prayers, riots, and the most serious federal-state conflict since Lee and Grant met, presumably to settle the issue, at Appomattox Courthouse.

The "Little Rock Crisis," as it would be known, began when Governor Orval Faubus defied a federal court order by calling out the Arkansas National Guard to block the racial integration of Central High School. Faubus, regarded up till then as a "moderate" Southern governor, needed a bump up in the popularity polls and rightly figured he'd get the same from his defiance.

"I'm just a country boy," Faubus said of himself. Born in a rough plank cabin along Greasy Creek, Faubus came to the relative urbanity of Little Rock from an Ozark Mountain county so poor it did not get a paved road until 1949. He didn't want to go back without one more term in the statehouse. When under another court order Faubus withdrew the National Guard, President Eisenhower faced a moment of truth: either do nothing to enforce the law of the land or send in troops to control angry white mobs and pass nine black teenagers through the schoolhouse door. The president did what he had to do—he dispatched units of the 101st Airborne Division to Little Rock.

Reporters flocked like eagles to spawning salmon, an inordinate number from England. "Not since the Chartists riots of 1860 have the British used troops against their citizens," explained Patrick O'Donovan, the well-tailored, well-lubricated correspondent of the *London Observer*, the best practitioner of the English language in journalism. John Chancellor and Frank McGee, excellent reporters, became mainstays on NBC-TV with their nightly news.

INS, a wire service geared to "the big story," opened a bureau in the Albert Pike Hotel where the peerless Bob Considine wrote A.M. and P.M. "leads" (fresh stories) and Bill Theis of Washington, a Presbyterian elder on Sundays, kept sidebars and insights flowing and reporters pointed in the right directions.

The mobs, nearly all male—Southern gentry would describe them as white trash, perhaps a clue to their motivation—came with tire irons and bike chains and ebbed and flowed in front of Central High School. Their numbers varied between 30 and several hundred, declining as they recognized the troopers meant business. They never charged the paratroopers. Reporters filed to their bureaus from a pair of telephone booths on the mob side of the street opposite Central High. Once while I was dictating to Considine, the ugly mass swelled and surged toward my telephone booth. I had seen their faces and heard their racist pejoratives once before, as a lad in Obion County, Tennessee, observing a mob intent on lynching a black prisoner in the county jail. The same faces in the crowd now closed on my dictation. Back at the hotel, Considine remained calm. I was about to lose my nerve and run when the INS ace said, "Got enough. Hang up and let's talk here." We did so, but not before Considine insisted on a stress buster from his well-stocked briefcase—"Bourbon, Scotch, or Gin?"

The back of Southern school segregation was broken that fall in Little Rock and not entirely due to the resolve of Eisenhower and the arms of the 101st Airborne. Newspapers and television, to the disgust of their Southern clients, reported a story slanted in favor of the nine well-scrubbed and polite black children moving impassively (well coached) past a jeering white mob to their studies. Who could not take sides with the black kids in this compact, vivid drama? More than black versus white, it was cowardice against courage.

One day, September 24, 1957, to be precise, the ever-present mob went into a frenzy when they spotted a black youth bearing groceries enter the home of Mrs. Fred Reutelhuber on Schiller Street near Central High. The woman was 70 years old and lived alone. I watched from the no-man's land between the troops and the white crowd. "Let's get that nigger!" one of them shouted and about 30 men rushed across a street onto Mrs. Reutelhuber's lawn. When she came to the front door, the white men demanded entrance. They wanted to get their hands on the black delivery boy. The composed woman politely told them "no." "What are you—a nigger lover," someone screamed. "I am a Christian lady, and you are trespassing," the woman replied, going back into her home and locking its doors. The mob, subdued, melted away. The black lad escaped a possible lynching, and in a newspaper sidebar story an old woman showed another side of the white South, one of fairness and moral and physical courage.

Considine and I took leave of Little Rock during a lull in the confrontation, he to New York to write a series on the "Anatomy of (Racial) Violence," I to Birmingham, Alabama, to do the legwork. We were inspired to this effort by the nearly fatal beating of the Reverend Fred Shuttlesworth, a black integration activist, and by the castration of a black named Aaron Judge, a victim picked at random for a Ku Klux Klan initiation ceremony.

I took a room at the upscale Tutwiler Hotel, where surely no redneck Klansmen dared lurk, and interviewed Alabama's racial headliners, Reverend Shuttlesworth ("Man was I scared—I thought I was dead"), Asa "Ace" Carter, leader of North Alabama's violence-prone White Citizens Council, John Whitley, head of a more moderate Birmingham Council faction, and retired Admiral John Cromelin, a World War II hero. Cromelin, an Ace Carter with a college education, cultured accent, and cotton plantation, was most voluble.

"You and your Yankee news service aren't going to print a word of what I'm going to say but I'm going to say it anyway." Integration, he said, was a Communist plot, insidious as it was ineffective. Blacks were inferior creatures and would never go to Alabama schools, and if they so attempted there'd be violence to pay. Considine printed every word of my interview with this crackpot, all of it and other news of Birmingham racism filed through the Western Union office at the Tutwiler's front desk.

These dispatches from Birmingham got through to New York, despite the odd, suspicious stares I began to get from the hotel clerks. I found myself a special guest of sorts, "Yankee nigger lover," one of them muttered late one evening. The stately Tutwiler panned out like the rest of Birmingham, racist and hostile. I appealed to Milt Kaplan, the INS national editor, for a return to the relative safety of Little Rock.

The heavy hitters had gone back to New York, Washington, and Chicago when I returned to Arkansas. Matters had gone from turmoil to routine under the guard of the 101st Airborne. Gene Schroeder, a veteran, and I staffed the Little Rock bureau. I watched the statehouse while Gene wrote, edited, and filed. At night we ate hamburgers and played the pinball machines at a local hangout favored by reporters and several leaders of Central High's racist observers. After all, we had news in common. One evening over beers one of these gents told of a plan to gun down a *Life* magazine photographer they tellingly named "Nig." "We talked about it, but decided against it," he said. "Those Feds were too much. Nobody but a fool would mess with them paratroopers." Maybe this good ole boy was boasting. But I doubt it. The wonder of Little Rock that autumn is that, so far as is known, nobody got killed either by accident or design.

Governor Faubus had a swaggering personal staff, country boys in the main with one Little Rock slicker, Jimmy Aram, as his right-hand man. Aram stuck out because he dressed like an Oaklawn racetrack tout. They delighted in the notoriety attending this historic crisis, proudly showing me letters approving and cheering the governor's stand on behalf of racial segregation. Letters came from all over the nation, and one of them from College Station, Texas, said the entire Texas A&M football team was ready to come to the governor's aid if ever he called. It was signed by Paul "Bear" Bryant, the Aggie coach. Later, coaching 'Bama, he came to appreciate at least the football skills of black citizens.

One crisp Saturday morning I went along with the political reporter of the *Arkansas Democrat* to the governor's mansion to get his reaction to a federal court's summary dismissal of a suit filed by a claque of middle-aged women, Mothers for Central High Segregation. They sought an end to the occupation of their school by federal troops. We drove through a cordon of state troopers with only a few "howdys." The man from the *Democrat* was recognized as friendly, a contrast with newsmen from the liberal *Arkansas Gazette.* Faubus came out to greet us through the kitchen door at the back entrance to the mansion. He was shoeless and had a streak of buttermilk above his upper lip.

"Howdy Orval," said my escort. "Howdy John," said the governor. "The courts turned down that writ from Mothers for Segregation," said the newsman. Faubus paused a few seconds, placing a hand on his hip and shifting his weight, before responding, "Well, I'll be a sonofabitch." "Can I quote you on that, governor," joked the reporter, meaning he would never quote a cussword from the lips of his political buddy, but would, instead, write that the governor appeared stunned at the federal court decision. And so he did.

I mark that brief summation as the beginning of the end of the conflict between state and federal rights as it took form in Little Rock, fall of 1957. In early November, I went back home to bureau routine in Dallas. Faubus, the public official who started the conflict, would win one more two-year term as a result, then return to obscurity in the Arkansas Ozarks.

"GOVERNOR FAUBUS seemed to have a bright future as a Southern liberal in Democratic politics—Mrs. [Eleanor] Roosevelt spoke highly of him," said my companion in the coffee shop of Love Field, two weeks after my return to Dallas. My companion was Senator John F. Kennedy, a Massachusetts Democrat and member of the Foreign Relations Committee. He was eager to return to Washington for his first sight of a newborn daughter, Caroline. But first he wanted to strip a reporter of his insight into the Arkansas statehouse—the personality and background of Faubus and his advisers, legislative leaders, the economic and social forces underlying the capital. It was a pleasant inquisition and we had plenty of time to talk. Kennedy's flight was delayed for two hours.

It did not begin with such cordiality. I was doing an INS feature, "Interview of the Day." Kennedy was the subject du jour. Previous subjects had been Lyndon Johnson, the Senate majority leader, and Dr. Willard Libby, of the Atomic Energy Commission (both of them alarmed that the Soviets "beat us into space" with the Sputnik), Frank Lloyd Wright, an architect of genius, and T. S. Eliot, a poet I described as a "crowd-pleasing, intellectual heavyweight," not yet being reconditioned from the sports beat. Dr. Edward Teller, a right-wing Hungarian who helped build the atomic bomb, I viewed as a twentieth-century Dr. Frankenstein, arms widespread, hair on end, eyes bulging as he shouted "It's Alive!" that monstrous dawn at Alamogordo. Dallas, a city with Birmingham folkways and K-Mart charm, was a crossroads for such celebrities.

Kennedy was on a sweep through the South in search of potential delegates to the 1960 Democratic National Convention. He wanted to be president. We met in the lobby of the Adolphus Hotel, where he had slept after spending the previous day in Montgomery with John Patterson, a segregationist who defeated George Wallace in the race for governor of Alabama. ("Nobody will ever out-nigga me again," the loser promised. He would keep his word.) Kennedy suggested we continue the interview en route to Love Field.

The hotel provided a limousine and a public relations chaperone. My questions were marshmallows until I asked about the effect of the current state of domestic race relations on U.S. foreign relations. He politely declined to answer. When I persisted, he insisted, "I'm not discussing the race issue." We rode a few miles and I came back to the subject of race—no sooner uttered when Kennedy wheeled about from his front seat, thrust out his right arm, as if to strike, and half-shouted, "Ask this one more time and I'm stopping the car. You can walk back to Dallas." His face was red with anger and I could see the veins in his neck. Our embarrassed chaperone looked devastated. Since we were only halfway to the airport, the rest of the ride was silent. I didn't aim to walk back to town.

Once at the airport's departure entrance, I jumped from the vehicle, satisfied that the interview was blown. I had pushed too hard and was sorry for having angered a politician I'd come to admire, at one time himself an INS reporter. I didn't bother to say goodbye, rushing toward a cabstand. Before I got away, a hand grabbed my shoulder. I turned and looked into the somewhat relaxed face of Jack Kennedy. "I'm sorry," he said. "I apologize for losing my temper. Let's go have coffee."

The rest was off the record. All we talked about was Little Rock, symbol now of the nation's crushing burden of racism. The president-to-be explained his predicament in the hunt for Southern convention delegates. He had to deal with the Pattersons and the Faubuses, and thus mute his comments on the race issue. Hypocritical, of course, but conventional politics. Odd as it may seem today, there was no question in the politician's mind that I would honor his confidence, which until this writing I have done. Such was the unwritten compact between reporter and source in those days. As Kennedy continued, he left no question about the need to resolve the dilemma of a nation with two classes of citizens; no question about how he would act on segregation should he win the White House.

Indeed, Kennedy, like Wallace, would keep his word; Kennedy by submitting to Congress the Civil Rights Act in August 1963, Wallace by doing his damndest to defeat the legislation. This legislation went to Congress three months before President Kennedy's assassination in Dallas. The act, forbidding racial discrimination in public accommodations, was pushed by President Johnson in the White House and Washington State's Senator Warren Magnuson in the Congress and became law a year after its introduction. It changed the shape of American society. Racism still exists, but no longer in its malignant, legally sanctioned institutional form that so bothered the senator and the reporter in the coffee shop that November morning at Love Field.

Despite my dislike for the city, free to roam from the press box and country clubs, I liked the work. As the Dallas bureau's marginally qualified "theater critic," I interviewed Anne Baxter of *All About Eve*, an excessively nervous chain-smoker worried about her wrinkles, watched Greer Garson of *Mrs. Miniver* at the Margo Jones Theatre—I can't recall a thing about the play, not even its name—and witnessed the stage debut of the celebrated Candy Barr.

Ms. Barr's vehicle was *The Seven Year Itch*, which wasn't too bad when she got offstage. You didn't have to be Brooks Atkinson to see that Candy was awful. An East Texas country girl (née Juanita

Jo Slusher) with a twang to match, Ms. Barr had gained fame as the star stripteaser in a nightspot run by the thuggish Jack Ruby. Tough as mesquite, what Barr lacked in theatrical talent, she compensated with a gorgeous body—and there was a helluva lot for which to compensate. But she starred without clothes. I speak with authority. During my post-play interview she was clad in a hand towel, oblivious to my embarrassment.

Ruby's star, Candy Barr, was the artistic and cosmetic creation of one Abe Weinstein, who ran a school for stripteasers in Big D. I got $75—that was three more than my weekly salary—from the *American Weekly*, a Sunday newspaper supplement, for a 350-word story on Weinstein's skin academy. He proudly showed off his latest creation, a shy country girl fresh from a chest surgeon, "the next Candy Barr! Tutti Frutti." "Abe," I asked, "why do you give your strippers these names?" "Because people like to eat food," he beamed, pleased as Professor Higgins with Eliza Doolittle after the ball.

Outside show biz, my friends were political liberals like myself, a small, endangered species in the Big D of those days. Jim (her given name) Aiken, the cigar smoking, down-to-earth daughter of a sharecropper turned oil millionaire, ran what passed for a liberal political salon. It was never very crowded. She went to Washington during the Kennedy administration and later wed Congressman Richard Bolling, a Missouri Democrat once touted as a future House Speaker. Pavel (Paul) Brod, a slight, self-effacing Polish refugee, wound up the war fighting for Berlin with the Red Army—"gun battles on one street corner, lovemaking on the next, all within sight." Every member of his family perished in concentration camps. Brod stayed after the war to work with Bertolt Brecht and his Berliner Ensemble. In Dallas he worked as a bookkeeper for Dr. Pepper, a soft drink company.

OLD MAN BAER, as he was called in the neighborhood, lived a few blocks from my cheap apartment in a two-story, rundown house advertised by a lawn sign as "The Baer Memorial Art Gallery." The neighborhood, Oaklawn, was lower middle-class white, not yet slum but gaining on that station. Baer was kindly regarded as eccentric by neighbors who gathered at the cut-rate cafeteria near the art gallery for a lunch of bread, fried spam, pie, and coffee, 99 cents. Less acute observers called him a nut case. He dressed in tatters barely concealed by a worn-out topcoat into which he would tuck the unfinished portion of his cafeteria meal. He was stingy, but I liked him, and enjoyed his conversation, which was sophisticated, not only for Big D, but for any civilized city. He had studied art with the Bauhaus group in Munich in the early days of the Weimar Republic, and told of the artist's life in Schwabing, the city's bohemian district. I figured he had a lot of unused spam around his broken-down mansion along with his paintings. One day after lunch he invited me to come and look. I did, pretending to be impressed because I enjoyed our talks. The house looked a mess like its master.

That's as much as I could tell about my unusual friend until one morning I found him splashed all over the arts-entertainment page of the *Dallas Morning News*. The man who wore pawn shop rejects for clothes and who saved his uneaten spam sandwiches was donating a sweet piece of prime Dallas real estate along Turtle Creek Drive to the Margo Jones Theatre, the site of a new playhouse to be designed by the master architect, Frank Lloyd Wright. Wright, the story gushed, was coming to Dallas in person to consult with the theater's benefactor, Sylvan Baer, a St. Louis native and heir to a fortune from the St. Louis department store, Stix Baer & Fuller. Cagey old fox, I thought. The land he was giving away was worth millions.

Before I had the chance to talk with Mr. Baer, the press agent in charge of Wright's pending visit asked if I would be so kind as to join Baer at his home at the date and time of Frank Lloyd Wright's calling. Delighted, I replied. He lived only two blocks away.

I arrived a bit early, anticipating an explanation. "He's a pretty formidable old coot, I'm told, and I want a witness to our discussion," said Baer. The great man arrived in a limousine, attired, as in his photos, in a long black cape with a cane and black porkpie hat. He left the press agent in his car.

"Memorial art gallery?" he noted with a wave of his cane at the crudely lettered sign. He employed the cane like a sneer. "Looks more like the Baer In Memoriam art gallery." Baer was cordial, nev-

ertheless, showing Wright paintings scattered upstairs and down-
stairs in his house. The architect kept shaking his cane at the pieces
of art. His comments suggested neither disdain nor appreciation. I
guessed he felt the former. He wanted something, and apparently
Baer had already been so apprised.

"That rock at the top of this little rise where I will place the
theatre must be removed," the architect announced after the easy
talk and social proprieties were fulfilled.

"No," said Baer. "The rock must not be removed. The rock
must stay where nature has placed it."

The two old men, adamant, unshakable, stared at each other.
I watched, thinking that the future of the Margo Jones Theatre, if
not the theatrical future of Big D, hung in the balance of this conflict
between the two men, one with the real estate, the other with the
artistic genius to create a landmark.

"Look at this painting," commanded Wright, pointing his
cane. "What would you have done had I stood over your shoulder
as you created this work of art and said, 'No, Baer, don't put the
brush there. Move it to the left and use more purple.'"

"I would have dismissed you from my presence," said Baer.

"But now you are, in effect, looking over my shoulder and trying to tell me how to create this theater," Wright shot back.

"You cannot remove that rock," answered Baer, and the visit,
the consultation of the mighties, ended. Wright retreated to his limousine and drove away, leaving me and Old Man Baer standing on
his walkway.

"Well," said Baer. "I told him and you heard me and that's
that. There's nothing more to say of it."

I didn't stick around Dallas long enough to see it, but Wright
did design the new theater and my guess is that he did so around or
over Baer's rock. Some things, like a man's character, are not to be
moved.

NONE OF THESE Dallas friends was more colorful than Ben
Phelper, a prewar carnival diver, middleweight prizefighter, and
pilot of racing airplanes. A ball-turret gunner on a B-17, Ben fin-

ished the war as a prisoner in Stalag 17, the German camp for downed airmen made famous by a play and movie of the same name. Phelper claimed both were based on the diary he wrote and then smuggled out of the prison camp, although he never got any Broadway credit. An examination of the weathered document indicated either an extraordinary forgery or that Phelper was egregiously denied his due. Phelper had a wife and three kids when he lost his job writing manuals for a nearby aircraft factory. He needed a steady payday and fast. For laughs he invited the eminent "INS drama critic" to go with him for a job interview at the apartment of Jack Ruby, the Selznick of strip in Big D. Ruby needed a bouncer for one of his honky-tonks. Ben certainly had the credentials. This was in June and sweltering Dallas heat. A tall, gaunt gent with a pallor that suggested solitary prison time met us at the door. He wore a buttoned-up double-breasted suit that bulged a bit under his left shoulder. He must have been right-handed. Inside Ruby's apartment, the nite-club king, clad in pants and an old-fashioned tank-top undershirt, sat in a pool of discarded newspapers talking on the telephone. He was short, fat, and balding and had a house cat in his lap. I did not like his looks or those of his companions, one of whom boasted of swindling small-town merchants with what he called "my pots and pans scam"—perhaps to distinguish it from his practice of other forms of larceny. He took the merchant's money but never gave pots and pans in return. The other fellow, the man in the double-breasted suit, took his seat in the apartment's mezzanine— the better, I guessed, to observe his boss and the unusual guests.

Ruby was a showoff. He made no attempt to disguise his string of telephone calls. On the contrary. They went to Chicago, Los Angeles, New York, and New Orleans. Between these calls he instructed Phelper on the gentle art of "handlin' rowdy broads." The trick was to cinch the lady's upper lip between your thumb and index finger and then pull. He used me, not Phelper, to demonstrate, and it hurt like the dickens. "See what I mean?" said Ruby, returning to the telephone. "Gotta deal," he said, without explaining what. We drank a few of Ruby's beers and left. Barely beyond earshot, I turned to my friend and commanded, "You can't take a job with that creep. He's bad news. He's a gangster. For the sake of your kids, forget Ruby. Find another job."

International News Service folded a few weeks later, the summer of 1958. They called it a "merger" with United Press. If so, it was a merger like the cat with the canary. I was one of a few INS staffers retained by the new agency, United Press International. So were Bill Theis of Washington and Harry Trimborn of New Orleans. For a month I worked the Dallas bureau under the eye of Preston McGraw, the day editor, and Ward Colwell, the Southwest supervisor. McGraw was a gifted writer. Colwell was a wire service bureaucrat working the bush leagues.

The hot story for a couple of days that month was a "top secret military" meeting at the otherwise wide-open Hilton Hotel in Dallas. The placed "crawled with brass, mission unknown." The hotel's second and third floors were closed to civilians, guarded by military police. There wasn't even enough infomation for newspaper speculation. The *Times Herald* and *Morning News* played it front page, anyway.

One day, for the hell of it, I bet McGraw a beer I could lift the sheets off the secret meeting during my noon lunch hour. He accepted. I rushed to the Hilton, walked past a bored MP by flashing my retired Army credentials, and up stairs to the mezzanine. There, like a candy store display, was a long table almost sagging with scientific papers prepared for the meeting. More papers were in wastebaskets outside conference rooms. I helped myself. Back at the bureau I read enough of the purloined papers to dash out a story. Its lead read something like this: "Top Air Force commanders and civilian scientists are meeting in secrecy behind barricades at the elegant Hilton Hotel to discuss exotic metals needed for rocketships to take an American to the moon." This was a decade before our first moon trip.

McGraw promptly filed the same—a scoop—on the UPI wire. Colwell came to look over the editor's shoulder, frowning: "Can't we spark up that lead?" The supervisor was serious. McGraw looked at me and rolled his eyes. I was assigned to the New Orleans bureau a few days later. McGraw still owes me a beer.

JOURNALISM

THE NATION WOKE UP in the 1950s to a nightmarish hang-over. Two centuries of racial injustice toward blacks burst from the recesses of our culture, and the pages of post–Civil War apartheid laws, into the mainstream of American politics. For sure there was also the Cold War, the vividly perceived possibility of a Soviet inva-sion of Western Europe, and a hot war in Korea. The more imme-diate issue, however, was right in front of us at our schoolhouses, dime-store counters, streetcars, and public parks. It was the inte-gration crisis which became, in 1957, an echo of the Civil War—the crisis over federal and states rights.

The nation would not adopt laws that opened voting booths and public accommodations to all citizens until the 1960s. But in 1954 those historic strictures limiting full participation and access were bending under the weight of the U.S. Supreme Court decision in *Brown v. Board of Education*, the ruling against segregated com-mon schools.

Nowhere was the heat greater than in the "Great (pronounced Gret) State of Louisiana," the origin of *Plessy v. Ferguson*, a Supreme Court decision of the 1870s fixing blacks as second-class citizens, due "separate but equal" accord. Earl Kemp Long was gov-ernor, the White Citizens Council flourishing and violence antici-pated when I took a desk in the UPI office in the back of the *New Orleans Item*. The *Item* was not flourishing. It was about to die. The newspaper had been publishing daily since the days of its star reporter-editorial writer, Lafcadio Hearn, in the 1870s. Hearn looked strange, had trouble with deadlines, but wrote like an angel. The high walled city room had changed little since his time. Some of the city was the same, but not our work routine.

Lafcadio Hearn described his typical day at the *Item*: "Have coffee, slip into the office, rattle off a couple of leaders [editorials] on literary or European matters and a few paragraphs based on telegraph news. . . . Work over and the long golden afternoon welcomes me forth to enjoy its perfume and its laziness . . . a delightful existence without ambition or hope of better things." Restless, he wound up as professor of English literature at the University of Tokyo, having discovered Buddhism, as well as coffee with chicory, in New Orleans.

UPI shared the backroom with the *Item*'s news wire teletype machines whose heat more than offset the single, overworked air conditioner. Frequently in the summer evenings of 1958 we worked shirtless with heads bound in bandanas to prevent sweat from soaking our copy. A visitor might have thought us workers in a Congo diamond mine. Sad to say, the *Item* folded that summer, but as a result of this death in our journalistic family, UPI would soon get cooler quarters in a cheap office building on Poydras Street.

I shared the four P.M. to midnight shift with an ex-Marine platoon leader named Muller. We worked breaking news—it was hurricane season and we had a big one, a dozen dead, millions of dollars in damage—and rewrote the afternoon and evening file for the early editions of P.M. newspapers, mainly the *Item*, a newspaper in death throes but not quite finished. The night's work done, we crossed Canal Street to the Napoleon House bar on Chartres Street in the French Quarter to join reporters from the *Times-Picayune*, the state's leading newspaper, drink Regal beer, and swap stories until dawn. (The place had been built for Napoleon's exile, but the ousted French emperor never showed up.) Muller told about Marine Corps training when he was inevitably matched against Jim Mutscheller, the next Marine in the company alphabet, in hand-to-hand combat and bayonet drills. Muller was fiesty but of slight stature. Mutscheller came to the Marines from a starting position on the Baltimore Colts, professional football champs. Muller got battered with regularity until his unit ran a house-to-house combat course. This involved scrambling two stories up a rope secured at the top by a fellow Marine. Muller went first, holding the rope with his giant comrade at the other end. "I held on until he got to the top, when I just couldn't hold any longer," my UPI partner explained. "I had to let go." Mutscheller got flattened. Muller had evened the score either for real or in his fantasy of vengeance.

At dawn we went home for sleep.

News kept us hustling and New Orleans abounded with material for feature stories. Claire Chennault, creator-leader of the much publicized Flying Tigers, Chiang Kai-shek's air arm in the fight against Japan, lay dying in a local hospital and Clay Shaw, a suave, handsome World War II hero, director of the International Trade Mart, was turning the waterfront into a modern port of call. Shaw brought Edward Stone, a latter-day Frank Lloyd Wright, from Manhattan to design a new trade mart building, a 33-story rectangle with straight-line columns and interior decoration inspired by the Moghul rulers of India—rather exotic for an office building. I went to interview Shaw, an eminent New Orleanian. Before I called, a trade mart public relations man went way out of his way to warn that, ah, Shaw might make some funny, extremely personal, moves during our talk. "You mean he's homosexual?" I tried to clarify. "Ah, yes," said the PR flagman. Shaw did no such thing. Instead, he was impressive in speech and dress and, at least for one hour, a gentleman. We discussed the work of Edward Stone and the current prospects for trade. On both topics Shaw was enormously informed.

Among newsmen, our talk, speculation, and gossip never strayed far from politics, which meant it never got far away from "the Longs": Huey, deceased, and Earl, the incumbent governor. Coming into Louisiana politics midway in 1958 was akin to entering *Hamlet* midway in the second act. It meant a lot of catching up. It helped being a Southerner, thus accustomed to the politics of race and graft and having friends who knew Dick Leche, who became governor after Huey's demise. Long was gunned down outside the governor's office in the statehouse. Leche was convicted of using the office for private gain and jailed. Being charged and convicted of abusing public office in Louisiana during the 1930s and 1940s was not terribly unusual.

Huey and Earl came out of Winn Parish (county), a poor part of the state with a populist, anti-Confederate flavor. Each began work as a salesman. Earl went about the country hawking Calumet baking powder and then Dyanshine shoe polish. He took his share of plunder as a state official under Governor Huey and later as lieutenant governor. He was never convicted and never, not even down at the pathetic end, did he repudiate racial segregation. On the contrary. Earl demagogued on race with the best of his white Southern peers. Nevertheless, by the time I came to know and observe him, Long was the nearest thing to a liberal Southern politician, which may indeed tell you more about John Patterson, Orval Faubus, George Wallace, and William Fulbright than it tells about Earl Long. His was not a conventional, darkness-to-enlightenment political epic. He was not an ordinary man.

According to the Louisiana political primer, there were two parties in state: "Longs" and "anti-Longs." This was useful as a general description, but not entirely accurate. Like the personality of the Bard's Danish prince, the relationship of the people of the Gret State to the Longs was ambivalent—no, damnably complicated. Sometimes the "anti-Longs" were "Longs" and vice versa— no better example than the seminal brothers themselves. Earl turned against his brother when Huey went to the U.S. Senate to prep for a run for president. Huey still ran the state from Washington, the nearest thing yet to an American dictatorship, through puppets other than Earl in Baton Rouge. I mean he ran schools, courts, highways, graft, and, of course, the legislature. Another cliché, one more reliable, is that Louisianans liked to vacillate between governments by Longs and governments by anti-Longs. All of them were white men and Democrats.

Earl and his brother became allies again before the senator was murdered in the art deco skyscraper built by Huey and consecrated as the state capitol, if not a de facto monument to his dictatorship.

It has never been formally established who shot first, Huey's guard of state troopers or Dr. Carl Austin Weiss, who bore a grudge from an offense by Long against his family honor. Huey was said to have alleged they had black blood. The troopers carried Thompson submachine guns. The coroner found 61 bullet holes in Weiss. Maggie Dixon, the well-informed reporter-editor of the *Baton Rouge Morning Advocate*, who visited Huey on his deathbed, said the fatal slug was flattened, suggesting a ricochet. Huey died the day after Maggie's visit, September 10, 1935. Dick Leche replaced Huey's puppet, O. K. Allen, as governor. Earl was elected lieutenant governor and then governor in 1948 and reelected in 1956 after a four-year hiatus.

With Earl in the statehouse, the Long machine stayed lubricated with kickbacks and payoffs. Earl made friends with a couple of newcomers from New York, Frank Costello and Meyer Lansky, gangsters who muscled out local smaller fry running whores and illegal gambling in and around New Orleans. Offshore they had business ties with the Batista machine running Cuba. Good government groups were shocked—shocked!!—by Earl's errant behavior. In fact, save for its scale, it did not differ greatly from the acts of other Southern governors of that era. There was a tradition of men coming barefoot to the statehouse and emerging wearing Italian shoes and silk suits. Dick Leche spoke for most of them: "I did not take a vow of poverty when I entered the governor's office."

What set Earl Long apart from the rest, at least by the time I began to cover him for UPI, was his willingness to fund schools, colleges, and welfare for Louisiana's black citizens and to welcome their right to vote. For sure this was expedient—blacks voted for Long. Equally certain, unlike his peers, Long could see all the way to Washington, where a new wave was building. At crunch time in 1958, he refused to "interpose" the state's National Guard between black students and Louisiana schools.

"If the feds are behind the niggers, I'll be damned if I'll make a fool of myself like Faubus," explained Earl in refusing to prevent 200 blacks from enrolling at the newly opened Louisiana State University, New Orleans, in September 1958. There were threats of violence, and twice I rushed to the campus, a surplus U.S. Navy base on Lake Pontchartrain, on tips of a pending clash. Nothing much happened—a few racial slurs shouted and rocks tossed, but no casualties. Earl and the reasonable people of New Orleans prevailed. A historic footnote: LSU-NO became the first public college in the South to be racially integrated.

Louisiana politics, however, reshuffled, polarized on race— that is, a division between those who would fight to stop school integration and those, like Earl Long, who would acquiesce in the laws of the land and the mood of most Americans, even a few Americans in Louisiana. This new dichotomy would quickly become a small piece in the emerging fight for the 1960 Democratic presidential nomination.

State Senator Willie Rainach, a partial hunchback with a disposition to match his looks, led the fight for segregation. Willie headed Louisiana's White Citizens Council, a white-collar Ku Klux Klan which was supposed to be nonviolent, but was never of a mind to raise a calming hand if trouble did stir. He also chaired the Joint Legislative Committee on Segregation—that was its formal title— the prime source of legislation to disenfranchise blacks already registered to vote as the result of backstage politicking by Long. Months before the opening of the 1959 state legislative session, Rainach brought the conflict to center stage, a meeting of the Democratic State Central Committee. The venue was the floor of the state House of Representatives in Baton Rouge, where I had been transferred as UPI correspondent.

Allied with Leander Perez, a micro-Huey as boss of Plaquemines Parish across the Mississippi from New Orleans, Rainach led the purge of Camille Gravel as Democratic National Committeeman. Gravel, an elegant, handsomely attired attorney from Alexandria, attracted segregationist fury by echoing a declaration of the New Orleans Catholic Archbishop Joseph Rummel: "Segregation is morally wrong and sinful." Neither cleric nor Catholic layman would back down from that judgment. Gravel carried another burden into the confrontation. He was known for his support of John Kennedy for the presidential nomination and rumored to be angling for a place as attorney general in a Kennedy cabinet. Worse, he had lost, at least temporarily, the support of Earl Long, the buffer between himself and the racists. This was punishment for Gravel's support of Harold "Fishmouth" McSween in a congressional race that summer of 1958. Earl gave McSween his sobriquet and delighted in a crude imitation of the schoolteacher's manner of speech. Perez, a Long supporter until the racial reshuffle, regarded Kennedy as one becoming the "Henry Wallace of the 1960s," a creature of that "hotbed of sedition" Harvard College. Perez overshadowed Rainach in the fight to purge the apostate Gravel—and a fight it was.

Seated at the press desk in the well of the House, I damned nearly got up and ran when Leander Perez tried to yank the microphone from the hands of Edmund Reggie, the elegant, articulate attorney from Crowley, Gravel's friend and defender in this extraordinary hearing. Reggie, calm as a courtroom master, was making the case for Gravel and against the miscarriage of party procedure. Leander was screaming his objections over Reggie's refusal to give him the microphone. They were pulling and wrestling, and, I feared, about to fall on my head. Suddenly, Reggie shouted into his adversary's ear, "Sit down Perez!" and to his astonishment, the boss broke off their scuffle and returned to his seat. But Gravel lost the day. He was stripped of his credentials by the state committee. When, a few months later, the Democratic National Committee restored Gravel as National Committeeman, Perez allowed that it was acting under "secret orders from the Kremlin."

Camille Gravel was smart, witty, sophisticated, and ambitious. As such he attended the 1960 Democratic National Convention in Los Angeles. Kennedy won the presidential nomination, and whether or not he offered Gravel the cabinet post was much discussed in Louisiana at that time. The president-to-be had a bait-and-switch tactic he used to attract critical support. He tempted several senators, including Washington's Henry Jackson and Missouri's Stuart Symington, with the offer of the vice presidential nomination, only at the end to withdraw the temptation and give the nod to Lyndon Johnson. It's not unlikely that he did the same with cabinet posts. Regardless, the matter became moot as far as it concerned Camille

Gravel. Kennedy would name his brother Robert to head the Justice Department.

Almost four decades later, I talked with Gravel, and Reggie, whose daughter had married Senator Edward Kennedy, about this dramatic public showdown over Louisiana's racist mores and the new laws of the land. In broad terms it engaged arguments of the Old South against the New South. Gravel and Reggie were unpopular proponents of the latter. Had Gravel been frightened by the racist hostility? "No. I was called a yellow Nigger-lover, but never physically threatened." Had Jack Kennedy tempted him with a cabinet position? "No. Jack Kennedy never talked to me about becoming attorney general. Ted Sorensen said something to me. But I never had a discussion with Jack Kennedy himself." (Sorensen was Kennedy's speechwriter and confidant.)

MEANWHILE, come Saturdays that fall of 1958, it was back to the press box fighting the Associated Press in coverage of the Louisiana State University Tigers, the best college football team in the nation that year, according to both the AP and UPI. LSU had an undersized defensive unit and a professionally equipped halfback. The defense played over its head, perhaps inspired by its sobriquet "Chinese Bandits." Billy Cannon, the halfback with a bad-boy reputation, was too big and too fast to be easily stopped. The team went undefeated, winning the Southeastern Conference championship and a trip down the river to the Sugar Bowl on New Year's Day. It was the best college football team I'd witnessed up to that time, but that designation deserves an asterisk: the conference talent pool was limited. No blacks were allowed on the all-white teams. Conference rules. Given black competition at his position, who knows if Cannon could have made the first team.

The press box battle for display in the Sunday sports pages was intense and refined. My AP competitor was Ed Tunstall. He was not merely worthy, but almost too much—the fastest and most aggressive wire-service man I ever encountered and later editor of the venerable *Times-Picayune*. To win, I began to write the story in advance of the game's ending. I'd dictate to a staffer in New Orleans, who would punch it into teletype tape with gaps provided for the final score and vital statistics, such as how many yards Cannon ran for against 'Bama. At the final gun, the staffer would run the tape through the teletype, punching in the final touches and sending the peerless prose to peerless UPI clients. The process usually went smoothly. It allowed UPI to at least break even in the football coverage competition.

To celebrate Billy Cannon (but not our coverage), Leo Peterson came down from New York to address the LSU football banquet. Cannon was UPI's "Player of the Year." Peterson was the UPI national sports editor and I, as the agency's provincial correspondent, was host to the emissary from headquarters. He was accustomed to service from underlings, and the first thing he wanted from me was a bottle of whiskey. I got it and he drank. Leo talked from the side of his mouth like they did in movies made about 1930s New York's demimonde. He talked incessantly, usually in a negative mode:

"They came to see me about this Cannon. He was a fuck-up, you know, a delinquent and they wanted me to tell them what to do with him. Do with him! You silly sonofabitch, give him pads and hand him a football and play him. Imagine that. They got a guy, 210 to 215 [pounds], runs the hunnert [yards] in 9.9 [seconds] and they ask me. Reminds me of O'Meche. [Alan Ameche, running back for the Baltimore Colts circa 1958.] They said O'Meche's got problems. Well, so he ain't a Boy Scout and so he don't attend Sunday School. So what. He can carry a football, can't he?"

He could and so could Cannon. On reflection, Billy would have made the first team regardless of the talent pool. Peterson never identified the hapless "theys" who needed his help in what to do with Billy and Alan. Nor did I, the reporter, pursue the suggestion about Cannon's private life. Another maxim forged in iron: the private lives of politicians or other celebrities were not the stuff of mainstream journalism unless it could be proved that it affected public policy. The sex life of randy pols was the stuff of *Confidential* magazine, not of daily newspapers and wire services. How times, even *The Times*, have changed. Cannon's private life had nothing to do with the final score for LSU. They always won. Enough said.

There were tales about Earl Long and women friends, probably true, but unrelated to his performance as governor. Read it in *Confidential*, the sleaze magazine 40 years ahead of its time. In the journalism of the 1990s that maxim on private lives is turned upside down. What we regarded then as sleaze may now be read on the front pages of family newspapers, which might be excused if the paper also reported acts of the politician on behalf of those he was elected to serve. There's far too much of the former, precious little of the latter, which is expensive to produce—the journal needs professional reporters, not gossip mongers—and flirts with threats of libel. Besides, sex sells. Betrayal of the public interest may not.

Leo stayed sober enough to mount the banquet platform, hail the Tigers, and tout Billy Cannon as an example for the "youth of America—our nation's greatest resource." He'd made the speech before, so, like my press-box copy, all he had to do was fill in the blanks—name of college, name of player, etc.

Peterson went back to New York, I went back to New Orleans on his assignment to cover the Sugar Bowl, LSU vs. Clemson, January 1, 1959. It is always a festive event for fans and tourists, drunks all over the streets of the French Quarter, especially Bourbon Street—"famed, aptly named," I noted in my best Timese for UPI. New Orleans was a behavioral free-fire zone for tourists who came from places where drinking in public and fornicating without the benefit of marriage are dangerous dreams, difficult of fulfillment. They came to gawk at stripteasers, lured into small lascivious dens by the slickest sidewalk shills this side of Ringling Brothers. The Cat Woman, a truly beautiful woman of a dubious sexual appetite, and Blaze Starr, who would soon try to hitch her wagon to a failing Earl Long, were still the major attractions.

The New Year's Eve party for press and greater dignitaries, hosted by the Sugar Bowl, started with a six-course dinner at Antoines with three wines and whiskey, the most lavish meal I ever addressed in 35 years of journalism and freeloads. It ended for me shortly before dawn at Galatoires, a superb restaurant favored by New Orleanians. A ranking city official with long-term plans for the statehouse in Baton Rouge and short-term designs on passion, manhandled my fellow UPI staffer, Ellen Hill, with more moves than a Civic Auditorium rassler. Wasted motions, as it turned out. At the dawn of the new year I went back to my room at the splendid Monteleone Hotel, drew the drapes and fell into a boozy stupor. The telephone rang in what seemed like a few minutes later. I was still drunk.

"What the hell are you doing sleeping. I tried an hour ago." It was the edgy voice of Harry Trimborn, a bureau chief in crisis. "Get the hell up and get down here immediately. The revolution has broken out in Cuba."

That last line was actually a relief. Becoming awake, I thought I had slept past the Sugar Bowl kickoff, blowing my chance at sports fame by failing to cover the Big Story. But it was Cuba, not football, and the time was 8:30 A.M., not 2 P.M. And it came as an utter surprise. AP's man in Havana filed a much used and much lamented story on December 31, which said Fidel Castro's revolution had fizzled: "Government forces backed by armor and warplanes hammered retreating Rebel forces today." That foreign desk boilerplate led the *Picayune* on January 1, 1959. Groggy, but unbowed, I got to the bureau. The place was pandemonium, like my head, especially my vision. There were two of Trimborn, a man torn between telephone calls to New York headquarters and to staffers already positioned at the docks and airports. The lovely Ellen Hill had shunned her amorous politician (and our generous benefactor) to interview Cuban refugees arriving from Havana by the hundreds at Moissant Airport. I was our man behind the typewriter, struggling to make coherent for our newspaper clients the story of Castro's revolution as it was coming into New Orleans. Our Miami bureau had the other running account of the revolution that dumped Batista, the American gangsters, shook the Western Hemisphere, and so does to this day.

I got to Tulane stadium in time for the kickoff, my head still buzzing, but from booze, not revolution. It was a dull game won by LSU, the winning score a touchdown pass by Billy Cannon. At the end of this ordeal by alcohol and wire-service journalism I wrote the "overnight" football story and went back to bed at the Monteleone wondering whether the "Player of the Day" was Fidel Castro or Billy

Cannon. They ran together like a surrealist painting by Dali. For the long haul, however, it was Fidel. After a career in the pros, Billy was convicted in a federal court on a charge of counterfeiting and jailed. When I read the news, I remembered Leo Peterson.

My real assignment, however, was back in Baton Rouge at the statehouse where the legislators returned in a tetchy mood over racial integration, curious about the new guy in the basement press office. "You ain't one of them Communist Bolsheviks like Warren Rogers Junior are you," the state Assessor inquired of me one day early on the beat. I overcame the urge to inquire of this statesman as to whether there was any other kind of Bolshevik. I answered "no," but for years afterward puzzled over what Rogers, an AP staffer at the statehouse and, later, a star for *Look* magazine and the *New York Herald-Tribune*, had done to warrant such a magnificent designation. "I was president of the local chapter of the Wire Service Guild," explained Rogers when I came to know him. I had held the same position for our Guild chapter in Dallas, a fact better left unsaid in the "right to work" atmosphere of Baton Rouge.

"Boy, where you from—Brooklyn?" inquired Senator Willie Rainach of this son of the Confederacy not long after meeting the Chair of the Joint Legislative Committee on Segregation. He had read something suspect of integrationist sympathies in one of my dispatches. Brooklyn, apparently, was just this side of Moscow in the minds of these backwoods legislators, the channel through which Kremlin commands, for, say, school integration, were routed. I'm at a loss to explain the rational connection. The hunchback's suspicions, however, were on point.

Rainach came to the 1959 legislative session with a heavy agenda, legislation not only to prevent integration but to purge black citizens from voter registration rolls. The opposition came from Governor Earl Long, and his fight would provide the penultimate climax to his career, and, some say, the most uproarious legislative session in state history. I would miss it—UPI's "Story of the Year."

Earl Long, like Shakespeare's Brutus, was a man of mixed elements—to name a few: scoundrel, parable-ist, gambler, friend of the poor and the disenfranchised, as well as to Mafia Lords Frank Costello and Carlos Marcello, and the unequaled maestro of Louisiana politics both at the capital and elsewhere around the state. But he was wearing down even before this showdown over voter rights, and it showed. The maestro looked frayed. He appeared tense, and, for a man who liked to talk a lot, almost uncommunicative at a Christmas press reception in the governor's mansion hosted with style by his wife, "Miss Blanche." His demeanor was uncharacteristic—perhaps, I thought, due to the starched white shirt, subdued tie, and three-piece black suit he was attired in for the occasion. When I inquired, in parlor small talk, about his tastes in music, he looked up, puzzled. When I pursued—"Do you like the symphonies of Beethoven?"—he seemed confronted with a trick question, perhaps never having heard of the composer. Sure, the question was out of sync with Baton Rouge politics, but, hell, this was a Christmas party, not a federal grand jury.

More telling were his summer campaign stunts on behalf of Lloyd J. Teekell in the race for a congressional seat against McSween. Earl took to the campaign trail like a hog to slop—as he might put it—that is to say with great relish and a stock of whiskey. He mocked McSween and called him "Fishmouth." Late one evening I got a frantic call from the editor of the *Alexandria Town Crier*, a client, saying I had to man the UPI wire—right now!—and report that the governor of the Gret State was advocating sedition! As best I could put the story together, as it was told by an overly excited newsman, Long, who had tapped the whiskey all day, told a crowd gathered in the evening near the courthouse that they should go release all the prisoners in the county jail; that the real thieves were there along Main Street, in the law offices and stores, but not in the county jail. You could call it sedition. You could also call it far-out campaigning even for Earl Long, a stretch even for his style.

Rainach and his racist ally, Leander Perez, provided discord enough for Earl. But in the background there were rumbles out of *Time* magazine and the *New Orleans Times-Picayune* about illegal gambling flourishing under Long's lax administration. Bob Wagner, the *Picayune*'s statehouse reporter, and I went to one such establishment along a creek in the woods near Baton Rouge, where a gent greeted us by name and organization even before we consumed our first glass of beer. He asked if our burial policies were paid up. We got the message, left, and subsequently asked Long what he aimed to do about this gross violation of state law. Rather listlessly, he indicated nothing. "Louisianans just naturally like to gamble," said the governor, and he wasn't about to interfere. But he was needled by the surprise attention over his cavalier regard for the law.

Earl was also looking over his shoulder at Jimmie Davis, the "singing cowboy" of third-string movie fame from Shreveport and a certain rival to Long for another term as governor. A bland political aspirant, Davis's greatest claim to the statehouse was that he wasn't a Long. His claim to fame—at least so long as there are singin' gee-tar pickers—is authorship of "You Are My Sunshine." One of Long's legislators ("The difference between me and Huey is that he owned legislators. I just rent them," Earl once explained), a good ole boy from Catahoula County, invited me for a drink at the Heidelberg Hotel bar with the promise of material that would "bust the governor's race wide open." A good reporter, incidentally, could cover the statehouse from this bar, and at least one I knew, the man from the *New Orleans States*, did so, nearly always a cycle ahead of the rest of us. The race for governor was nearly two years away, but time counted every day in Louisiana until the election. Politics was a 24-hour a day operation. I bought the drinks. The explosive material turned out to be two photographs showing Jimmie Davis dancing in the arms of Lena Horne, a woman beautiful and talented enough to melt the bronze statue of Huey Long on the statehouse lawn. Race mixin'—get it? I didn't know whether to laugh or to cry. More to the point, I didn't know if the photos were real or rigged composites. I left him with an unfinished drink.

The politics of race, not the real or doctored image of Jimmie Davis race mixing with Lena Horne, busted the statehouse wide open. Ole Earl went into Rainach's Segregation Committee hearing on bills to wipe blacks off the voter rolls. He was cussing and screaming, incoherent and irrational in his speeches, they said. He was out of control. He acted no better in a speech to a joint legislative session. He had cracked up. It was national headlines. What got lost in this sensational news of a governor going bananas is that he was defending, and not very well, the rights of black citizens to vote and, so doing, defying majority white opinion in Louisiana and its racial enforcers, the Klan and the White Citizens Council. This was May 1959 and Earl wound up in a state mental hospital in Mandeville.

I read about it in the newspapers. In a spasm of good judgment and bad timing, I accepted an offer from the Associated Press in Oklahoma City in late April. It carried a raise of $10 per week plus relief from the drudgery of typing my copy into teletype tape and sending it on the UPI wires. I gave the agency two weeks notice and conferred with Harry Trimborn. With some reluctance, we agreed that an advance obituary on Earl Long was now in order. It was my last assignment for UPI.

What I wrote about Long was that for all of his sins, his gambling, shakedowns, Mafia connections, and personal indiscretions, he was a very good governor. He never tried hard to hide the indiscretions. He did his best to take care of the health, education, and welfare of the poor, and he did this with an administration staffed by honest and efficient officials. He had the vision to see an end to the old Southern order, personified by Willie and Leander. ("Whatcha gonna do now Leander? The feds have got the atom bomb.") Earl had the courage to stand against them. It was politically expedient to encourage black voters, of course. They voted for Long. But good policy and good politics are not always in conflict. Besides, it might have been more expedient for Long to join the racist reaction. Contrast Long's record with that of other Southern "moderates," William Fulbright, Orval Faubus, George Wallace—it is a short list—and you see a paragon. The myth of Earl Long was one thing, mostly true. But the fact of his governance was something else. I wrote about his administration in this obituary. As for the man, I took a line that Earl had applied to his brother Huey: "He was sui generis." Earl "went crazy" about one week after I sent his prepared obit to the New Orleans bureau ready for use on demand, and left Baton Rouge for Oklahoma City.

Over the years I've attracted funny looks from political sophisticates for offering this view of the governor I covered. So it is somewhat surprising to discover a similar judgment rendered by scholars Michael Kurtz and Morgan Peoples in their biography *Earl K. Long.* Most surprising is a valedictory by Earl's racist nemesis Willie Rainach who precipitated, as much as any individual, the fall of the House of Long. Willie, as quoted in the Long biography, said he was a good governor, "Earl Long was not vindictive. . . . One of Earl's good qualities was that he wanted everybody else in his administration to be honest. He didn't permit any level beneath himself taking money and he conducted a relatively honest administration."

NEWSMAN

LIKE SALMON DETERMINED to swim upstream, no matter the opposing current, it has been the biological impulse of minor league baseball players and wire-service newsmen working the boondocks to "make the majors"—to move up in class in competition and rewards. Unlike baseball, however, the "majors" for wire-service reporters working in Oklahoma City, Bismarck, Dallas or Des Moines were limited. There was Washington and New York or, almost beyond hope, a desk in a foreign bureau—Paris, London, Rome, Moscow, and, as it would come, Saigon.

The way up for youngish newsmen was no less difficult than the passage of salmon through the Bonneville Dam. Openings were lean and narrow and it was a zero-sum game, a few winners, many losers, a struggle far easier to fail than to pass.

The regional bureaus meant a steady, numbing routine of rewrite: first the local newspapers, then a rewrite of these rewrites for the radio wire, prose even more stripped down than the stuff we furnished small-town newspaper clients. Office work. Oklahoma City at least had a state capitol to go along with tornados, cattle stampedes, and occasional man-made disasters such as one I got out of the office to cover. It happened when the roof of a meat packing plant collapsed, leaving a sight akin to that of the bombed-out Murrah Federal Building decades later, though short—thankfully—of as many casualties.

The Associated Press, my new employer, was strict about accurate body counts, almost as demanding as it was of fairness in reporting. This accident happened in early morning. By noon bureau chief Wilbur Martin, a crackerjack destined for bigger office, wanted an "update"—the word we used meaning current status— of the death toll. I went down into the wreckage to verify the police report of a dozen dead. Fifty feet down I could see below me one poor workman alive, moaning, but barely visible under a ton of rubble; clearly he was doomed. I scrambled up from harm's way to a telephone in the plant office, oblivious to two women in a corner of the room. "Make it thirteen dead," I told the guy on rewrite. "Cops say twelve," said rewrite, reciting names of the dead. "They missed one," I said giving the name of the man I'd seen buried in concrete. With that sentence, the two women burst into hysterics of sobbing and screaming, the sound of profound pain. "Oh Daddy, Oh God," one shrieked. For a moment I thought they might strike me, the inadvertent messenger of their grief. Instead they put arms around each other while I slipped from their sight, crushed by their suffering. The memory still haunts.

Most of the bureau work could be filed under "drudgery" and "dull," but the AP was a graduate school in writing with accuracy and fairness. The dull drudgery kept hammering these fundamentals into the journeyman reporter. I learned another critical lesson in that provincial bureau: the need to listen, no matter how loopy the message and its purveyor might seem. It came from a single experience, a call one Saturday evening just as I came to my 5 P.M. shift as night editor. Wire-service bureaus, at least until the coming of "talk" radio shows, attracted nut calls and inquiries like cattle to a salt lick. Laugh if you will, but it can be proven that such calls accelerate with a full moon—just as murders and suicides increase at Christmas time. The caller, sometimes drunk, nearly always accompanied by beer-hall cowboy music, usually wanted verification of a piece of trivia. ("Hey AP, my pal says I'm full of shit. I say Garagiola caught for the Cards in the '46 series. Right?" Right.) Sometimes they made less sense, such as the one I caught that summer night in Oklahoma City.

"They are all after me," said the caller. "They want me out of it, on the street." I listened but kept my mind focused on reading the day file. Clearly this was another nut call. "Who is *they*," I asked, pro forma. "Gulf, Shell, Humble, Texaco, Standard—Big Oil," he answered. Psycho, I thought, still preoccupied with the day file. But I didn't hang up: "In that case you don't need me, you need a lawyer." "I got one," he replied. "Then you ought to go to court," I replied. "Been there," he said, "three days ago, federal court in Tulsa." At that moment I dropped the day file and quit playing games. "If that's true, if you filed a legal brief, you can bring it down and show me," I said and hung up the telephone.

An hour later, a youngish man dressed in cowboy boots, Levi's, and a straw ranch hat came through the bureau door. A bit of bulge around his midsection showed he hadn't spent all of his time in a saddle herding cattle. He walked straight to my desk and delivered a 250-page legal brief. "It's all there," he said and left. It was. Quality Oil, the cowboy's small oil company, versus Gulf Oil, Texaco, et al., a half-pound blockbuster of an antitrust action alleging these major oil companies had ganged up and conspired to price his company out of business.

Over-the-transom stories like this are as rare as Pulitzers. Why it had been overlooked by beat reporters in Tulsa on the day of its filing is most strange. I made the most of it, digesting the brief, writing and filing 450 words on the AP wires. The story led every Sunday paper in the Southwest and kept them busy months afterward covering the federal court trial. I got it, and a nice note from the bureau chief, because I hadn't brushed off a "nut." Listening to callers became a career policy, although never again with such a remarkable payoff.

I suffered no culture shock moving from coverage of the Louisiana legislature to the Oklahoma legislature. In both bodies, some legislators were very bright, others quite stupid. Venality was not unknown. The votes of at least one or two Oklahoma lawmakers could be bought with a new pair of shoes. Following the 1961 session, several went to jail, one of these being the House Speaker, a cunning fat man who ran the House and took money under the table from two competing interests—those seeking to legalize horse racing and those who aimed to legalize dog racing. The dog boys learned about the horse money and called the Feds. Sure enough, the speaker had an income tax problem. In sum, the Oklahoma legislature was about average. It brought me halfway to an understanding of Winston Churchill's description of democracy as the worst possible form of government, except for all the others. I'd learn the rest working the statehouse in Cairo, Egypt.

The most impressive member of this august body, state Senator Fred R. Harris, was a sharecropper's son from Walters with a brilliant record from the University of Oklahoma. He was honest, funny, and my age. Along with jokes, we shared ideals and became friends. Ideals? Indeed. There are cynics in both professions. But they are few. Forget the stereotype. Most newsmen and politicians want to do good. They have a notion of what "good" is about, and when performance fails to come up to their ideal they respond to correct the anomaly. It is pursuit of ideals, not wages or prestige, that kept most reporters of my generation on their beats and at their desks. Without those ideals of democratic government, the reporter is as hapless and ineffective as a combat infantryman without a rifle.

Years later, as a U.S. senator, Fred Harris was named Democratic National Chairman, compensation from Hubert Humphrey, the 1968 Democratic presidential nominee. Humphrey selected Ed Muskie instead of Harris as his vice presidential running mate. I was assigned by Hearst's Washington bureau to write a profile of my Oklahoma buddy. "Everything I know about politics, I learned in the Oklahoma State Legislature," Harris began our formal interview. I immediately closed my notebook, put away my pen, and demurred, "Fred, I can't let you say that—you'd be libeling yourself."

I LEFT OKLAHOMA for Harvard College on a Nieman fellowship in the summer of 1962, but not before a final trip to the statehouse to bid farewells. I'd come to feel affection for the place and several of its people. One of these was Joe Bailey Cobb, the squat, shrewd chairman of Senate Highways Committee from Tishomingo, a small town in the Oklahoma nethers where book-learning may have been looked down on as something fit only for city slickers.

The well-shod Cobb had the squinty eyes of a skeptic, a wheezy voice, and a fine way with the trucking lobby.

"I'm leaving Oklahoma for Harvard," I told the senator. He looked up, scrunched his face like Gabby Hayes and asked, "Wher's that at?" "You know, Harvard College, back east." He shook his head, utterly puzzled. I repeated, "Harvard College—back East." His face relaxed: "Oh, Hartford. I heard of it—that place back east where they have all them in-surance companies." We parted.

One evening on the night desk before I moved upward to the higher reaches of Journalism, a convict escaped the state prison in McAlester, got a gun, and returned to near his home in the woods of southeastern Oklahoma. There he bushwhacked and shot to death his wife, son, father-in-law, and mother-in-law. There was a man-hunt, a posse with dogs and deputies, to scour the impoverished scrub oak hills for the killer. I had an immediate vision of an AP "exclusive"—an interview with the prisoner from his jail cell. I assumed his capture. Accordingly, I promised the county sheriff "a little something extra" (a bribe) if he would arrange the interview and refuse the same to UPI. He agreed, but without any excitement. "What kind of a man is he," I asked to arouse some interest in the sheriff. "A paranoid? A psychotic?" There followed a significant pause. Then: "No. He ain't none of that psychology. He's just a mean sonofabitch." A more fitting description of evil is yet to be uttered. The dogs tracked him, the posse caught him, but he did not come back alive to the jailhouse. The sheriff didn't even apologize. "Shot trying to escape," he said. Of course. I hadn't bribed the whole posse.

Nine months in Cambridge had to be about the best time of my life, expenses paid, the company grand, the teachers—John K. Fairbank, Arthur Schlesinger, Louis Hartz, Stanley Hoffman, Henry Kissinger—examplars. I sized up the arrogant, brilliant Kissinger as a survivor of the German Army's General Staff, not a refugee from the Holocaust. The time for reading and talking was unlimited and there were bars in nearby Somerville where we could get in touch with the world outside academia. We did a lot of this. In fact, as

Larry L. King once noted, the year at Harvard was so much fun he'd like to go back and do it again sober. My friendship with fellow Fellows, Patrick Owens, Bernard (Bud) Nossiter, Bill Eaton, Dan Berger, Saul Friedman, Jack Kole, and Gene Graham, endured.

We were good professionals, at times unruly. Most of us had worked all of our lives. Now "work" was participation in a full college class load, reading, and talking—but no deadlines or clock punching. Our way was prepaid by the Nieman Foundation. Several of us, I felt certain, were selected from the American boondocks and brought to Cambridge for education in the same fashion as ancient Chinese emperors brought promising peasants to the royal court to be trained as Mandarins. At times we exasperated Louis Lyons, the Nieman curator. Once he assigned Owens, late of Pine Bluff, Arkansas, and me to meet and escort the featured speaker, A. J. Liebling, to our weekly Nieman dinner at the Signet House, a Harvard dining club. Liebling, the best writer in American journalism at that time, and the author of a classic book on Earl Long, had a room in a Cambridge Hotel. We met him in the hotel bar and promptly got carried away in drink and talk. He and I had a mutual friend, the "Black Cat," race horse handicapper for the late *New Orleans Item,* one of Liebling's sources in Louisiana. It was a splendid evening until someone realized it was past dinnertime. We stumbled into a taxi and drove through a raging snowstorm to the Signet House where, on the street outside, was a furious Louis Lyons waving his arms to express his wrath at Pat and me. He blamed us—not Joe Liebling—for the tardy arrival. We had earned his ill-will, but there were no reprisals.

In the main I studied Chinese history and Soviet politics and wrote a 7,000-word paper on the yawning political split between Communist China and the Soviet Union. Although much of the data came from CIA translations of foreign broadcasts, it would be almost another decade, and a Vietnam War, before the State Department reached a similar conclusion about the "Commie Monolith." But for all of this learning, talking, and drinking, Harvard was also the rocket shot to lift a newsman from the boondocks to the majors, in my case the foreign desk of the AP in Manhattan's Rockefeller Center.

NINE MONTHS EARLIER, enroute to Boston via New York with my wife, Peggy, and year-old daughter, Jane, I'd paused on the Jersey Palisades and looked down upon the Manhattan Towers. My heart sank. Save for one green rectangle in the middle of the tall buildings, there were no trees, only unending acres of concrete, a spectacular achievement for human enterprise, but disquieting for a country boy. I knew at that moment I could not long endure such a place and made a decision to stay in the big leagues no more than one year. And so it would be. Whatever it was—ambition or that odd biological quirk shared with salmon and ball-players—it had driven me up a dry creek.

The people were so strange and impolite, I felt lonesome for Joe Bailey Cobb. They lived in small boxes stacked on top of each other in tall graceless buildings and treated each other with less civility than we treated farm animals. But, here I was, one of them, with a wife and baby daughter in a middle-class apartment in Queens, alongside the Long Island Railroad tracks. Sleep came in lulls between passing commuter trains. Lulls were brief in early mornings and evenings. The work followed a formula so fixed one might now wonder if it could not be done with a well-programmed computer: incoming cables were edited or rewritten. The usual clichés sufficed. For example: "Revolution broke out tonight in (fill in name of country). Rebel forces with armor and artillery seized the capitol (blank) and the radio station and urged calm. The rebel leader (blank) said order was restored and promised normal relations with the United States. Washington declined immediate comment."

To my naive amazement early one morning an overnight (midnight to 7 A.M.) editor, too drunk to walk straight, took over the foreign desk in the midst of one such breaking story. Wobbling in his chair, he filed paragraph by paragraph on the AP's main national wire, a running account of this revolution. Bare facts came from a correspondent, or, more likely, a part-time stringer in the capital city. The editor's prose came naturally, as if encoded on his brain. I cannot recall the country, but it was big enough to make the "A" wire. As for myself, alas, I couldn't do as well sober. I lacked the skill of that intoxicated editor or imaginary computer. The night editor, a sour man with ulcers named Charlie Grumich, disdained my work much as he disliked my lack of appreciation for urban life. I think he regarded me as a cowboy, too wild and unfit to learn the skills of major league journalism as practiced by America's prime transmitter of news. There would be no promotion and I would keep to my word: one year in New York, no more.

Before leaving, however, there was a brush with history. My political hero, Jack Kennedy, now in the White House, had gone for the "domino" theory, an adjunct Cold War thesis which held that if the Kremlin, in cahoots with Red China, could take over one country in Southeast Asia, the surrounding territory would tumble into the Evil Empire's Communist web. Whether Kennedy really believed this theory—in 1963 there was much evidence to the contrary—or accepted it as a political shield against Republican charges of "soft on Communism" will never be known. He surely recalled the catastrophic fallout in the 1950 elections from the Republican charge that Democrats (through treason) had "lost China" to Communists. Could he survive the 1964 campaign having "lost Vietnam—and maybe the rest of Southeast Asia?"

A postwar remnant of French colonialism, Vietnam was threatened by a Communist revolution led by a charismatic, one-time U.S. intelligence operative, Ho Chi Minh. The Vietnamese wanted their country for themselves. All of my instincts as an ex-soldier and observations as a seaman in Southeast Asia said this was the flowering of another nationalist movement, and we should steer clear. This was a strong personal judgment which I expressed privately, but never allowed to enter the thousands of words I would come to write about Vietnam. Such were the journalistic strictures of that time. If a rationalization was required for such constraint, it was this: the people have elected Jack Kennedy (and subsequently

Johnson and Nixon). No democratic constituency has elected me to anything.

As seen by Washington hawks, Ho wanted the rest of Vietnam for the Commie empire. His troops had already dumped the last of the French mercenaries and taken control of the northern half of the slender tropical country. President Kennedy dispatched U.S. advisers to help save the rest, the friendly government ruling South Vietnam from Saigon. In response, AP, UPI, the *New York Times*, and other journals beefed up news bureaus in Saigon to report the action, a story brilliantly told by William Prochnau in his book *Once upon a Distant War*.

Our man in Saigon was Ngo Dinh Diem. His title was president of the Republic of South Vietnam, but his rule was that of a Mandarin despot, and a rather weak one at that—a Catholic in a Buddhist country. Our CIA and embassy were on hand with constant advice, along with our military advisers. Their big job was to get the South Vietnamese troops to fight against Commie guerrillas. Whether our men in Saigon, or Diem's own generals, decided he wasn't fit for the job is another matter for scholars to argue. What was to come of the puppet suggests all of the above.

Saturday nights were the quietest nights of the week on the AP foreign desk. Sunday papers, except for those on the West Coast, were mostly closed. I shared them with Stanley Johnson, an AP veteran of Moscow and London, who seeemed to wish that he had never left the latter. He would take charge at 4:30 P.M., read the day's news file, and soon take leave of the quiet office for a watering hole on the other side of the Avenue of the Americas. This left me alone to handle the news of the world, of which, at those hours, there was but little. I read the New York newspapers. There still remained eight of these in 1963, each distinct, all interesting—a feast for readers. Then as now the *Times* was the *Times*, a paper of record; the *Herald-Tribune* was gracefully edited and written, especially when you got to Red Smith on the sports page; the *Post* had kick-ass reporters and Murray Kempton; the *Mirror* had Winchell and Wilson, dispensers of gourmet gossip; and the tightly edited

Daily News (pronounced Daily Noose) had the acerbic Dick ("Young Ideas") Young who couldn't even be sweet to Mickey Mantle, the Yankee slugger. Saturday, November 1, 1963, was of this same routine until about 10 P.M. EST when the telephone rang. Instead of a request to settle a barroom bet ("Was Chiang Kai-shek ever a Commie like Mao whatszis name?"), the call came from Saigon. The AP reporter, Roy Essoyan, asked for authorization to spend several hundred dollars for photographs of the bodies of Diem and his brother-in-law/gray eminence, Ngo Dinh Nhu. I dropped a *Daily News* story about a mob killing in Brooklyn's Cobble Hill and bolted upright: "The bodies of who?" The reporter repeated the names and his request, sounding a little woozy, as will befall soldiers or reporters with too much work and nerves and too little sleep. "Hell, yes. Get the pictures, but for God's sake first give me the story." Diem and Nhu, victims of a coup by their generals, were taken for a ride, Cobble Hill style, in an armored personnel carrier, and shot to death.

I filed the story, each paragraph as a separate bulletin, on the national wire, apparently getting the news to our clients before his men in Saigon could notify President Kennedy. The biggest foreign news story of that autumn was done when Stanley Johnson returned from his hiatus shortly before quitting time, 11:30 P.M. He read the dispatch, recognized what he had missed, and discolored. I thought he might have a heart attack. In any event, he sobered on the spot.

President Kennedy did not have long to live after the passage of President Diem. At one P.M. (CST) November 22, he was pronounced dead at Parkland Hospital in Dallas, victim of gunshots by an assassin or, as likely, assassins, as he rode through the city streets in a motorcade. I heard the death bulletin on a radio in my bathroom in Queens, where I was trying to heal a killer hangover from the previous evening on the town. Like most Americans, I cried. But not all. The night on the town was spent with well-to-do friends from Kentucky, socialite car dealers in New York for a convention. Part of their conversation was to tease me and disparage the president as "Nigger lovers." Knowing the temper of American racists, and aware of Kennedy's historic civil rights legislation still before the Congress, I figured him as a martyr to racial integration. The heart of this legislation would prohibit discrimination in public accommodations—no more "whites only" designations for hotels, toilets, and drinking fountains. It would become law the following summer due to the will of President Johnson and the legislative skill of Warren Magnuson, the modest senator from Washington State. Some say it was tribute to the martyred Kennedy.

The assignment of this evil to racists lasted about 48 hours. At noon on Sunday I sat in my kitchen, listening to the play of steel on wheels from the adjacent railroad track and watching television coverage of the alleged assassin, Lee Harvey Oswald, as he was being moved from the Dallas jail. With policemen on both sides, Oswald's face came clear on the TV screen. He had the look of a snarly infantryman, compensating for a lack of heft with a scowl and swagger. As I watched, a figure loomed from a clot of bystanders bearing a snub-nosed revolver. In an instant he fired into the prisoner's stomach. Oswald folded at the midsection, his scowl twisting into an expression of excruciating pain. He was dead shortly thereafter.

Once composed from the shock of a "live" murder, television began to talk of the man who came out of the crowd, the killer. They soon had a name—"Jack Ruby," a nightclub operator, police buff, well known as a character about town. And then a picture—a balding fat man with a ferret's face. Jack Ruby. Damned if the name didn't sound familiar, and there was something about the face and his occupation. My coffee got cold as I watched the television and, without thinking why, I discovered myself pinching my upper lip with thumb and forefinger. This happened unconsciously and continued until I made the connection: Ruby was the gangster with whom I'd spent an evening in Dallas, the striptease entrepreneur who wanted to hire Ben Phelper as a bouncer; the guy who showed Phelper how to handle "rowdy broads" using my upper lip as an instructional tool.

With that realization, I dressed, ran to the subway station in Queens, emerged on 54th Street, and ran three more blocks to the AP newsroom in Rockefeller Center. Sam Blackman, the tall, gray general news editor of the Associated Press, stood in its center, presiding over a corps de news editors, filing on a half dozen different wires with variations on a single story, the Kennedy assassination. He was calm. I was not. The vast room was rather noisy when I burst into its midst and grabbed Blackman from a telephone: "Sam, Jack Ruby is a gangster. I think—I have good reason to think that he's hooked up with the mob." Blackman calmed me before I could say more. "It's okay," he said. "We've got Bernie Gavzer going to Dallas to get the story on Ruby." Gavzer was an ace on the news-features desk where new clichés were tolerated. But he did not know Big D. His story on Jack Ruby reflected a Dallas party line: a harmless character who hung around the cop shop and presided over stripteasers Candy Barr and, more recently, Tutti Frutti. It was not convincing. When the Warren Commission reported that Ruby killed Oswald in order to spare Mrs. Kennedy the ordeal of bearing witness in a trial, I laughed. So far as I could tell from an evening with Ruby in his lair, the only sign of a gentleman's sensitivity was a display of affection for his cat. Women were "broads," flesh for his nightspots. Jack Ruby's involvement in the crime of the century suggested mobsters, not racists. I remain convinced, although shy of further evidence.

Four years later after I'd left New York for Hearst's *Seattle Post Intelligencer*, I was stunned by a page one headline: Clay Shaw indicted by a New Orleans grand jury for conspiracy to murder President John Kennedy. To put this mildly, the man I knew as director of the New Orleans International Trade Mart did not appear capable of conspiring to kill a rabbit, despite an exotic lifestyle. But there it was and behind the headline an investigation by the prosecutor, Jim Garrison, resulting in charges wild enough to inspire Hollywood film director Oliver Stone, if not to convince a New Orleans jury. Shaw walked.

Jim Garrison wrote a book about this bizarre side of the death of the president, *On the Trail of the Assassins*, which quotes former CIA director Richard Helms as saying Shaw had, indeed, been a "parttime contact" person for the agency traveling in and out of the country. This was information Garrison didn't have at the time of Shaw's trial. Otherwise, it would have added substance to his charge that rogue elements of the CIA played a role in the killing of Kennedy, the contention in Stone's film *JFK*.

The film has been widely condemned as blasphemy and Stone scorned for its execution. But in the last analysis, the book upon which it is based—in this man's judgment—has more credibility than the official Warren Commission report. That is sad to say, because it suggests the Kennedy case has yet to be closed. For that matter, the grief of many Americans over Kennedy's loss is unfinished. Our political optimism has never recovered.

An artistic—if that's the word for it—failure in New York, I took a writing-editing job with Phil Bailey, publisher of the *Argus*, a weekly in Seattle. Driving away from the city toward the Pacific was about the happiest day of my life. The compensation for having struck out in "the majors" would be overwhelming. "If you want to go West, head East," said the Chinese sage Lao-tse, an ironic lesson I didn't think much about until I got past Chicago and onto the plains and up to the mountains. After a false start, I was heading home.

I had a marvelous two years with Bailey, a political maverick who ran a weekly publication to suit his own eclectic tastes: politics, business, and arts. Bailey greeted dissent, and its camp follower, argument, with something akin to joy. And there was a lot of joy around this sheet because he never employed writers who agreed with his sometimes conservative opinions. Instead he had Ron Abel in Portland, Murray Morgan in Tacoma, Mike Layton in Olympia, and myself—all shaped by the Depression and western liberalism. We raised hell in the 1960s by promoting trade with "Red China"— a heresy just short of treason—but we never raised enough money for a significant pay hike. Accordingly, I went back to work for Hearst as political writer on the *Seattle Post-Intelligencer*, my home base for the next 27 years between stints in the Middle East, Washington, D.C., and the state capital, Olympia.

OLYMPIA

THERE WAS MUCH to expose when I debuted in Olympia for the *Seattle Post-Intelligencer*, nothing like the relatively open pay-offs in Louisiana and Oklahoma, but a more subtle, thus more interesting, kind of game between politicians and the special interests.

All statehouses and their legislatures have much in common— a rough mixture of altruism, venality, petty feuds. They move fast, when they move at all, almost all of the significant moves out of sight until final action. Good reporters learn to divine their plays by carefully watching their players, the way a defensive football line-man watches a pulling guard's twitches to signal the direction of an offensive play.

More complicated is the matter of what makes a good reporter in such an environment. It is a complicated mix of curiosity and zeal of the hunt based on a will to try to do good for the less powerful in our democratic society by keeping them informed of the forces that would do them ill. The good reporter has a calling, not a profession, and conducts himself within the severest strictures of fairness and factual accuracy. Otherwise, he is a stenographer or, worse, a propagandist. He must develop sources and, to do so, he must be trusted and he must be fair. It is no place for an ideologue or a back-stabber. The relationship between reporter and statehouse workers and politicians is symbiotic: They have stories they want to place in print; the reporter seeks news to inform his readers, the democracy. He must care about the democracy and he must work hard. Given those "musts," sources will gravitate to his confidence. Tricky as this relationship may be, a reporter without sources is at the mercy of handouts and press conferences, the apparatus of a self-serving politician or special interest.

Tricky? Unless he comes with sufficient written documents, the source is merely the first step to a news story. The tip must be verified and refined, depending on the size and breadth of the information, usually a matter of several weeks of interviews and record searches. The reporter must always keep in mind that the source he has come to like or admire may be the person he will later be forced to uncover and send to jail. That sobering recognition tends to inhibit close friendship between reporter and source. To my embarrassment, I stepped over the unwritten line once, briefly investing hard-earned cash from a book-writing project in an investment club which included one member of the state legislature. The legislator had his money in a blind trust. My editors were informed and had no objections. Nevertheless, hostile legislators made an issue of it— an embarassment and doubly so since the investment never earned a penny.

Olympia's shady business often had the cover of real estate deals or, more exotic, a Chinese money laundry—either Seattle's Chinatown or across the Pacific in Hong Kong. In Olympia as elsewhere, the key stories began with leads from sources. Politicians aiming to make a financial killing from their public trust do not issue press releases. Good reporters treat handouts as no more than an introduction to a story and, as such, probably misleading. If handouts provided the whole story, the Creator would not have given us wastepaper baskets.

In 1970 working off a tip from an official in Seattle government and working with an aggressive TV reporter, Don McGaffin, we uncovered a land scheme by three members of the state Legislative Highways Interim Committee, all proper and respectable Republicans. This was a time before TV "news" abandoned any pretext of statehouse coverage. The committee had authorized construction of a "Dream Freeway" in a fast developing suburban area east of Seattle. This much was public knowledge. But the Republican trio had quietly purchased for $243,000 a ranch that would be close to the dream road. The purchase was hidden to the general public and to their constituents.

The state had yet to adopt public disclosure laws in 1970, so connecting the new ownership of the Alder Springs Ranch and the three legislators took luck and weeks of courthouse research, since ownership was recorded in the name of a fourth partner, not a member of the legislature. Alas, one of the partners, a pompous, teetotaling state senator, had signed his name to a note on earnest money for the land. He literally recoiled, unbelieving, when I told him of the lapse. The story headlined the *P-I* a few days later. All three legislators brayed innocence at the charge of a conflict of interest. Two of them sued for a $4 million libel judgment, a case subsequently dropped. And curtains, too, on all three political careers.

Even more complicated, and instructive of the ways of the legislative demimonde, was the investigation leading to the downfall of state senate Majority Leader August Mardesich, a Democrat. It began in all innocence when Paul Kraabel, a Republican representative from Seattle with an eye for the curious, showed me a three-line amendment to a measure dealing with garbage haulers. The amendment was proposed by Senator Mardesich, a legislator of charm and brilliance. Kraabel asked if I could decipher the amendment's significance. I couldn't—it looked as innocent as Kraabel himself. "But the Republican House caucus [a majority at that time] has locked up on it," he said. "It must pass." Equally puzzled, I put the amendment in a coat pocket and, for a year, forgot all about it.

The mystery began to unravel in the 1973 legislative session when a tape recording of a meeting of state garbage haulers leaked out of a power struggle between Mardesich and Senator Robert Greive, both Democrats, for control of the state senate—in real politics, a struggle for control between business and banks (Mardesich) and the state's powerful labor lobby (Greive). Public policy rides on the outcome of such legislative struggles; in this case, less regulation and taxation for business, or more labor-promoted accountability for business. Big stakes for a relatively small state.

The tape was at least a year old when it came to the hands of Mike Layton, my *P-I* colleague, a peerless statehouse reporter. It captured garbage haulers discussing plans to raise $20,000 to pay Mardesich for passage of that innocuous looking, three-line amendment. The micromeasure would have required cities to buy out all equipment of an operating authority if it chose to take over garbage hauling from a private operator. Its effect would be to make the price of a takeover prohibitive. The little measure had a lot of lives. Approved in 1971, it was vetoed by the governor. Resurrected in 1972, the Republican House majority agreed to move the measure into the Senate where Mardesich was now majority leader—but only for a price.

That price, a source inside the House GOP Caucus told me, was the majority leader's support for a Republican-based redistricting bill, the measure that draws new legislative district lines to fit the new federal census figures. As a rule, such lines will result in bringing about Democratic or GOP majorities in the legislature. They also may determine the political life or death of incumbents—and nothing is quite so dear to a legislator as reelection.

Our story, January 12, 1973, blew the deal wide open, probably resulting in a change from redistricting by the legislators to redistricting by a select commission and nonpartisan geographers. It also resulted in a federal indictment of Senator Mardesich for filing a false income tax report. His trial revealed contributions to a "dump Greive" campaign fund, some of it stashed in a Cutty Sark whiskey box. Mardesich was acquitted, but before he left the courtroom Judge Charles Renfrew told the senator and the court: "Mr. Mardesich, you are a very fortunate man. There is sufficient evidence in the record to convict you of the charges." Lucky in court, the once powerful senator was not lucky enough to win reelection. Whatever his sins, I greatly admired Senator Mardesich's skill as a legislator.

And I never wasted much time puzzling over the motivation of sources. They varied from case to case—from abject revenge to righteous altruism. Two stories stick out. Lenny Boeckelman, a hustler on his way to a federal prison to serve a felony conviction, paused to give me documents describing deals between state Speaker of the House Leonard Sawyer and Papua New Guinea. Sawyer set himself up as "the man to see" in order to do business with the new Pacific nation. Star Kist tuna paid him a sum to prevent New Guinea natives from hurling spears at their South Pacific fishermen. When his business with Sawyer went sour, Boeckelman repeatedly stated he aimed to "get even with the little sonofabitch." He did. The news stories prompted Sawyer's retreat from the legislature after he was deposed as House Speaker.

At the other motivational extreme, a government worker gave me documents sealed by a Superior Court judge detailing the flawed construction of a fleet of Puget Sound ferryboats—the stuff of a dozen columns and the call for a grand jury investigation which, alas, never materialized. This person felt a responsibilty to the taxpayers rather than to those providing immediate employment. It was a daring person, risking the loss of a job, if not bodily harm. I maintain the trust.

In 1975, House Bill 435 cast a klieg light on the dark side of legislative life, along with a cascade of federal indictments and jail terms. The measure would have allowed the state's privately owned utilities to charge ratepayers, instead of stockholders, for the cost of construction in progress. It anticipated the extravagant cost of building nuclear power plants. HB 435 rushed through the 1975 legislative session in Olympia as though gifted by the Gods of Democracy, or perhaps by something more earthly: payoffs.

Don Brazier, a former legislator turned brave chairman of the state's Transportation and Utilities Commission, the body regulating private utilities, called the bill a "consumer ripoff." He had noted the undue haste with which it passed the legislature. With ample reason to suspect a fix, Mike Layton and I began to ask questions. We got no answers, not even the hint of a leak from a federal grand jury, until the indictment and flight from a federal charge by Representative Robert Perry, de facto leader of the House Democratic Majority. Like Mardesich, Perry was brilliant and effective and a figure far less than a model for honest government. Despite this I liked him.

A rough and tumble union strongman, Perry was, like myself, an ex-merchant seaman. As a seafaring mercenary, he had been hired to transport survivors of European concentration camps into Palestine, where they would help create the State of Israel. We had several conversations about the fate of Israel and the plight of those dispossessed by its creation, the Palestinians. He warned me of the danger of dealing with Palestinians. This was an unusual background for the making of a state politician. More improbable was Perry's taste for classical music—a rarity among politicians, I've observed. (Jack Kennedy preferred Lerner and Loewe.) His office resonated with the concertos of Rachmaninoff and études of Chopin. Perry was the prime mover of HB 435. You didn't have to be Sherlock Holmes to understand that whatever happened to speed the passage of HB 435, Bob Perry was the key. He was also, as I came to know, a flawed crook—that is, a crook with a conscience.

I knocked on doors from Seattle to San Francisco searching for Perry, who had skipped out on a half-million-dollar bail. Ex-girlfriends, former political handymen, and the business agents of the Marine Engineers along the West Coast professed ignorance of the fugitive's whereabouts. At least one of these is certain to have passed the word that I, like the FBI, was in pursuit.

The call came in the midst of the *Post-Intelligencer*'s morning editorial board conference. I took it on a telephone in the city room. The caller identified himself as Bob Perry's friend and bodyguard and said that under certain conditions the legislator wanted to return to Seattle and surrender himself to federal authorities. What conditions? For openers Perry wanted me to meet him at an airstrip near Port Moody, British Columbia, listen to the tale of his flight, make a deal for his security, and accompany him to the federal courthouse. It took me a few seconds to agree to those terms, another hour to arrange wherewithal from the newspaper and charter a private airplane.

Why me? He trusted my ability to report his confession, and to cut a fair deal with federal officials on his postsurrender security. Having authored with Layton a series of news articles on the monies spent and strategies employed by the private utilities to overcharge consumers and mold public opinion to their private interests, Perry knew of my knowledge about the darker side of the utilities business. I needed no education. Nor did my newspaper, which printed these unflattering pieces in the face of potentially powerful opposition from the business community. He needed a good newspaper as well as a good reporter for what he was about to do.

Jack Doughty, a newspapering holdover from *The Front Page*, and the *P-I*'s executive editor, agreed to come along and witness this unusual journalistic business—a federal fugitive surrendering to a newsman, but not before telling all. Telling all was Perry's way of taking out a life insurance policy; the tale told to a newspaper would lessen the need for his assassination. With ample reason, according to his bodyguard, Perry feared an attack on his life from past associates out of Baltimore or Chicago.

The outlaw was sitting in the back seat of a car parked alongside the airport at Port Moody, a small concrete-block office, pay telephone, and Coke machine about 30 miles east of Vancouver, where we had to clear Canadian customs. A big, serious looking man, in a waist-length jacket escorted us from our rented Cessna to the auto. The jacket bulged too much on one side, not a smooth fit for an Uzi submachine gun. This was Perry's bodyguard, and his eyes kept moving around the airstrip like the headlight on a high speed passenger train. He said there had already been two attempts to kill Bob Perry.

While the gunman stood guard, we listened to Perry's tale: Washington Water Power, the private utility based in Spokane, put up the payoff money for HB 435, which Perry proceeded to launder in Hong Kong and then return to Olympia via Vancouver. There he handed the cash to Jerry Buckley, Water Power's corporate secretary and Olympia lobbyist. Perry was complex. So was this money laundry. As Perry explained: Tyee Construction, another firm with which he was affiliated, kicked back ten percent of its contracts with Water Power to the Spokane utility. Perry would carry these checks to Hong Kong, where his main contact, one Sammy Lee, would convert them to cash. Lobbyist Buckley used about $30,000 of the laundry haul to speed passage of HB 435.

After 18 months on the fly, apparently all of it in Costa Rica, where, according to his bodyguard, persons unknown made two attempts to kill him, Perry said he was coming home to let the public know he had "whored and sold his soul" for Washington Water Power and for Knoerle Bender Stone, a Baltimore construction outfit building the new West Seattle bridge across the Duwamish River, under a contract greased with kickbacks to at least two public officials: "I've screwed the public long enough. They need to know the whole story. . . . I was a tool in the hands of some very sophisticated people. Now I'm here because I'm sick of it. I don't mind spending [prison] time for it, but I want to let the public know."

He talked of his public sins for two hours with only one interruption, another condition to be met before his surrender: Perry wanted assurance of federal protection, a safe jail, and a fake name. He also demanded that I accompany him into the courthouse and through the surrender process, mugshot, and fingerprints. I used the idle pay telephone to negotiate with a high federal official, who agreed to meet Perry's terms of surrender.

"Let's go," he said when I returned to the car. The bodyguard, still wearing his jacket despite the May heat, walked me to the airplane: "He's now in your care. If anything happens to him I'll hold you responsible." I lied to get Perry past U.S. Customs officers at Seattle-Tacoma International Airport. They were skeptical about his lack of luggage. "He's a civil engineer returning from a job in Central America," I lied. "You know how it is with these high priced engineers. They don't have to carry luggage." The official then wanted to know if Perry, the liberal legislator with a touch of larceny, a fugitive wanted on a federal arrest warrant with bail set at $500,000, brought in any "fruits and vegetables." I had to fight the impulse to laugh.

Having slipped past Customs, strictly speaking whilst harboring a fugitive, Doughty and I had to bang on the door of the federal courthouse and shout for guards to let us inside. It was early in the evening. Even Perry laughed at the spectacle. When finally aroused, I thought the two marshals would faint at the sight of their captive. But they recovered, handcuffed and booked Bob Perry. The Feds stuck to their agreement, a safe jail, up Interstate 5 in Everett, and a false name for their chief witness in the trials and convictions of officials of Washington Water Power and Seattle officials connected with Knoerle Bender Stone's building of the West Seattle bridge. A case of payoffs galore.

Perry pleaded guilty of income tax evasion and prepared for prison. At his sentencing the judge asked if, in fact, Perry had not come home to surrender because of the attempts on his life in Costa Rica. Fred Tausend, the brilliant attorney working to secure a lesser prison sentence for his client, thought he saw chances melt. Before Tausend could reply, Perry interrupted to answer, "No sir. I decided to surrender in order to come home and clear my conscience by telling the truth." The judge was convinced. Perry got two years at a white collar prison in Pensacola, Florida.

The former legislator had also come home with the allegation of a payoff by two Asian bagmen of $20,000 in the usual $20 bills to himself and the House Speaker Len Sawyer. They wanted help for a Japanese chemical factory in Seattle. Perry was specific in details of the bagmen's visit: time, place, and accuracy of the sum, carefully counted. Layton repeated each specific when he questioned the Speaker: Did you in the company of Representative Perry on the night of April 21, 1975, at 205 Plum Street, Olympia, Washington, receive $20,000 in $20 bills, then proceed with Perry to the bathroom to count the money, and, if so, have you any comment? There was a pause before my colleague hung up the telephone.

"What did he say," I asked.

"He said, 'It doesn't ring a bell,'" Layton answered. Indeed, the legislative leader was never charged.

THE FLIP SIDE of such political scandal could be summed up in one legislative session in Olympia in 1970, when an exceptionally effective governor, Dan Evans, proposed and then got the legislature to approve the heart of the state's environmental protection laws. In the same session Evans's fellow Republicans worked a kind of democratic magic by winning passage of the nation's first law legalizing a woman's right to an abortion. It all happened in 32 days. So much for legislative lethargy.

Senator Joel Pritchard, a Republican, introduced his bill legalizing abortion on January 13, 1970. The unsympathetic presiding officer assigned it to the Judiciary Committee, or, as the newspapers put it, "assigned it to oblivion"—the fate of about 99 percent of all bills introduced. William Gissberg, an abortion foe, chaired Judiciary. So observers noted. What they did not perceive was the popularity of this radical measure, or the zeal of its proponents, liberal churchmen like Seattle Unitarian Pastor Peter Raible and organizations promoting women's rights. Nor did they recognize the legislative skill of Pritchard, a rare politician, one able to subsume his ego into his work, staying shy of TV cameras, giving credit to others, and emerging with legislative victory. An upbeat, extroverted college athlete and infantry veteran of World War II, Pritchard worked quietly behind the scenes while others raged pro and con over the abortion issue. The arguments are now clichés.

The "woman's right to chose" won the battle in the House of Representatives over the "voices for the unborn." Getting it through the Senate and its muscular bloc of Catholic members required all of Pritchard's guile and the muscle of his friend, Evans, the state's chief executive.

At the peak of the debate, two legislative staffers, veterans of the Vietnam War, and, of that evening, too many bottles of beer, argued how to reform the legislature's upper chamber, thinking not only of Senator Mardesich and other wheeler-dealers, but of a sizable bloc of whiskey soaked drones. The solution: one 60-pound TNT satchel charge inside each caucus chamber to be detonated after select, incorruptible members were invited outside. Several Democrats made this hypothetical list and quite a few Republicans, including Pritchard. A few days later when I privately informed Pritchard of this honor, he did not smile. He frowned. "Not when I get through passing this abortion bill," he said, an apparent reference to backroom deals. "They won't ask me outside."

Whatever this great legislator did, it worked. The nation's first law to allow an abortion on the consent of the woman and her doctor passed the Senate 25 to 23 and went on to win approval of a referendum of the people by an overwhelming majority. "I've been put through a wringer," said Senator Gissberg, one of the more skilled legislative operators, when the matter was finished. Pritchard rarely mentioned his legislative achievement and never boasted of it.

Israeli bombing raids on Cairo shared a front page of the *Post-Intelligencer* one January day with names of legislators who voted behind closed doors in the House Natural Resources Committee to kill Governor Evans's shorelines protection bill. Closed doors or open doors, nothing is ever really secret in a state legislature if it is watched by a tough inquisitive press. That's a mammoth "if" in these days of soft journalism and hard-core entertainment. Next evening Evans went on statewide television to chastise the "no" voters. A few days later the committee reconvened to reconsider its vote. Message received, Shorelines Protection emerged "do pass" from committee and became the law protecting the state's thousands of miles of shoreline from predatory commercialism.

Evans was an effective governor through the use of his office muscle—to be crass about it, the power to appoint judges and members of commissions—and his use of the public pulpit, television and newspapers being most effective. If Huey Long "owned" legislators and his brother Earl "just rented them," Evans used the tools of his office and his power to arouse the public to its better senses. There was another difference. Evans was incorruptible.

And so are an overwhelming majority of legislators I've encountered covering state capitals, the most challenging and rewarding work a journalist can undertake. Unlike the Congress, a most deliberative body, legislatures tend to move pell-mell, giving the observer scant time to watch, the conniver ample opportunity for mischief. Even worse, the current newspaper neglect of statehouses—barring a sex angle—is a journalistic scandal. As disdain of federal government grows, the importance of statehouses increases, a sad fact forgotten or ignored by newspapers. Never mind television, which long ago discovered that "news" is entertainment, in marginally different wrapping.

Fortunately, most citizens come to the state capitals to "do good" as they see it, more given to altruism than personal greed. In general they are practical and flexible within their personal beliefs. In almost all the cases I've watched, those who are exceptions to the rule of pragmatism are shunted to one side of the body to exercise their one vote. To borrow a metaphor from football, legislatures are no place to regularly perform the 98-yard touchdown run. Joel Pritchard's remarkable achievement is a rare exception. To get back to the line of scrimmage without being thrown for a loss is to do well. To gain an inch—help pass a piece of favored legislation—is to do very well. Legislators learn this, or get out.

I remain a politician lover and a lover of their game, especially as it is played in the "bush leagues" of state capitals. This is why: for most legislators, politics ceases to be personal and egos tend to subdue rather than swell. There are obvious exceptions, witness Earl and Huey Long. But most of them quickly learn that the fellow or lady opposing their bill today may be a vote in their favor on the next roll call; that, smart as they are, there is another individual— maybe more than one—with equal or better knowledge and skill.

This general relinquishing of personal politics works for the common good. It is the essence of democracy. From time to time, ideological absolutists gather a legislative faction of sufficient size and zeal to sway, if not dominate, public policy. Fundamentalist Christians—or so-called Christians—had such influence in the 1990s. But they also go, giving way to pragmatists—or so we must hope at the century's end. We've suffered enough from their zeal in the past hundred years.

1968

"WILD TRIP," says my notebook at the end of it, March 6, 1968. Air Force One had just landed at Andrews Air Force Base near Washington, D.C., disgorging its human cargo, President and Mrs. Lyndon Johnson, the chairman and members of the Joint Chiefs of Staff, all four-star generals, and a half dozen reporters, representing newspapers, magazines, and television, the White House press pool for the last leg of the wild trip.

We had flown in from Ramey Air Force Base, Puerto Rico, having left Washington, D.C., a week earlier, then flying to Houston, Texas, Beaumont, Texas, and Marietta, Georgia. Each time we boarded the two Boeing 707s, one bearing the president, another the press, we were left ignorant of our destination. Each time we figured almost certainly that it would be Vietnam, until we got the straight word after "wheels up." The trip was not only wild. It was bizarre, a function of the tormented whim of President Johnson, himself a hapless victim of events already unfolding in 1968.

The press pool's task was to travel a bulkhead away from the president on Air Force One, talking with Johnson or his aides and, finally, to brief the other reporters, flying behind on the other 707. This last leg gave the pool something prophetic to relate. It came straight from the president himself and when it did we all laughed. It was inconceivable on March 6, 1968, that Lyndon Johnson would not be a candidate for the Democratic nomination to the presidency. So, we were foolish.

I had come from Seattle early in January on temporary duty in the Washington Bureau of Hearst Newspapers, a crackerjack news group headed by Bob Thompson, a Capital veteran, and starring Marianne Means and Leslie Whitten. Elsewhere, the nation was in turmoil over Vietnam and growing violent with protests against the war and against racial discrimination. It was already an ugly time. Johnson's administration was anguished and uncertain about what to do. We had no inkling that the anguish and uncertainty would accelerate until the November elections; that the wild ride would become a metaphor for one of the wildest years in American politics.

Since I was the lone Washington staffer without family to tend, and able to take leave on an hour's notice, Thompson assigned me to the White House beat soon after Johnson began making what he called "surprise" trips. The first of these came on February 18 when the leader of the free world went to Fort Bragg, North Carolina, to tell our soldiers "it is your duty to defend freedom."

By that dubious phrase he meant fight in Vietnam on behalf of a U.S. puppet government. There, two weeks earlier, the Tet offensive by Viet Cong and North Vietnamese troops had penetrated the grounds of the U.S. Embassy in Saigon and shattered American confidence in our conduct of the war. It would never be restored. Yet this apparent defeat seemed to brighten Johnson's candle. He became more belligerent. His generals called for a U.S. commitment of another 206,000 troops to back the war as a "strategic reserve." News of this quickly leaked into print.

Tet was a catastrophe. The North Koreans' seizure of our electronic spy ship, the USS *Pueblo* on January 23 was a major crisis. The ship's master and crew were imprisoned. Trouble began to avalanche the administration in January. The talented singer Eartha Kitt left Mrs. Johnson in tears at a White House ceremony when she denounced the Vietnam War as a source of the nation's racial turmoil, the force driving young Americans to drop out of school and smoke dope.

From the press gallery in the House of Representatives we watched President Johnson walk through his state of the union address like an actor with bad lines and little enthusiasm. He called for $10 billion for a war on poverty. He looked tired. The newspaper columnists were writing about a feud between the president and Senator Robert Kennedy and, as its corollary, a possible Kennedy run for the Democratic presidential nomination.

Why not? Distress over Vietnam, most visible in street protests against it, fertilized American politics in 1968. Out of this came nine serious contenders for the presidency. The themes of their campaigns reflected the conflicting attitudes of the people, as in "Peace Now" and "Law and Order." We were tugged between "doves" and "hawks." One of the latter candidates, we overconfidently assumed, was Lyndon Johnson.

As a reporter, I have rarely been so well positioned as during the first three months of 1968. I had a seat on the press bus covering the New Hampshire primary election, and a desk, telephone, and typewriter in the White House East Room. It was not an ordinary time. Teddy White, a great reporter and sometime companion, had made campaign coverage glamorous with his account of the 1960 presidential race, *The Making of the President*. Those of us following candidates had Teddy's model reportage in mind. It made us adhere to campaign details that otherwise might have been dismissed. But nothing I would experience in campaigns before or after could match travels with President Johnson.

The manic quality of those trips matched the confusion in Washington, D.C., about what to do with Vietnam. A year earlier the question came under intense discussion in the Oval Office between the president and his Senate Democratic leadership. William Fulbright said "get out." George Smathers said our troubles came from "dissident voices here which encourage our enemies to resist." John Pastore, a liberal's liberal, said if negotiations don't work Johnson should use his "Sunday punch"—presumably atomic bombs. Vice President Hubert Humphrey, in a hint of his campaign to come, is recorded as having said nothing. During this meeting, the president kept his own counsel.

There was no such silence elsewhere. Vietnam created a mixed chorus of rhetoric, nowhere more vocal than in New Hampshire, battleground for national convention delegates, the nation's first presidential primary election in 1968.

Richard Nixon, arising from the political dead in California, arrived in Manchester, New Hampshire, on February 1, mingling that evening with political reporters sent to cover the primary. He was most cordial, drink in hand, addressing all questioners. These included George Packard of the *Philadelphia Bulletin*, Haynes Johnson of the *Washington Post*, Bob Semple of the *New York Times*, and me working out of Hearst's Washington Bureau. When last seen on a public stage Nixon had been a loser in the California governor's race. "You won't have me to kick around anymore," he told reporters, some of whom actually had so treated "Tricky Dick." He was not popular. Now he was mixing with the enemy, allowing, "I must demonstrate [in New Hampshire] that I can win."

The former vice president also said he had a plan to end the war in Vietnam. Packard pursued the issue, noting an article on Vietnam in *Foreign Affairs* magazine, October 1967, under Nixon's byline. The candidate told the reporter that Dwight Chapin, an aide, and not himself, had written the piece. "He's standing right over there," said Nixon, pointing across the hotel ballroom. "Go ask him about Vietnam." If Nixon had a plan for Vietnam, it was much the same as the current administration's theme pushed by Secretary of State Dean Rusk and vigorously supported by Senator Henry Jackson: The world wouldn't be safe until China turned from imperial ambitions. Nixon was saying that the war in Vietnam wasn't a civil war, but an extension of Chinese imperialistic adventuring. It was not, but American policy at that time generally agreed with Nixon. Nor did Nixon's ideas contain any semblance of a plan to get our soldiers out of Vietnam.

Nixon's main pitch was a soft-ball, white collar appeal to law and order and its faintly disguised sidekick, racism. The raw, unvarnished approach to racism and "law and order" came a few weeks later when Alabama Governor George Wallace entered the race, as he put it, "shaking the liberals to their eyeteeth." Wallace promised to "indict every person advocating a Viet Cong win in Vietnam on our college campuses" and to "let the Joint Chiefs of

Staff win the war militarily." The nation was polarized, or worse. As the March 1 landmark report of the Kerner Commission on race declared, there were two societies, "white and Black."

Yet that night in Manchester was a good start for Nixon, a pleasant evening for all of us. We would see little of the Californian thereafter. He introduced a new campaign style, appearing before select audiences once a day in closed studios suitable for television. It was campaign hide and seek as far as the press was concerned. Nixon wasn't that concerned about the press. TV carried his message with the image of approving audiences around the state. Much of the time he rested. Covering Nixon was so relaxed, I took off one day, rented skis and slid around on New Hampshire's ice slopes. Bob Semple wrote about the "new Nixon," a line that stuck beyond this campaign and into later decades, as the "new, new Nixon."

Senator Eugene McCarthy, a leading war critic, a major "dove" in newspaper lexicon, brought his antiwar crusade through the snow and over the hills across New Hampshire. He was clever, charming and a natural press attraction. Imagine television live from the showdown between Little David and Goliath. But the candidate who made the most sense and gave the most prescient analysis of the American crisis of 1968 was George Romney, a former car maker turned Michigan governor. A handsome Mormon with the energy of an avalanche, Romney was also the most ignored. The press of America owed him an apology. This is mine.

I followed Romney, and his chief aide, Travis Cross of Oregon, into country houses, country clubs, and small-town social clubs. Our day began before sunrise and ended just short of midnight. After one such exhausting day, I suggested to the governor that he might wish to lead the press in a couple of laps around the Manchester airport, where our small plane had just landed. He smiled and winked.

The word with which Governor Romney, presidential aspirant, will always be remembered is "brainwashed." He blew his chances by remarking, with astounding innocence, and no less accuracy, that he had been "brainwashed" by the administration on Vietnam. Thereafter "brainwashed" followed in the second or third paragraph of every Romney story—pack journalism at its destructive peak. It was a shame. In the style of Teddy White, I rank Romney with Morris Udall and Fred R. Harris as at least one of the best presidents we never had.

While Johnson, his chief military advisers, Generals Earle Wheeler and William Westmoreland, Defense Secretary McNamara and his successor, Clark Clifford, wrestled over what to do about the undoable—Vietnam—Romney precisely defined their dilemma. This was not behind the closed doors of the Oval Office but out front before ordinary people in New Hampshire.

No theoretical dancing and pussyfooting by Romney. He said: "What's happening in Vietnam shows the power of people [Vietnamese]. We're off on a military kick in Vietnam that is going to end in disaster. Either we lose the war in Vietnam or we start World War III." Fortunately for mankind, if not the American psyche, it was not the latter. We suffered the loss, but did not drop the nukes.

Trailing George Romney, I reported his words from those farm houses and Rotary Clubs to the Hearst newspapers. Yet I dimly remembered the candidate and had forgotten his verdict on our war in Vietnam until reviewing my notes for this memoir. He has deserved better.

In fairness, there was a nonmilitary side to the struggles for the hearts and minds of the Vietnamese, a push by the administration to get our (I use the word advisedly) government in Saigon to redistribute farmland in South Vietnam. It was a noble idea, indeed a copy of the Viet Cong's great success with the peasantry. It had as much chance to succeed in Vietnam as efforts by politically enlightened Southerners to repeal slavery in 1864. Slaveholders and their economic system were the foundation of the Confederacy. Large landholders formed the backbone of indigenous South Vietnamese government support. Land reform might have saved South Vietnam. Repeal of slavery might have allowed the Confederacy to become a separate nation. As realistic choices, however, both ideas were as farfetched as a squared circle.

If prescience and honesty accounted for much in politics, Romney would have won Republican votes in the New Hampshire primary. But they don't, and two weeks before the primary election the Michigan governor withdrew from the race, a candidate slain by a single word. Gene McCarthy, the "peace" candidate, went further but never spoke with such blunt force.

THE *NEW YORK TIMES* broke the story of General Wheeler's request for a 206,000 troop buildup. Wheeler called it a "contingency force of strategic reserves." But it was interpreted as more cannon fodder for Vietnam. It would be in addition to the half million American soldiers already deployed in Vietnam. The story followed General Westmoreland's declaration to the Associated Press that Tet had been a big victory for the U.S. troops under his command. This was Alice in Wonderland.

A parade of cabinet secretaries walked away from the Johnson administration in this hectic first month of 1968: Clark Clifford succeeded McNamara as defense secretary; John Gardner resigned as health, education and welfare secretary; Alexander Trowbridge quit as secretary of commerce. McNamara said the situation was out of control. It was a busy time for the White House press, usually a body under tight control. Sometimes almost surreal.

In the midst of cabinet resignations and the USS *Pueblo* crisis, Johnson entertained the Boston Red Sox baseball team, winners of the 1967 World Series. It was pro forma—a visit to the Oval Office and a photo op outside in the pressroom. But Hearst's *Boston Record American*, a blue-collar tabloid, wanted 350 words dictated fast for its early edition. I obliged and got a page one byline big enough for a blind man to read. The *Pueblo* and Trowbridge played deep inside.

More surprising than the cabinet disenchantment, we now know that ranking Democrats on the Senate Armed Services Committee, including a leading "hawk," Senator Henry Jackson, sized up political consequences of a 206,000 man buildup and said no. Jackson described their rejection as a critical influence on Clark Clifford, the new secretary of defense.

Four days on the job, Clifford, a St. Louis lawyer turned Washington lobbyist-legal meister, spent a day quizzing the Joint

Chiefs of Staff and departed "appalled" at the weakness of their military case for war in Vietnam. This too was an obvious influence on his decision against the troop buildup. Johnson met with General Wheeler on February 28 and said he was delaying a final decision.

We knew Johnson carried the weight of that decision onto Air Force One when, on a one-hour notice, we assembled at the White House to take off for parts immediately unknown. The press party included Packard of the *Bulletin*, Ted Sell of the *L.A. Times*, Max Frankel of the *New York Times*, Dan Young of the *Chicago Tribune*, Carroll Kilpatrick of the *Washington Post*, Dick Saltonstall of *Time*, Harry Kelley and Frank Cormier of the Associated Press, and me, the temporary Hearst bachelor.

Unlike earlier press trips to the Johnson ranch near Austin, where we could kill time by playing touch football (Packard's team consistently beat the one I quarterbacked), the only games we played on this bizarre expedition were at night, stress-busting parties with White House secretaries and Secret Service agents. Hangovers hung around Air Force One and its companion 707 like jet fuel fumes.

The Texas hiatus in mid-January was instructive, however. Johnson had to escape via a back door from Gregory Gym at the University of Texas to miss the wrath of protesting students: "Hey, hey, LBJ. How many troops did you kill today!" In a surprise visit to an association convention in Dallas, his first visit to that city since the slaying of Jack Kennedy, Johnson spoke of "our unshakable resolve in Vietnam." Delegates gave him a cheer, but protestors outside the hall forced Johnson and his police escort to leave through another back door.

The president of the United States, a Texan, the most progressive chief executive and effective politician since Franklin Roosevelt, had been humiliated by his own people. The lesson must have resonated with the White House as it did with reporters. The natives were restless. The nation was tearing apart.

Suspense, as well as surprise, hung over this final helter-skelter trip with the president. Would he order up another 206,000 troops? Would we go on from the Houston Space Center, our first stop, to

Vietnam? We did not. Instead, we flew 100 miles east in a 550-mph jet to Beaumont, Texas, where Democratic loyalists filled a motel banquet hall to raise money and honor Representative Jack Brooks. The room was murky with smoke, and noisy with loud talk. LBJ was with his kind of folks, and maybe he had pulled on the jug a few times before arriving. It didn't matter. He was home and he could speak his gut as well as his mind in cadences and vernacular in a place where there were no eastern snobs to sneer at him as a rube.

"We're going to find peace with honor," he roared. No need to explain peace where. No need for mechanical amplification. The drinking slowed, the drinkers got quiet, perhaps from respect. "We're not going to be a Quisling [sic]. We're not going to be appeasers. We're not going to cut and run! Mr. Ho Chi Minh! He was never elected to anything in his life. Now he is determined that his might makes right! That he can take that little country [South Vietnam]!" I didn't know whether to laugh or cry. Coming shortly before midnight, it was too late to file copy. Newspapers had closed their final Sunday editions. There wasn't time to report his comments on Ho Chi Minh, and how could anyone explain the misplaced reference to (Vidkun) Quisling—not an "appeaser" but worse, a Norwegian traitor and Nazi puppet—without speculating on Johnson's apparent tug on his jug?

We got three hours of sleep before a call for the next flight, which, again, did not end in Vietnam. Monday's editions of the *New York Times* corrected the president and enlightened the reader: Ho Chi Minh had, indeed, been elected to an office, chairman of the Communist Party unit in Batavia, Java, Dutch East Indies, in the 1930s before the fall of colonialism.

A much subdued, heavily guarded president christened the first rollout of a Lockheed C5A, the world's largest transport aircraft, from its factory in Marietta, Georgia. Reporters got but a glimpse of Johnson at the next stop, Ramey Air Force Base, Puerto Rico, where Air Force One parked alongside B-52 strategic bombers packing hydrogen bombs—but no war protestors. He was as secure inside this highly restricted military compound as an Iraqi dictator in Baghdad. Our stories from this travel, thus far, had labeled our unusual outing as Johnson's campaign tryout. Their content varied little: allusions to pre-Broadway theatrical previews in Boston and fourth-paragraph speculation about the military call for more troops in Vietnam. There was no hint, however, that Johnson might quit a reelection race. On the contrary.

We had a pleasant time inside this armed Lotus Land, swimming on its lovely beach, partying in its subsidized barroom. Outside, things seemed to be going to hell. Viet Cong rockets were blasting our base at Cam Rhan Bay, and the strategic city of Khe Sanh was under siege. James Reston was writing in the *Times* that the "war is going badly." And my notes kept reminding me "LBJ looks tired." I got a glimpse of him at a photo opportunity, dressed out in brown slacks, two-tone shoes, and sporty golf hat. He was heading off in a self-propelled cart to play golf. He still looked tired.

At home Gene McCarthy was gathering steam, and leading Senate critics of the war were charging the president with "deception." Ominous to the hopes of both Johnson and McCarthy, Robert Kennedy, the senator from New York, the late president's brother, was reported on the verge of a presidential race. "It is immoral and intolerable to continue the way we are in Vietnam," said Kennedy. "We should negotiate with the National Liberation Front [Viet Cong] and halt the bombing of North Vietnam as a prelude to peace talks."

Back-page news stories told of meetings in Phnom Penh between Cambodia's leader, Prince Sihanouk, his prime minister Son Sann, and the U.S. representative, Chester Bowles, who pledged our government to honor Cambodian neutrality and sovereignty and to respect its border with Vietnam. The Cambodians were distressed by U.S. incursions across that border in hot pursuit of Viet Cong. Some pledge, as it turned out. So much for honor.

At least the press was rested when roused for the next leg of this journey with Johnson. Packard and I had been selected as newspaper reporters for the press pool on Air Force One. So had the fawning Dan Young (the regular White House beat led to lucrative speaking engagements, an inducement to bootlicking). It would be my first chance to question the president face to face. Soon after takeoff, bound—surprise again—to Washington, D.C., we were invited to the airborne Oval Office, a small compartment amidship in the 707. We took the places of the Joint Chiefs of Staff. "Get up and let that boy have your seat," the commander in chief ordered a sluggish general with four stars over each shoulder, the Air Force commander. I sat in his place.

Johnson sat against the port bulkhead, beneath the seal of his office and the hovering presence of his wife, Lady Bird. Neither looked as if they had enjoyed a vacation. They looked strained, worried. The questions we asked were unsettling, dealing with opinion polls that reflected the acute unpopularity of the war in Vietnam. Johnson dismissed them as inaccurate. He was tense. So was the mood inside that compressed space. The two television poolsters, aware of the side money to be made speech making as a consequence of their status as White House correspondents, began to look as uncomfortable as the Johnsons.

The *Tribune*'s Young tried to change the subject from Vietnam to something more pleasant. His voice betrayed a case of nerves: "Mr. President, now that you are running for re . . ." He got no further. Johnson, a big man, leaned over the small office table and into the reporter's face: "Who said I was running! I never said I was running for anything!" Everyone in that 560-mph Oval Office laughed, except the president and his wife. Why laugh? Every story written about this week-long journey had called it a modified campaign trip; a road show, not a testing of waters. Johnson had just made out the elite of the capital press corps as fools. Of course, no one believed what he said.

We would not become believers for another two weeks, a period in which General Wheeler described Johnson as "wavering" on the troop request and "emotionally upset." The president was terrified of political implications coming from a lost war. Yet, as his aide Harry McPherson said, the troop request was "unbelievable and futile," with domestic consequences that meant either inflation or a huge tax increase—or both.

Johnson got more votes than Gene McCarthy (48 percent vs. 42 percent) in New Hampshire, where his name was on the ballot but where he had never actively campaigned. McCarthy, however, won the fight for delegates, 20 to 4. Having drummed George Romney out of the Republican primary two weeks earlier, the press effectively declared McCarthy the New Hampshire Democratic winner and national heavyweight antiwar champion. Four days later, March 16, another fast rising antiwar contender, Senator Kennedy, joined the race for the Democratic presidential nomination. "The race is just beginning and I can win," he declared. And well he might have.

Governor Wallace turned up the volume on his "law and order" bombast—arrant racism with a little verbal gravel tossed on for concealment—by promising to place 30,000 troops with fixed bayonets standing 30 feet apart on the streets of Washington, D.C., if needed to eradicate crime. I left those streets and adjacent offices in Washington, D.C., to watch the political spectacle from Seattle and to cover the presidential primary in Oregon.

A few days later, March 31, 1968, Johnson appeared on a television set in the Hunt Room of the Sorrento Hotel, where I was having a homecoming luncheon. He still looked tired, but his speech was deliberate: "I will not seek, nor will I accept my party's nomination."

After Johnson, the deluge.

On April 4 a gunman shot and killed Dr. Martin Luther King, Jr., the most influential apostle of nonviolence since Gandhi, a shaper of the American conscience on racial justice. Riots, fires, and looting, mainly in Washington, D.C., and Chicago, followed the murder. Thirty-four people died in these riots, the worst outbreak of domestic violence since draft riots of the Civil War. Federal troops and National Guardsmen soldiered them to an end. Still a pall of smoke hung over Washington, D.C., and Hearst's Bob Thompson wrote, "Not since the Civil War has the nation been so bitterly divided." No end to the division was in sight.

SENATOR ROBERT KENNEDY, slight, intense, and too fixed on his goal to spread charm, came to Oregon in mid-April for an antiwar contenders showdown with Senator Eugene McCarthy in a critical primary election. Bobby, as he would come to be designated in campaign shorthand, reminded me of a B-team football player who goes into every game as if the Rose Bowl was on the line. Mc-Carthy seemed to detest his fellow senator for reasons surely having as much to do with 1968 politics as with the younger man's personality. After all, who had got the antiwar ball rolling—and who now was trying to take it away?

Kennedy's nominal state campaign manager was Sid Leiken, a state legislator, self-made lumber mill owner, and a friend of mine. Sid came west during the Depression with the Civilian Conservation Corps. Despite his success in Oregon business and politics, he still showed grit brought from the streets of New York. He did not take kindly to his candidate's Boston bag handlers and bodyguards. They were rude to Sid and overbearing to me when we went to meet the Kennedy party at Portland's airport: "No fuckin' reporters—unnerstan."

Leiken fumed and drove me—not Kennedy—back to town. We had a drink at the old Congress Hotel before walking down Broadway to the elegant Benson Hotel, where the candidate and his team were staying. It was nearly sundown and Kennedy, alone, was standing on the steps at the entrance to the hotel. Sid was still steaming. He walked up the steps, straight past the senator's outstretched arm and into the Benson, refusing to accept the proffered handshake. The formidable and cocky Bobby Kennedy looked utterly forlorn. I couldn't help myself. I felt sorry for the candidate. But not for long. We joined two of his attractive female staffers for a drink and forgot the unpleasantness.

After a few days around Portland, Kennedy boarded his campaign entourage on a train for a whistle-stop trip down the Northern Pacific line to Eugene. At every stop—Albany and Salem being most conspicuous—Kennedy finished up his speeches with a line from George Bernard Shaw: "Some men see things as they are and say 'why?' I dream of things that never were and say 'why not?'" It was the signal for the working press to drop their trackside interviews or tavern beers and rush back to catch the train. Usually everybody got back aboard. Those small-town crowds were impressive, a tribute to the candidate's zeal as well as good advance work by his Oregon handlers. All of us—staff and press—felt good about Kennedy's campaign, even if some were dubious about the person. No one doubted his message of racial and, frankly, class reconciliation—an end to the war in Vietnam, racial and economic equity at home. Bobby talked with the passion of a new convert. Saint Paul must have preached this way. Sometimes he softened it with a passage from the poet Robert Frost: "The woods are lonely, dark and deep, but I have promises to keep and miles to go before I sleep . . . miles to go before I sleep." I could imagine Gene McCarthy brooding: First he steals my campaign issue, now my way with poetry.

The last time I saw Kennedy he was preaching his message to a young crowd in the old Haywood Stadium at the University of Oregon, a lovely day of warm sun and green grass where I lay and listened. Two weeks on the road and eager to get back to Seattle, I got a car and driver from Kennedy and rushed to the airport in time for a flight home. The candidate went south to campaign in California's primary.

Oregon's primary continued in force. Governor Ronald Reagan came up to ride a conservative wave generated four years earlier by Barry Goldwater. Nixon continued to lead Republicans but Reagan was pressing. Back on the Oregon beat, I sat beside Gene McCarthy on a prop hop from Portland to Pendleton. He spent most of this time grousing about Bobby Kennedy, a man he did not like who had refused his offer to debate. He seemed more churlish than poetic and in his speech to an approving audience in La Grande, he said Kennedy was under pressure "to defend the old mistakes" in Vietnam. Presumably he meant the mistakes of Jack Kennedy as well as those of Lyndon Johnson. There was a food fight on the press bus carrying us back up Interstate 80 to Pendleton. It had been a long campaign for reporters as well as candidates.

McCarthy won that Democratic primary. More to the point, Kennedy lost it in rural Oregon, where it was (and is) politically incorrect to advocate gun control. He did. He lost. Nixon beat Reagan three to one, but hold the predictions. There remained the

California primary with its larger haul of delegates and the formal entries of Vice President Humphrey and New York Governor Nelson Rockefeller. Kennedy had been working California overtime, perhaps to the neglect of Oregon. Sid Leiken had shunted his considerable skills into local congressional races.

Another political show, the Western States Republican Conference, pulled into Portland shortly after the primary election. Governor Rockefeller made a speech and late on the night of June 5, I joined Buehl Berentsen, the GOP Senate campaign coordinator, and C. Montgomery Johnson, the Washington State Republican chairman, in a hotel room to watch returns from the California primary. Both men were talented professionals. Kennedy won and we watched his victory address to a rally in the Ambassador Hotel in Los Angeles. He left the platform and minutes later, in the ballroom's kitchen, was fatally wounded by an assassin. We were too stunned to cry.

Vice President Humphrey inherited a sorry mess, a war in Vietnam, a political party as bitterly divided as the nation itself. The murders of King and Kennedy left a residue of cynicism, grief, and indifference. You could hear people saying "what's the use." It was a mood out of sync with the relentlessly upbeat Humphrey, the sort of fellow who could spend a year in a Syrian prison and come out raving about the swell jailhouse cockroaches. Besides, he entered the race aiming to prosecute "Johnson's war" in Southeast Asia.

The "New" Nixon—thanks, Bob Semple—would win the Republican presidential nomination, despite an eastern press favoring Nelson Rockefeller, and a conservative wave carrying Ronald Reagan (yes, movie fans, even then, 1968). Bob Considine, a beautiful column writer, my Hearst colleague, had his lead paragraph written before balloting began that night at the convention in Miami beach. It said "New York Gov. Nelson Rockefeller defeated a comeback by Richard Nixon for the 1968 GOP Presidential nomination." It is not at all unusual for a deadline-pressed journalist to start his prose in advance of the actual event. Saves time. In this case, I took a seat alongside Considine and told him Reagan had a better shot than Rocky. The great global strategist Henry Kissinger,

my tutor at Harvard for a few months, had looked distressed a few
hours earlier when I warned that Rocky was already out of the running. Unique insight? Not at all. Any one of two dozen reporters
who had followed this campaign season would have told him the
same. Rocky's foreign policy adviser, a more flexible player than his
students had reason to suspect, switched to Nixon a few days later.
The rest is diplomatic history, for better or worse.

Republican-friendly *Time* magazine put handsome Dan Evans
on its preconvention cover. He was a possible vice presidential nominee and he would deliver the keynote address. The fall of Rocky
doomed his shot at a place on the ticket—a prospect that would rise
and fall again in 1976. His speech fell flatter than a balloon out of
helium, an undeserved fate, given its content—possibly a case of
right message, wrong place.

"Time to shift the nation's priorities," said Evans to the preoccupied delegates, "from the war front to the home front, time to
reach inward and touch the troubled spirit of America." The governor stopped just short of saying it was time to quit Vietnam. Three
decades later he remembered and said, "looking back, I wish I had
had the courage. I wish I had taken one more step. I was not yet sea-
soned enough." The nation was greatly troubled as it has not been
since. Without being explicit, the keynote was surely a suggestion
that it was time to get out of Vietnam. But this wouldn't happen for
another six years, despite Johnson's withdrawal from the race and
the opening of negotiations. It would not happen until another
30,000 Americans came back from Southeast Asia in body bags or
coffins.

Democrats, by contrast with Republicans, entered their arenas
at war with each other. The Washington State Democratic convention in Tacoma made Republican Miami seem like a beach party.
One newspaper lead summed it up: "The Humphrey machine met
the McCarthy Crusade and the winner was Richard Nixon." And
Tacoma was a mere preliminary to the main Democratic event in
Chicago in late August.

The party nominated Humphrey as its presidential candidate
in the stockyards coliseum, a pool of relative calm in the middle

of tear gas, billy clubs, and riots in the streets of Chicago. While Mayor Richard Daley's police were crushing war protests, the Soviet Army invaded Czechoslovakia to quell an outburst of democracy in its Warsaw Pact satellite. Senator Warren Magnuson, a magnificent old liberal of the congressional establishment, bemoaned the hell these street riots played with civil procedure.

Humphrey won easily, as expected. There was suspense over his potential running mate. Speculation, the sidekick to political indecision, fixed on Senators Edmund Muskie of Maine and Fred R. Harris of Oklahoma. At Harris's invitation, I spent most of August 29 in a suite of rooms at the Conrad Hilton (née Stevens) Hotel with my friend and his family, all of us awaiting a call from Humphrey. We fidgeted for several hours. Fred told a few stories, one about the confusion and dismay that overtook his older sister, a segregationist, when she learned that her favorite country-western singer, Country Charlie Pride, was a black man. The Harris family had sharecropped.

The call came in the middle of an old movie on TV. Humphrey asked Harris to nominate Muskie for vice president, which he would do that night. Fred took it like a soldier. Minutes later Harris answered a call at his door. Senator Walter Mondale entered and embraced his colleague and said he too was disappointed. The curse of Chicago and Tacoma, the image of street riots and angry cops, fell on the Democratic ticket, Humphrey and Muskie.

Worse than Chicago, Humphrey couldn't shake the curse of Vietnam. If Nixon really had no plan on how to extract our soldiers from the warring Vietnamese factions, Humphrey had no plan on how to remove himself from the shadow of President Johnson. Was he intimidated by Johnson? Probably. The double curses gathered force in the early fall. Nixon looked like a man walking to the White House.

In late September, I got on the Humphrey campaign bus in Portland, joining, among others, my old comrade from Harvard and the 1967 Mideast War, Bud Nossiter of the *Washington Post*. The polls showed us traveling with a sure loser. His subsequent campaign appearances were even worse for the embattled vice president. In Portland, an ugly young crowd, bent on disruption, angered the gentle candidate, who said, "These American style Hitler youth have decided to destroy my candidacy." Did they prefer Nixon? Apparently.

The next night in Seattle, war protestors arose in the middle of Humphrey's speech to declare the candidate "guilty of war crimes against humanity." These were organized disruptions, initially tolerated. When Humphrey offered a gesture of conciliation, one agitator stood up in the Seattle Center Arena and shouted, "We have not come here to talk with you but to arrest you for complicity with deaths in Vietnam." That cut it. Humphrey supporters struck back against protestors with their fists. Police moved quickly.

"It's a riot," said R. W. Apple, the *New York Times* reporter who raced me to a telephone bank to dictate bulletins for the late editions in Manhattan. Perhaps alerted by previous incidents, Seattle had sufficient police on hand to stop the fights and safely exit Humphrey—shades of LBJ—out a back door. It must have been the last straw, the last evening in which the curse of Vietnam and the shadow of Johnson dominated Hubert Humphrey's run for the presidency.

Next day, a Sunday, I was assigned to the press pool. Humphrey and his entourage were staying at the Olympic Hotel, sometime home of Senator Magnuson and the master creation of Magnuson's friend William Edris. It remains a Seattle landmark. His schedule called for the candidate to go fishing up Puget Sound off the *Thea Foss*, a classic beauty of an early steam yacht, one well suited for J. P. Morgan. But Humphrey didn't show up. Instead, Fred Harris, his wife LaDonna, a couple of Secret Servicemen, and the pool, four newsmen, and fishing rods motored (fuel had replaced steam) to the base of Whidbey Island, where nobody got so much as a strike. All of us wondered, where's Hubert? If Harris knew, he said nothing. We all knew the rumor that George Ball was to join Humphrey.

Ball, a Chicago lawyer, was a "dove." The day before the outburst in Portland, Ball had resigned as U.S. ambassador to the United Nations. He already had expressed doubts about Johnson's conduct of the war and he favored U.S. recognition of what everybody in those days called "Red China." After we arrived back, fishless in Seattle, word spread that Humphrey had spent the day preparing a speech to be delivered the next day in Salt Lake City. Inside the Olympic that Sunday Bob Considine got the scoop for Hearst's Monday morning editions.

For once, there were no hecklers in the Mormon city, where Humphrey met Ball and took a step away from Johnson toward his political freedom. The vice president said he would halt the bombing of North Vietnam in order to punch up negotiations under way in Paris between the three parties, North Vietnam, the United States, and Viet Cong (Viet Minh) representatives. He would make "an honorable end to the war" his first priority. He would reduce the U.S. force in Vietnam. But he would not unilaterally withdraw.

North Vietnam was not moved by Humphrey's Salt Lake City speech, but the candidate made a big jump up where it counted most—American opinion polls. Suddenly, his campaign took life. Had the November election deadline not been so close, he might have overtaken Richard Nixon and won the White House.

It did not happen. His step away from Johnson's conduct of the war may have been too little. It was certainly too late. But it left a question mark—what if?—over that year, 1968—a year that already was wild and unforgettable.

MORE HAPPENSTANCE

UP TO 1967 everything I knew about the State of Israel and conflict in the Middle East came from Fox and Hearst movie news-reels and two acquaintances of disparate personalities: Gallagher, a man about the University of Washington campus, 1950 to 1954, told tales of Israel's War of Independence in 1948; David Hirsch, whom I knew and admired as a civil rights activist in Dallas in the late 1950s, lobbied for the anti-Zionist organization, the American Council for Judaism.

Gallagher was somewhat unusual among my circle of working students. His first name is missing from my memory bank, but not his campus presence. He had a Plymouth convertible, smoked a pipe, and wore a tweed coat with leather patches at the elbows. He also drank beer at the Blue Moon Tavern, a free-thinking place fre-quented by students, the painter Morris Graves, poet Ted Roethke, several notable professors, and once, it was said, by the Bolshevik writer Maxim Gorky, later liquidated by Josef Stalin. Gallagher claimed he did a stint as a mercenary gunman for the Stern Gang, shooting up Arab villages in an early, unauthorized version of eth-nic cleansing. As he told it, with Irish gusto, this was an updated version of Cowboys versus Indians. True or not, these tales made noble the return of Jews from Hitler's holocaust to their homeland of antiquity. The tales excused the excesses of this return. Arabs who were dispossessed, like Indians, had no standing in the Ameri-can conscience of that time, a result of ignorance, and no standing in our social life, a result of their absence from it.

The Jews of my youth in the agrarian South were professionals—merchants, lawyers, storekeepers—and thus of the same social
rank as the town and country gentry. Although it may have been different in the city, these folk drank together and laughed together; humor is the grace of people who have been whipped and lost. Despite
the difference in religious practices, we were spared the special curse
of anti-Semitism, although, Lord knows, we compensated with the
most rigorous economic and social discrimination against blacks.

Arabs? Palestinians? One might have learned something about
them from State Department briefing papers. The department,
headed by the most exemplary American, George Marshall, opposed U.S. recognition of the Jewish state in 1948. President Tru-
man decided otherwise and most Americans applauded—and still
do with some qualifications.

When he wasn't picketing segregated facilities in Big D with a
handful of liberals, usually the sum of their numbers in that redneck,
reactionary city, Dave Hirsch quietly preached an anti-Zionist gos-
pel: the creation of Israel was a grave, even tragic mistake, a case of
victims (Jews) victimizing others (Arabs) with no good to come to
any of us. Because I admired Hirsch as much for his courage as his
intelligence, I listened and, respectfully, argued; the westernized Jews
would, in time, elevate backward Arabs from their wooden plows
and donkeys to a higher economic level—tractors and Fords. Besides, Jews deserved the land of Palestine as compensation for their
suffering in World War II.

In a manner perhaps too gentle for his lobbying craft, Hirsch
countered: Zionists were placing a religious state in a region where
population numbers overwhelmingly favored Arabs and Muslims.
He could only forecast wars and tribulations, in place of peace and
accommodation—accurate unto this day, of course, but a forecast
insufficient to affect the support of Americans for the State of Israel.

This was all long behind me when I went to Olympia to cover
the state legislature for the *Seattle Post-Intelligencer* in 1967, my
third state capital beat as a reporter. The legislature was in the heat
of battle over Governor Dan Evans's proposed income tax that winter when Gideon Saguy, the stately Israeli consul-general in San Fran-

cisco, came to the statehouse with an invitation: an all expense paid trip to Israel, where I could travel, observe, and, naturally, write anything my heart and mind desired. No strings, of course. I jumped at the invitation. So did my editors. There are two schools of thought on such government-paid freeloads: okay and no way. Jack Doughty, a conservative relic of the *The Front Page*, and Louis Guzzo, the *P-I* editors, held the former view. Reporters live in a world of attempted mind rape—propaganda—and not only from foreign or domestic governments. They are the constant targets of a multi-billion-dollar industry, public relations. In pluralistic societies, such as ours, this is not as sinister as it might seem to a layman. For every propaganda force, there is a counterforce. The newsman caught between has a fundamental criterion: what is best for most average citizens. Is it, for example, a tax break argued by Boeing's lobbyists, or a hike in welfare payments sought by Boeing's opponents.

(In a closed society, such as the Soviet Union or Egypt, it's another matter.)

In Doughty's view, if a reporter wasn't smart enough to resist the entreaties that go with a freeload, and to balance the countervailing arguments in favor of average Americans, he wasn't smart enough to work for his newspaper.

There was a catch, I told Saguy. I couldn't leave my post in Olympia until completion of the legislative session, time unknown and unpredictable. He got nervous as matters ran on though March and April, insisting I should make the trip in springtime before the Holy Land of my biblical upbringing got uncomfortably hot. By that he meant the weather.

By mid-May 1967, when I went to New York for an El Al flight to Tel Aviv, I knew it was not the weather. A crisis loomed. Gamal Abdel Nasser, the Egyptian president, had moved a 100,000-man army into the eastern Sinai Desert, near the Israeli border. U Thant, the United Nations secretary general, had removed peacekeeping troops from the Gaza Strip. Then, the day I took flight on the El Al 707, Nasser closed the Strait of Tiran, blockading Israel's lone Red Sea port, Elat. I didn't know much about the Mideast. I did know that blockading a nation's port was cause for war. So did most everybody. The El Al flight was virtually empty of passengers.

The freeload lasted two days.

I checked into an assigned hotel on the edge of Tel Aviv and then into the government public information office, a compound of low buildings opposite the Israeli Defense Ministry. It looked like a Seattle elementary school. There I met my driver, guide, and propagandist, Yitzhak Austrian, an Israeli with a barrel chest, docker's fists, and scars of combat from three wars. It took about two hours before we became drinking buddies and boon companions.

Yitzhak made it out of Poland to Palestine ahead of the German death squads in 1939. He had a survivor's sense of humor and disdain for formal religion. When I explained my Southern Presbyterian upbringing, he almost snickered. "Look, Christian," he said the first day out of Tel Aviv when we pulled alongside the Sea of Galilee at Tiberias. "This is where your Savior walked on water. Some tricks, huh?" And a few miles further on a hill overlooking Capernaum on the so-called sea: "And here is where your Savior turned stones into bread, water into wine. Where is he now that we need him, being hungry and thirsty?"

"My guess, Yitzhak, is that Jesus is careful about the Jewish company he keeps. Maybe if I dump you I can get an interview and a few tricks."

"No way, thanks God. I've got two weeks to fill you full of booze and Israeli bullshit or I lose best job I have since killing Afrika Korps Germans."

Above Capernaum we reached the "horse ranch," the Israeli version of a Western dude ranch run by an ex-GI from Chicago, Yahuda Avni (née Eddie Schneider). Yitzhak had been around this circuit a few times before—once, he said, with a veddy stuffy Brit writer, Lawrence Durrell. Eddie broke out the local beer, Gold Medal, good stuff made in Haifa, and told me about the shellfire coming from Syrians in the hills on the other side of the Jordan River, several miles to the east.

"Something has to be done," said Eddie. "A farmer can't get on his tractor up in the valley without risking his life. If it isn't a

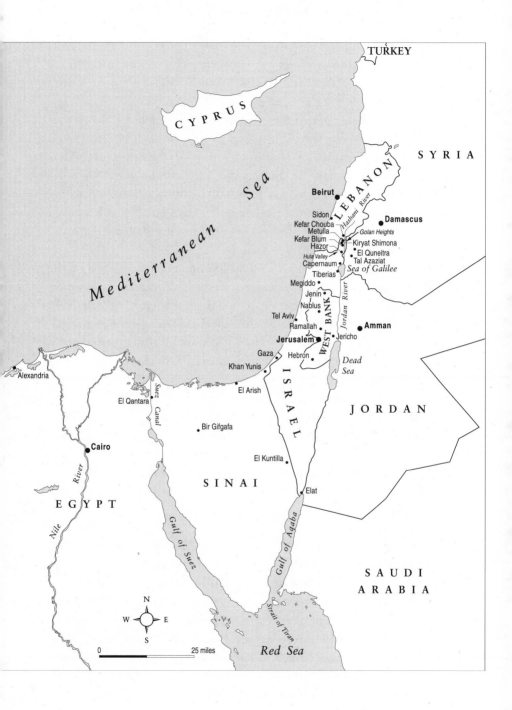

TURKEY

CYPRUS

SYRIA

Mediterranean Sea

Beirut

LEBANON

Sidon
Kefar Chouba
Metulla
Kefar Blum
Hazor
Hula Valley
Capernaum
Tiberias

Hashani River

Golan Heights
Damascus

Kiryat Shimona
El Quneitra
Tal Aziat
Sea of Galilee

Megiddo
Jenin
Nablus
Tel Aviv
Ramallah
Jerusalem
Gaza
Khan Yunis

WEST BANK

Jordan River

Jericho
Amman

Hebron

Dead
Sea

El Arish

ISRAEL

JORDAN

Alexandria

El Qantara

Suez Canal

Bir Gifgafa

Cairo

SINAI

El Kuntilla

Nile River

EGYPT

Elat

Gulf of Suez

Gulf of Aqaba

SAUDI
ARABIA

N
W ✦ E
S

Strait of Tiran

0   25 miles

Red Sea

shell, it's a sniper. Last week they planted land mines on the road north and detonated them by remote control. I ran over one, but my junk truck wasn't worth the TNT. Somebody else got it. That stuff can't go on."

In Washington at this time, they worried about global consequences—World War III?—of a war between their clients, the Israelis, against the Soviet clients, Arabs. At the horse ranch they worried about farmers getting shot off their tractors. My polychrome visions of a haloed Jesus walking on water and preaching the Sermon on the Mount, all of which I was taught had happened right near where I sat drinking beer and talking of war, faded away like memories of Sunday School.

"Blessed are the meek," said Jesus that day to a crowd on the hill above Capernaum. "And the peacemakers." Where are they now, I wondered. Up the road in the middle of the fertile Hula (Huleh) Valley we talked with the English-speaking farmers at Kefar Blum, a commune prospering from its adjacent fields of cotton and apple trees, but under the watch of Tel Azaziat, a Syrian fortification on the slope of the Golan Heights.

I felt an immediate kinship with the men and women of Kefar Blum. They lived simply and worked hard with an ethic we once defined as "Protestant." Food and books were ample, creature comforts spare. Most of the men had already fought in one or two of the wars with Arabs to create a new nation. Now they talked of another as we sat in an apple grove in the evening cool beneath the silent guns of Tel Azaziat.

THERE WAS A TWO-WEEK HIATUS before the planes and guns commenced the Six-Day War that reshaped the politics and borders of the Middle East for the rest of the twentieth century. My freeload, however, ended when we returned to Tel Aviv from Kefar Blum. Due to an imminence of war, foreign nationals were ordered to Lod Airport for return to their homelands. A great shuffle from the Tel Aviv hotels ensued. A telex from Hearst in New York gave me new orders for the Mideast: I would remain in Israel as the newspaper chain's one-man bureau, pending arrival of Serge Fliegers, the

Paris correspondent who had covered the 1956 Arab-Israeli gunfight. I checked into the Dan Hotel, smack against the Mediterranean beach in downtown Tel Aviv, my home for the next six weeks, some of the time even for sleeping.

Into the vacuum left by departing tourists came reporters, most of them British, masters of their craft and subsequently constant companions in our "bomb shelter," a small bar below the hotel lobby with reinforced walls, a large stock of refreshments, and Max, their genial dispenser. Patrick O'Donovan of the *Observer*, a veteran of Little Rock, greeted me like an old friend, insisting that he buy the first round. He looked older, more whiskey-worn, than at our initial meeting a decade earlier. But Patrick would set the tone of our one-sided coverage of this war on the day that it commenced, June 5, 1967. Wrote Patrick: "Today I am ashamed that I am not a Jew." Jimmy Cameron, a prose stylist, Donald Weiss, of the *Mirror*, a war lover, Johnny Wallis of the *Telegraph*, a veteran of the 1948 War of Independence, Christopher Dobson of the *Daily Mail*—one could never find better English-speaking company. The U.S. contingent of newspaper and TV reporters was coming in to stay up the beach at the new Hilton.

It was an anxious time—unnecessarily so, we may now understand. There was no question of a war. The question was whether the small state could ward off the Arab armies that surrounded it from the north, south, and east. Soviet armed and trained, the Egyptian Army poised in the Sinai Desert close to Israel's border loomed most formidable. Could Israel defend itself, thus sparing another potential holocaust? Arab brutality, myth or not, lay at the core of this anxiety. We shared this with the Israelis and one night in the Dan bomb shelter discussed whether we should bear arms while covering the war. The consensus was "no." We would leave our fate to Israeli arms, about which, in comparison with Arab forces, we knew very little. Never in these discussions did I hear Weiss, Wallis, or Cameron, the most war-tested of our lot, suggest Israeli arms were superior, and thus would carry the field in quick order. At best, we figured, the Israelis could stand down their opposition and spare us all. And if, like Patrick O'Donovan, the bulk of our coverage tilted in favor of our hosts, the Israelis, the fault lay with our ignorance of the Palestinian diaspora of 1948 and our fears of the immediate future at the hands of Arab armies. We knew of the Holocaust, however. Thus we were only half awake historically. Never again would I take a war out of its historic context.

War, or its threat, is the great aphrodisiac. People need to get next to each other, and my hunch (I've seen no figures) is that a disproportionate number of 30-year-olds hold Israeli passports. While we waited, we dated and observed the native population. I found a different mind-set among the company at the Alaska Cafe on Jaffa Road a block away from the government press office in Jerusalem. It was a hangout for left intellectuals, all of them nervous about the prospect of war but also with strong sympathy for the plight of dispossessed Palestinians. The latter, we would come to see, were living on the United Nations dole in refugee shacks in camps scattered from the Gaza Strip on the Mediterranean, across the West Bank of the Jordan, to Amman and Damascus.

Jona Bachur, a poet and translator, an Alaska regular even though she lived in Tel Aviv, gave me a primer on the complex aftermath of the creation of Israel: the overwhelming and unresolved question of how to live in peace with a people of a vastly different culture and religion, many, if not all, of them embittered by their dispossession. We became close friends, mainly, I suspect, because she lived alone in a fearful time.

Mid-hiatus, Bernard (Bud) Nossiter of the *Washington Post* and Bill Mauldin, the triple threat—writing, photography, and cartoons—from the *Chicago Sun-Times* showed up at the bomb shelter, having just arrived on one of the last flights from New York. Nossiter was a boon companion from our days at Harvard. Mauldin I knew, like about every other American of our generation, as the philosopher-cartoonist of World War II, the creator of Willie and Joe, ironic, woebegone archetypes of American civilians conscripted into mortal combat. He had an imp's face and the journalistic gifts of an angel. We left for a restaurant in Jaffa, hometown of Jonah, turned Tel Aviv suburb, in Mauldin's rented German Ford. It was a superb reunion and carried over into an all night booze and girls joint run by Moroccan gangsters in Tel Aviv. Bud promptly fell in love. Yitzhak was there with a lady of the evening. He knew of and embraced Mauldin, a kindred skeptic. We laughed, drank, and danced all night.

Came dawn, I realized I had a 9 A.M. appointment with the mayor of Elat, the blockaded Israeli seaport at the top of the Gulf of Aqaba, which meant an 8 A.M. flight from Tel Aviv. I jumped into the Mediterranean in search of a clear head. I made the flight, dizzy with the excesses of the evening.

Elat had to be as hot as any place this side of a Christian's concept of Hell. I showed up at the city hall, a Quonset hut with a primitive air conditioner, only a few meters from the Egyptian border on one side, and on the other, a mile or so across a narrow strait from the Jordanian port of Aqaba. In other words sandwiched between two Arab armies. "You look awful," said the mayor, Joe Levy. I accepted a cold drink and went to work.

Can you survive here with the port closed by the blockade? "No," he said. Can they take you? "No," he said again. "As you can see we are ready. I expect an air strike first, so we've dug a lot of slit trenches." I was inclined to his optimism. The town reminded me of an Alaskan fishing village—albeit one with the thermostat turned to its peak—up a remote fjord, an outback where inhabitants rely only on themselves for security. All of the local population packed pistols or Uzi submachine guns and dressed in slacks or shorts and sandals, rough and ready. There was a one-story hotel-bar worthy of the mangiest Mexican village but named for a female saint—"I slept with St. Catherine last night and it was dreadful, she had fleas," is a lead that topped more than one newsman's story datelined Elat. The guns were loaded and locked.

There is a beautiful beach on the clear blue waters of the Red Sea at Elat, now transformed into a major tourist resort. I went down for a swim and a talk with a dozen young international hippies living a free life on the sand. They wore little clothing, showed no money or care about what might happen when (not if) Egyptians roared in with MIG-21s or Jordanians began lobbying 105 mm shells across the strait. They were mostly Europeans, several Americans. Some were high on dope, which might have been a practical method of handling anxiety, if any were so afflicted. All were utterly carefree.

Later at St. Catherine's blessed bar I joined His Honor, Joe Levy: what about your transient hippies?

He shrugged: "It's their ass."

THIS RUN-UP TO WARFARE was valuable to me as a time to learn about these people and their new nation. Obviously they had come here to work; to "make the desert bloom," as their publicists boasted—"overendowed with the Protestant work ethic," I wrote for Hearst, never minding the religious irony. The work was essential to make the nation. but it also may have been compensation for an old, murderous European notion that Jews shirk physical labor. Four hundred years before Adolf Hitler, the Protestant revolutionary Martin Luther said of German Jews: "They hold us captive in our own country. They let us work in the sweat of our noses to earn money and property for them while they sit behind the oven, lazy, let off gas, bake pears, eat, drink, live softly and well from our wealth."

Soft living in Israel, circa 1967, was harder to find than a snowball in the Sinai. It was impossible for one raised on Southern Presbyterian screeds against sloth and waste not to like these people, even cheer their cause.

On Sunday, June 4, Jona Bachur and I took a bus from Tel Aviv to Jerusalem up the narrow road built to bypass the Jordanian stronghold of Latrun and winding up from the sea to the cooler mountains. Along the roadside were relics of the 1948 war, shot-up half-tracks and old trucks jury-rigged with steel plates to simulate armored vehicles. These were reminders of the heroic effort to feed and arm the Holy City during its siege by Arabs. I wanted to see the Dead Sea Scrolls, housed in a new museum near the Israeli Knesset (parliament) building. Jona aimed to visit a friend's ceramic display at a shop on Jaffa Road near the government press office and the Alaska Cafe. The city had a bad case of the nerves.

Machine-gun chatter across the Green Line dividing Jewish

from Arab Jerusalem stimulated nervousness. At the Alaska, we met a friend of Jona's, a government official privy to a just completed meeting of the Israeli cabinet. He looked all shook up and kept repeating "ein brera," meaning "no alternative." No question about an alternative to what. These folks were not of a mind to surrender. I bought a beautiful ceramic bowl from Jona's friend in the shop on Jaffa Road. The woman's hands shook so badly I through she might drop the sale. Then Jona caught the shakes. We took the next bus back to Tel Aviv.

I figured war was but a few hours away.

A message awaited at the Dan. Serge Fliegers had arrived from Paris to take charge of Hearst's coverage, and a party in his room had commenced. I joined a reporter's equivalent of a class reunion, Fliegers chairman, the procurer of Johnny Walker Black Label, Perrier water, and several attractive ladies. Flieger's entourage included a suave—make that too suave—columnist from *Newsweek* magazine, Arnaud de Bourchgrave, and Russ Braley, the *New York Daily News* man in Bonn by way of Lincoln High School in Seattle, plus several of Flieger's Israeli pals, one the son of a cabinet minister. Several of the Johnny Walker bottles were empty.

I knew little of Fliegers, the International News Service correspondent in Moscow when I worked sports and rewrite in Dallas, reputed to be some kind of Russian count—Russkie royalty driven by Bolsheviks to France. He was pleasant, offering a drink and introductions, until I told him I aimed to skip the party and go file to New York that war in the Mideast was imminent, a matter of hours. He didn't like that idea. We argued a few minutes about my gut instincts until he reminded me that the Hearst wire was inoperative on Sunday, thus nothing would move from New York until Monday morning. For the sake of saving a big-shot journalist's face in the presence of his cronies, I agreed to wait until the following morning, June 5, 1967. But no longer. I skipped the class reunion and went to bed alone.

Around 7 A.M. I took my typewriter to the porch of my room at the Dan, looked out of the green Mediterranean, and began a report that said war between Arabs and Israelis would start "in a matter of hours, not days." I had written no more than six paragraphs when it did. There were air raid sirens and radio bulletins. I would like to recall it as relief from the tension of the previous weeks. It was not. It was scary. Had I the scantiest knowledge that the ensuing week would reorder the borders, politics, and sociology of the Mideast for at least three decades to come, and that it would leave the U.S. and the U.S.S.R. poised for an Armageddon over the protection of their respective client states, it would have been as despairing as it was frightening. Initially, my only thought was of incoming bombs or shells.

I pulled the six paragraphs from my Olympia portable, tossed them into a wastebasket, and left the room to report a war. I thought it would be—one way or another—the last.

BEFORE THE SIX DAY WAR, there was gunfire from both sides. Israeli Defense Minister Dayan claimed in a recently revealed interview that most of the shooting incidents in the North were provoked by Israeli forces eager to acquire Syrian territory. His claim came to light in 1997, thirty years too late to change history. Matti Peled, the dovish member of Israel's four-man general staff, told the author in an extensive 1992 interview that he opposed the Syrian invasion. But he said nothing about alleged Israeli provocations. If Israelis deliberately provoked those guns, it would have been news to the farmers and to Yahuda Avni.

THE SIX-DAY WAR

IT'S NOT SAD to say that there never will be another war like the one commencing that bright June morning, a clash without the use of nuclear weapons, open to all newsmen wishing to witness battle firsthand, and one with tactics from the now obsolescent playbooks of George Patton, Heinz Guderian, Erwin Rommel, and the daddy of them all, Nathan Bedford Forrest. Its technology was from World War II, not Star Wars. It was mercifully short, and surprisingly one-sided, a regional conflict with enduring global implications, proba-bly the hottest spot in the 40-year Cold War, "the cockpit of World War III," said one editorialist without exaggeration.

If news of "Desert Storm," our high-tech annihilation of Iraq's intrusion on Kuwaiti oil, was stage-managed by the military much like the introduction of a new software by Bill Gates, the six-day battle was as wide open. Come see, come report. The reporter needed only good nerves and a good car. There was a price for this, however: three newsmen killed, five badly wounded, while covering the action. This made it the most casualty intense war of modern times for journalists, given their few numbers—less than 50—and the war's short duration.

For other reasons, we have escaped much notice of the vicious wars between local guerrillas and U.S.-trained soldiers defending Central American dictators in the name of anticommunism. My col-league Mike Layton risked life and job security by reporting warfare in Central America. Not many Americans wished to be bothered, least of all the administrations of Reagan and Bush, whose propagandists told a different story from that of an honest reporter.

Unknown to most of us, a deadly jungle war engaged Cambodian guerrillas against Vietnamese troops occupying that benighted Southeast Asian nation. The Vietnamese lost 55,000 troops in the 1980s to the underpowered guerrillas, a death sum equal to U.S. losses in Vietnam. Any one of Liz Taylor's frequent weddings got more play in the press. The war was almost totally out of sight, but it did not carry the potential of an Armageddon between the superpowers as did the one I went out to cover on June 5, 1967.

I went directly from the Dan Hotel to the government press office, a twenty-minute walk away, in a group of one-story buildings on Bet Sokolow. The Israeli Defense Ministry compound, swathed by a razor wire fence, covered the block across the street. One wing of the press office featured a canteen, serving cheese sandwiches, beer, and *erak*, a Mideast liquor with a taste like licorice and a kick like Tennessee white lightning. A few slit trenches had been dug across the lawn for what we considered to be inevitable: an air raid. They would have been overflowing given the number of newsmen.

For one day I took the military handouts—"communiqués" is the euphemism—and filed a running report to New York, one studded with local color about the reaction of ordinary citizens, mostly calm, to the anticipated horror of bombardment. At midmorning the senior Hearstling, Serge Fliegers, bounded in to the maze of reporters and typewriters working in the pressroom, bearing the smile of a man reunited with an old love. Fliegers, a veteran of the 1956 war which took Israelis to the Suez Canal, gave orders to his underling: "Stay here and file to New York everything you get from the military spokesmen and everything you can steal from other reporters." Then he left for the Gaza front with an Israeli newsman and a cameraman for the Canadian Broadcasting Corporation (CBC). As Gene Autry would have sung it, Fliegers was back in the saddle again, and delighted. I would not see him again for ten days.

Tel Aviv was pitch dark, blacked out in anticipation of an air raid, by the time I broke away for the walk back to the Dan and food in the bomb shelter. Aircraft would not attack the city, but the explosion of several heavy artillery shells in a suburb announced the proximity of Jordanian guns to a large urban population. The shelling also announced Jordan's unwise decision to join the war.

The respite from work was brief. Around midnight all reporters in Tel Aviv were assembled in the auditorium on Bet Sokolow for the most extraordinary press conference I would ever witness.

Yitzhak Rabin, the Israeli Defense Forces commander, and his staff, including General Matti Peled and Air Force Commander Mordichai Hod, took the platform and used pointers against large-scale maps of the Sinai to show the swift advance of the Israeli Army across the desert and the rout, after one day of fighting, of Nasser's Egyptian Army. Rabin said El Arish, the oasis headquarters of Nasser's army, had fallen as had Abu Aguela, Khan Yunis, and El Kuntilla. In unison the local press gave audible gasps at the calling of each of those names. The rest of us had to check desert maps to know the implications of El Arish and El Kuntilla. When Hod, a tall angular fighter pilot, announced the destruction of 376 Arab aircraft, the desert battle came to a focus: The Egyptians were stripped of air cover and left naked to face Israeli panzers, tanks, and troop-bearing half-tracks. Israeli armor was World War II surplus, Sherman tanks refitted with larger (90 mm) cannon, and the partially armored half-tracks. The Soviet-supplied Egyptians had better equipment, but with ruined MIGs still smoking on their Sinai airstrips their cause was doomed. They were fleeing by truck or foot for the Suez Canal about 125 miles to the west. Only the strong and the lucky would make it home.

THE SIEGE OF ISRAEL (real or perceived) was over. But not the warfare. Despite 24 hours of reporting and filing to New York, via telex through Israeli Army censors, my work had barely begun.

Well past daylight on June 6, the last story on the desert battle dispatched, Milt Kaplan, the Hearst editor in New York, cabled fresh orders: I was to forget the running battle account and go cover the battlefield—or, in this case, battlefields. The war was moving from the Sinai to the Gaza Strip. Where next?

Bill Mauldin, the *Chicago Sun-Times* triple threat, the only other reporter besides myself left at Bet Sokolow, imparted a hunch that action would go to Jerusalem. He had a rented German Ford and suggested we team to work the battles. I liked Mauldin. Apart from his extraordinary talents, he was quick, aggressive, and he had been in battles before. So he was also careful—a perfect companion for this situation. We spent one day among troops on the Gaza front, watching aerial duels between MIGs and Israeli Mysteres, at one point narrowly missing hostile mortar fire.

Next day, not long past dawn, we headed up the hills toward Jerusalem on the road bypassing Latrun, the site of a monastery, an ugly reminder of the 1948 war. In 1948 the British-trained Arab Legion withstood three desperate attacks by Jews, many just landed from European displaced persons camps and bused into battle. They carried little or no arms. Latrun was critical to the relief of Jerusalem, the point where roads from north, south, and east joined in the Ayalon Valley to run up through the Judean Hills to the Holy City. Hundreds were killed in these assaults, the last on June 9, 1948, three days and 21 years before Mauldin and I stopped for a 7 A.M. breakfast, beer and cheese sandwiches, at a roadhouse on the narrow highway built to go around the Latrun salient. Still manned by Glubb Pasha's Legionaires, the salient ran like a dagger into the heart of Israel.

The breakfast was half-finished when the sound of battle—Hell's roar—broke out on the other side of a low hill behind the roadhouse. We took off, beers in hand, in a cloud of dust and rubber in the small Ford in that same direction over the Israeli equivalent of a Northwest logging road. At the crest of a ridge line we pulled up to look down on the lush green, fertile valley of Ayalon. It was as peaceful to behold as a Renoir landscape.

What unfolded in the few minutes it took to finish our beers was the Israeli assault and capture of Latrun, its monastery and police barracks. One column of armor came straight up the old Tel Aviv–Jerusalem road, troops spilling out of half-tracks to close for the kill. Another column came up the dirt road that brought us to the ridge line and then down into the valley, its commander screaming at us to get the hell off the hill. Forgive the cliché but there is no better description: it was like watching a Hollywood war movie. Arab troops, apparently including an Iraqi contingent as well as the Jordanian Legionaires, came out, hands up. And no one fired a shot at Mauldin or me while we gathered a world-class scoop.

An Israeli roadblock a few miles beyond the roadhouse brought us, along with an Israeli Army column, to a dead halt. Mauldin's hunch about a battle in Jerusalem now looked certain as a hooker's congeniality. Israel was going after the Arab half of Jerusalem, but we were going to reverse along this long stream of troops and vehicles and return to Tel Aviv—so the military police commanded. We did not. Just short of the roadblock, we spotted another back road twisting up into the hills, apparently, but by no means certainly, in the direction of Jerusalem. Up we went, the sawed-off Ford grinding and bumping but moving up and ahead. We surely crossed the border into Jordan on this uncharted route as we had done earlier in the morning. But no one—no army—came to stop us. Instead, several Arab farmers pushed their plows behind donkeys, a sight older than the Holy City down the road. We made it, an uneventful trip that ended on the western edge of Jerusalem within sound, if not yet range, of Jordanian artillery.

Meron (Ronny) Medzini, the government spokesman, greeted us with good and bad news when we reached his office in the government building on Jaffa Road. Two of our colleagues, Paul Schutzer of *Life* magazine, and Ted Yates of ABC News, had been killed—Yates just on the Arab side of the Green Line dividing Jerusalem. Medzini (and us) had yet to be told of a third death, Ben Oyserman, a cameraman working for the Canadian Broadcasting Corporation, and of serious wounds to two other journalists. On the other hand, the fight for Jerusalem, already underway, was looking good for his side—so good that Ronny forecast the capture of the entire city before sundown. Having witnessed the quick fall of Latrun, we were now to observe the bloody consolidation of Jerusalem under the flag of a Jewish state.

We took advantage of a lull in the shelling to drive through a buttoned-up, shut-down city, to the Histraduth Building, the town's tallest, normally headquarters for Israel's all-powerful trade union, now taken by the military as its command and observation post for the battle in East Jerusalem. Initially, we passed unnoticed to watch the orange flash of exploding ammunition amid khaki-colored assault troops in the battle around Ammunition Hill. Glubb Pasha could be proud of his Legionaires, fighting bayonet to bayonet to hold on to Arab Jerusalem. Then something about Mauldin and me, average looking Americans, caught the eye of a staff major. We were ordered to leave. With big news to file, no problem.

A decade later, during a lecture at the University of Washington, I mentioned observing the battle for Jerusalem from the top of the Histraduth Building. After the talk, a Jordanian exchange student approached me smiling and identified himself as commander of a 105-mm artillery battery in Jerusalem. In a pleasant, even light-hearted, manner he related that early on that fateful Wednesday afternoon he had been ordered to place all of his battery's fire on the top floor of the Histraduth Building—an order subsequently remanded as the struggle for Ammunition Hill turned critical. His guns were turned to other targets.

We had no inkling of this good fortune at the time that it happened. Instead, unscathed, we rushed through the comatose city to write reports on the fall of Latrun, and, given late-breaking word from Ronny Medzini, the capture of Jerusalem—the latter several hours premature. En route to the telegraph office across Jaffa Road we ran into Joe Alex Morris of the *Los Angeles Times* with a reporter for *Time* magazine. The latter looked shell-shocked, glassy-eyed from fear or fatigue or both. Morris reported that they had just walked through the Mandelbaum Gate from "the other side," the Intercontinental Hotel, a modern structure near the Garden of Gethsemane and the Mount of Olives. Bill and I decided to do the reverse—walk back to the Intercontinental in East Jerusalem. Quite safe, said Morris.

It took about 15 minutes to file our copy, an interlude that may have spared our lives. This is the way with wars. No sooner were we clear of the telegraph office when shelling commenced with a new intensity. This was no time to be outside a concrete shelter. Civilian casualties were reported. Back in the stone fortress of the government information office we met Yuval Elizur, already a veteran Israeli reporter, who invited us to watch the war from the balcony of his apartment building overlooking the Green Line. The fighting ended a few hours later, our stories on the reunification of Jerusalem only a few hours ahead of the fact. Yuval, a Sabra (a Jew born in Palestine, as was his father) has been a friend and a crack newsman ever since.

The shelling had quieted before we returned to the press office to file additional detail about the fall of East Jerusalem. While there we picked up a hitchhiker, Renata Adler, a reporter for the *New Yorker* magazine who was calm under shellfire. She wanted a ride back to Tel Aviv. Indeed, we found the back road running through a piece of Jordan and down to the sea and Tel Aviv. Mauldin was instantly smitten by our new companion, but there was still a war to cover, and new orders from Hearst: I was to remain in Israel, Fliegers was to exit to Cairo to report the war from the Arab side.

Fliegers wasn't going anywhere. Back at the Dan I found Hearst's Paris bureau chief bedded down in his room, an entourage and ample Scotch whiskey at his side. His vehicle had detonated a land mine near Gaza, killing Oyserman, the CBC cameraman, and wounding an Israeli newsman and himself. Fliegers was studded with steel shrapnel, damaged more seriously than he would let on, perhaps because of shock. He would spend his immediate future in hospital beds and thereafter trigger airport security alarms even with empty pockets. We spoke briefly and I went back to work after a few hours sleep.

Just past dawn, as we drove out of the Dan Hotel garage, a beautiful lady in a denim shirt and body-tight blue jeans came to my open window and asked if she could join us on our battlefield journey. Mauldin beat me to an affirmative answer. This was Dahlia, and she would become as valuable to our coverage as she was beautiful. Neither Mauldin nor I would question her credentials or motivation. We were overcome at the chance for her company. An Iraqi Jew, Dahlia spoke fluent Arabic, Hebrew, and English. She also had courage and a sense of humor. We loved her and so did the troops, rising out of slit trenches, we visited near Gaza and, later, on the

West Bank of the Jordan. Once past Jerusalem, the Israeli blitz had carried down to Jericho near the Jordan River, south to Hebron and north to Nablus and Megiddo. Guderian couldn't have done it better. Resistance was spotty or nonexistent. Under the lightning assault, the Legion had retreated across the River Jordan toward Amman.

Now we had a routine: drive to a selected front, catch the action, return to Tel Aviv to clear copy with the Israeli military censor, then file through government telex. With two notable exceptions, the censorship was light and reasonable, not worthy of argument. A bit of food, a few shots of whiskey, maybe an hour or two of sleep, then back to the front in Bill's rented Ford. After three days, Mauldin broke the routine, giving me no explanation. He flew back to Chicago, bearing a fat portfolio of photos and drawings. In a dispatch to the *Sun-Times*, he said he had been unable to move photos taken of troops entering the Sinai, "the most frustrating experience of my life." He told of our cross-border trips to watch the fall of Latrun and Jerusalem and asked his editor to "tell the family I'm fine." He left me the German Ford and Dahlia.

By now, days were blurring into one prolonged work shift. Too much had happened too fast and sleep came only in snatches. Calendars and timepieces, I learned in those days, are creations of the intellect—useful, but arbitrary. They are not absolutes. Fortunately, I marked the changing of dates in my notebook so that I could assign events to their proper day, thus maintaining what passes for an orderly sequence.

Russ Braley of the *New York Daily News* joined me for a swing across the West Bank—Ramallah, Hebron, Jenin, Nablus. Israeli military traffic on these back roads through what a day earlier had been Jordanian territory, was crowded, curious, and revealing: tractor-trailers hauling armor, two and a half ton trucks bearing soldiers. All of them bore the mark of the Sinai, brown dirt on the vehicles, sand and fatigue on the faces of the soldiers. Having slaughtered or driven Egyptian forces back across the Suez Canal, Israel was shifting its army to the north—moving them without much rest.

"They're going to invade Syria," I told Braley, remembering the farmers of Kefar Blum. "They're going to clean out those guns on the slopes above the Hula Valley."

So I surmised, and, back in Tel Aviv, I filed to New York without quarrel from the censor. And I sent another story, this one straight from the government press officer about a mistaken attack on a U.S. Navy vessel off the Sinai which had resulted, alas, in casualties. To my professional embarrassment, I filed this government handout without even a cursory question. This was a war of shoot first, reflect later, and I had no trouble imagining a hair-trigger artillery lieutenant calling down fire on a vessel that might have been an enemy. In fact, the USS *Liberty* was a spy ship, or, as the Pentagon called it, a "technical research ship." It was struck not by one inadvertent bomb but by a series of air and sea attacks that killed 31 U.S. seamen. The vessel stayed afloat but had to be towed to Italy for repairs. The reason for this odd assault has never been given by either our Pentagon or the Israeli government. The most informed speculation attributes the deadly attack to the Israelis' excessive zeal in keeping the United States ignorant of the shift of its army from the Sinai to the Hula Valley for an invasion of Syria. But that explanation is at odds with the government censor's release of my dispatch to New York detailing such an army movement and forecasting the invasion of Syria. If, after three decades, the attack is no longer a tightly keep secret, the reason why is still a puzzle.

Having filed all of this, the informed with the untruth, I found Yitzhak Austrian in the press office canteen, told him what I had written, and said I planned to go early on the next morning to the upper Galilee to witness the invasion. He did not dispute my speculation or my intent.

"I'll go with you," said the government press officer. "You may need official help."

Austrian, Russ Braley, and I departed Tel Aviv long before dawn in case my hunch was correct and the invasion kicked off in the morning twilight. The road ran through Nazareth in the hills and Tiberias on the Sea of Galilee, past Capernaum where Jesus turned water into wine and preached "Blessed are the meek," then into the fertile Hula. It was so quiet, Yitzhak cradled his Uzi sub-machine gun. The half-tracks and military trucks were long gone.

There was a bridge over the Jordan, a river no wider than the average Tennessee creek, less than a mile from Kefar Blum, the kib-butz where Yitzhak and I had journeyed on the second day of my visit to the Holy Land. The farmers, mostly from South Africa, were En-glish speakers. I reckoned it would be an ideal vantage for witness-ing action above us on the slopes of the Golan. There were just the three of us. Nothing else moved on these roads. Dahlia, probably forewarned of the danger, had taken the day off. Bud Nossiter said no to my invitation to the invasion, a grand show and a helluva story, if it came off as I expected.

"We go back to Tiberias," said Austrian when at dawn we turned off the main road and headed down a small side road to the bridge and to Kefar Blum. It was too quiet, not a farmer in the sur-rounding fields, not a vehicle, save our German Ford, on the roads. I said no. He shrugged and frowned.

Three grim looking farmers greeted us under the struggling shade trees at Kefar Blum. The other members of this commune were tucked away in bunkers. There was a field telephone, a radio hitched to one tree, and a slit trench a few feet away. Despite the lack of military uniforms or insignia of rank, it was an advanced artillery observation post. The radio frequently crackled in Hebrew. The sun and the temperature were rising, but the army had yet to move, the day had yet to stir.

The first sounds, like an orchestra warming, were screams from three Israeli Mysteres, slashing down with bombs for Tel Azaziat, the Syrian fortification a few hundred feet above and sev-eral kilometers away from Kefar Blum. The pop of antiaircraft fire followed, and then the boom of exploding 250-pound bombs; a crescendo at the close of the first movement. We stood and watched. "It's come," said one farmer-artillery observer. "Deliverance from Tel Azaziat."

Emptied of bombs, the aircraft broke away, their shrieks re-placed by the clank and heavy squeals of tanks, jeeps, and half-tracks on the road beside our observation post—a point where the road made a 45-degree turn to the north and to the bridge across the Jordan and into the Syrian hills. For several minutes we watched the invasion of Syria, knowing the impending horrors of steel and flesh, yet transfixed as though the whole matter was abstract.

The Israeli column reached halfway to Tel Azaziat before the first Syria shells came down on or toward Kefar Blum. I dove for the slit trench, banging my knee in the extreme haste. Braley and Austrian landed on top of me. The hour that followed was an unblended symphony of incoming shells—heavy artillery, light artillery, and mortars. They seemed to fall all about us, reaching for the nearby road and the Jordan River bridge apparently. Each species, like the pieces of an orchestra, had its own sound to accompany its trajectory. Some seemed to be coming directly into our slit trench. Austrian was calm—"nothing compared to Tobruk," said the British Army veteran. Braley, veteran of our Pacific War, said, "I never went through anything like this in the Philippines." My fright nearly caused a loss of physical control. Some relief came at not having brought Nossiter, the father of four, into this maelstrom. I held fixed to the belly of the slit trench for what seemed to be an eternity, the time it took the Israeli column to close on Tel Azaziat.

There was a pause in the shellfire. We jumped from the trench and ran toward the German Ford, still intact, slowing long enough to gather a souvenir, a razor-sharp piece of shrapnel curled into a nasty ball. I floorboarded the Ford, so we bounced over the shell-pocked byroad, then sped over the highway to Tiberias, where the government had a military censor and a telex ready to dispatch what Braley and I believed would be the first exclusive accounts of Israel's invasion of Syria.

"Thanks God we are alive," said Yitzhak Austrian.

"I've never been so exposed to shellfire, or so scared, in my life," I answered.

"No—not artillery shells. Thanks God for saving us from your driving."

NEITHER RUSS BRALEY nor I got that year's Pulitzer Prize for daring reportage. As it turned out, our accounts were not exclusive.

Al Friendly, managing editor of the *Washington Post*, had seen it all through binoculars from the Israeli Army command post in the hills on the western side of the Hula Valley. He won the Pulitzer. Obviously he had been tipped on the invasion by the highest authorities and escorted to the command post. As a result, his underling, Bud Nossiter, declined my invitation to an invasion and stayed in Tiberias. It would be Friendly's story, not Bud's.

There remained business in Syria and Nossiter did join me on a recoilless-rifle-mounted jeep in an armored column pressing up the Golan Heights toward El Quneitra, the largest city west of Damascus. We left the Ford on a dirt road at the bottom of the hills and fared well for several hours. Our hosts had "liberated" Jenin on the West Bank the day before and were still hopped up on adrenaline ("flushed with success" is the military euphemism) and ready for the next battle. As the sun set behind us over the Mediterranean, an incoming Syrian shell landed on a vehicle a hundred yards ahead in our column. As easily as we had been invited aboard, the company commander came back to order Nossiter and me to get lost. He did not want to risk the blood of American reporters on his company records. We didn't argue, despite a long downhill walk toward darkness to our car. There was copy to file in Tiberias, the first reports from inside Syria.

It was a stroll in the silky Golan dust until we reached the bottom of the hills. Quite suddenly, the night was pitch black, starless, given the dust stirred up by guns and vehicles. For reasons I can only ascribe to fatigue and the zeal to file copy, the danger of two men in civilian clothes walking down from the hated Syria did not occur until I heard the bolt of an old Enfield rifle slam a .30-caliber bullet into its chamber, metal on metal. An Israeli roadblock.

I had an immediate surge of fear and the vision of a young Israeli conscript, barely big enough to shoulder the World War I relic of a weapon, on his first night of field duty and even more frightened of the apparition presented by Bud and me than we were of him. It was a terrifying vision. It was close to reality.

"Journalist!" I shouted.

Bud tried French: "Journaliste! Américain!"

We both raised our hands.

"Schriftsteller! Wir sind Schriftsteller!" I cried out, desperate that he might know a bit of Yiddish. Neither of us knew a word of Hebrew, not even the word for journalist, a potentially fatal omission in our vocabularies.

He did not fire, but he was shaking, finger on trigger, when we approached, hands reaching even higher into the black night. Another gun came on us, the roadblock commander. Neither knew a word of English and neither lowered his rifle pending a resolution of this mystery: two civilians walking in the dark down the road from the hated Syria. They took our wallets and press cards. We waited while the commander went up the chain of command on his radio and got word we were "friendly." I have rarely ever felt such relief.

Next morning, copy filed and the Ford gassed, we barreled past an army roadblock and a sentry poised with rifle on shoulder (if he fired he missed) up the road and into El Quneitra, a few hours behind the Israeli Army but slightly ahead of United Nations peacekeepers come to enforce a cease-fire and stand watch on a new Israeli-Syrian border. The Six-Day War was officially over. The new border would later shift a few miles to the west after the 1973 Mideast War. Otherwise, Israelis still occupy the Golan Heights and their old fortifications—guns once aimed down on Israeli farmers who demanded their politicians bring a military solution to their exposure.

I felt neither relief nor elation, only fatigue softened somewhat by Beethoven's Seventh Symphony playing on the car radio as I drove back to Tel Aviv that night. Nossiter, exhausted, slept sitting upright.

There followed a fast turnaround. Bud went back to his Paris bureau. Russ Braley returned to his normal post in Bonn. I accepted an Israeli Army invitation to fly into the Sinai, an Egyptian air base at Bir Gifgafa, and thence by truck to El Qantara on the Suez Canal. So did a dozen other newsmen. I had time for a nap before the military transport, a Korean War vintage C-119, flew across the desert and landed near the burnt shells of MIG-21s, relics of Israeli air strikes seven days earlier. From there we traveled in a convoy, one half-track, one machine gun–mounted jeep, and one Tel Aviv city bus, bearing the journalist cargo.

Egyptian soldiers, from the air looking like black ants on the tan Sinai landscape, were straggling back across the desert to El Qantara. They were terrified. But they were not shot. Instead, Israeli troops placed them on a barge and shipped them across the canal to Ismalia and thence, presumably, to their homes. We looked across the canal to palm trees and brilliant azaleas. It was my first trip to the canal since passage through it as a 19-year-old seaman on a merchant tramp out of Seattle. At that time, 1952, Egyptians were fighting British soldiers for independence. Fifteen years later, different politics, much more killing.

"The Sinai," wrote T. E. Lawrence, who led an Arab guerrilla force to glory against the Turks out there in 1917 and himself into literary immortality by telling the tale, "is a jolly desert." That description has escaped my observation. Maybe the exotic soldier was being ironic. What I have seen is a vast sandbox, crossed down its middle by a low range of bare hills and laced east to west by a narrow-gauge railroad built by the Turks and two crumbling highways built by construction crooks. The highway robbers devalued their cement with sand and split the savings with Egyptian politicians. The same has happened in several of our own states where road contracts come dear and road inspectors are cheap. The Prophet Moses is said to have received the Ten Commandments in the Sinai. None of these imperatives, however, commands or even suggests that the Sinai traveler carry lots of water and warm clothing. By day the desert heats to a dehydrating temperature of 120 degrees Fahrenheit. At night it cools to 42 degrees.

On return, our three-vehicle convoy got halfway between El Qantara and Bir Gifgafa, where it stalled, the bus up to its axles in sand, the sun long gone behind the Egyptian desert. We were stranded under a clear host of stars, a crescent moon. We were surrounded by dozens of devastated Egyptian military vehicles still bearing the upright corpses of their occupants. Israeli warplanes, distributing napalm, stopped the western flight of these troops to the barges at El Qantara, leaving an unfinished graveyard. The

desert smelled heavily of human decay; the dead showed their pro-
files against the night-light from stars. A "jolly desert" where we
stayed the night.

Nothing spared us from the stench, very little from the cold.
The little was provided by taking turns sleeping, one on top of another, in the narrow bus seats. My companion was Robert St. John,
a radio reporter once famed for his coverage in World War II. Now
he was too old and too skinny to provide much comfort. It was a
long night. I have no idea what happened to the dead soldiers we attempted to sleep among. Presumably, they were soon stripped of
their valuables by Sinai Bedouin, the desert nomads, some of whom
got rich from the vehicular refuse of war, particularly the small
wheels and sprockets from tanks and half-tracks. Evidence of their
success quickly became apparent with the appearance in the Sinai of
Bedouins in Mercedes cars, the produce of Stuttgart, instead of the
indigenous camels.

Liberated from the sand and the dead by an army wrecker,
and flown back to Tel Aviv, I washed off the desert residue and rang
up Dahlia at what I presumed to be her home. She was ready for another field trip, this one to the West Bank, passage through the roadblocks secured by allowing an Israeli Foreign Office Arab expert to
come along as an observer. We drove straight to Hebron, an ancient
town with a split religious identity—then as now, a furnace of
Palestinian nationalism, but also the burial place of the Hebrew
prophet Abraham. Dahlia stood by me in a local pool hall, crowded
with idle Arabs, when I took on the resident shark in a game of
eight-ball. Our passenger, frightened beyond reason, stayed inside
the Ford, doors locked, and demanded an immediate return to Tel
Aviv. Dahlia laughed at his fear, and I won applause from the idlers
by defeating the local shark. It was the best game of pool I ever shot
in my life.

Relying on Dahlia's gift of Hebrew and Arabic speech and my
knowledge of the back road up the Golan Heights, we set out, sans
the Foreign Office passenger, to dodge army roadblocks and government red tape and go back to Syria. The road was steep and
dusty and we did not get far.

Midway up the slope we reached a Syrian Army camp, newly occupied by Israeli troops. No doubt it had served as a backup to the fortifications of Tel Azaziat just below it. While Dahlia bedazzled the troops, I interviewed a young lieutenant who told me Israelis had seized four Soviet advisers when they captured the camp a few days earlier. The Soviets were aiding their Syrian client's artillery fire, he said.

"Who commanded these troops," I asked, curiosity heightened by the fact that some of those shells came uncomfortably close to my personal flesh.

"I did," he answered. This information was freely volunteered and I accepted it as a matter of truth—until the military censor in Tel Aviv rejected not only my story but the accuracy of my facts. For reasons best known to their political leadership, the Israelis did not want the world to know about Soviet soldiers advising Syrian combat troops. It was the only time I was censored.

The German Ford, my inheritance from Mauldin, began laboring as we resumed the drive uphill. It coughed and sputtered and within a mile refused to go farther. We turned around. What the hell, I had what I thought to be another scoop, time to go back and file. My spirit was willing. The Ford was not. On the main road between Tiberias and the Lebanese border, the car gave one last, terminal cough, and quit. We pushed it off the road near a sign pointing uphill to the archaeological dig of Hazor. An omen?

Cars and wars may end, but nothing is ever finished. The events of the past month to which I had given all of my energy—events which would shape the boundaries and the future of this region for the rest of my life—would pass as the Hittites, Canaanites, Egyptians, Hebrews, Romans and Brits had passed through Hazor. The Hebrew warrior-prophet Joshua had burned Hazor to the ground. King Solomon had it rebuilt. Yet this city on a hill showed itself only as a hole in the ground; a relic.

Dahlia and I took hands, walked up the hill, and looked down into Hazor's past where soldiers, merchants, mystics like Jesus, salesmen like Paul, had camped. The remains of Hazor said nothing and everything, and for the first time in a month I felt exhausted and empty, as spent as the engine on our Ford.

An Israeli military truck graciously stopped, put a rope on our bumper, and dragged, at a wreck's pace, our disabled Ford back to the Dan garage. Dahlia went back to her home. I joined a party rejoicing in the Dan's bomb shelter, Max the bartender presiding with martinis. Patrick O'Donovan, Donald Weiss, Chris Dobson, Jimmy Cameron, a couple of Hungarians, and several others I didn't recognize drank heavily on the freeload. Hanon Barrone, a favorite from the Israeli Foreign Office, celebrated with us. We were happy for more than survival. This was it—peace in our time. The Israelis could swap territory conquered the past week for peace with the Arabs. Weiss urged me to skip straight from Tel Aviv to Vietnam. "A great war to cover. If you liked this one you'll have a ball in Vietnam." Barron, a slight, sandy-haired intellectual, reinforced our euphoria: now it was "land for peace."

I was swept away, the mood and the lesson of Hazor already faded.

A DECADE LATER in Jerusalem to cover a trip by President Jimmy Carter I paused after work for a drink at the Hilton Hotel bar. The White House press gang was there along with an Israeli attorney. He stood next to me. Carter had, in fact, fulfilled part of that "land for peace" prospect which we had celebrated at the end of the Six-Day War, pushing the Israelis and Egyptians into trading the captured Sinai for a peace treaty. I discussed this with the attorney, who otherwise seemed a little depressed. Woman trouble, he said. The talk moved on to the '67 war and his work for army intelligence.

"Ever work with a beautiful Iraqi lady, fluent in Hebrew, Arabic, and English?" I asked, with only an inkling of suspicion.

"Dahlia? Of course," he perked up. "Who could miss her. Not quite Iraqi, though. More English. She was called back from London to work with us during the fighting—a real comedown, I guess. She's a figure in London society, married to what you would call a fat-cat owner of one of England's largest department stores."

I wasn't much surprised, nor was Dahlia's character diminished by this knowledge of her role as a lovely sort of double agent. I doubt she was as valuable to Israeli intelligence as she was to Hearst Newspapers and the *Chicago Sun-Times*. Besides, as General Forrest once told a Yankee colonel he hoodwinked into premature surrender, "all is fair in love and war."

THE PALESTINIANS
THE "WAR
OF ATTRITION"

ON MAY 27, 1970, almost three years since the end of the Six-Day War, I took a taxi from the Intercontinental Hotel on Jebel Amman in Amman, Jordan, across a deep valley to a guarded compound on Jebel Hussein, only a high-powered rifle shot away. This was headquarters for the Palestine Liberation Organization (PLO).

It was a modest establishment, newly built concrete block structures, surrounded by old concertina wire and casually attired Fedeyeen—PLO fighters—bearing AK-47 rifles. From this compound, the PLO would share ruling power over Jordan with its king, Hussein, an awkward political arrangement brutally terminated four months later when the king unleashed his Bedouin Army on the PLO, killing thousands and scattering the rest over the hills into southern Lebanon. Unlike the Palestinians, settled people of towns and farms, Bedouins are nomadic people of the Mideast deserts, only lately come to modern social life—such as the Jordanian Army. Like a killer oil slick on a high tide, the Israeli-Palestinian conflict would spread over the mountains to the Mediterranean. The peace we had contemplated in the Dan Hotel at the end of the 1967 war had not materialized and might not do so in the time that our lives have yet to spend.

On the strength of my press card bearing the imprimaturs of King Hussein and the PLO, a guard let me pass into the compound and to the office of Abu Omar, the organization's chief spokesman, but not, so far as anyone could tell, the main object of my visit. Tipped by an informed source, I was in search of John Mikail, born Ramallah, Palestine, October 24, 1935, graduated from Harvard in chemistry and government studies. Until recent months Mikail had been an assistant professor of political science at the University of Washington in Seattle and greatly valued, according to his official university papers. Reluctantly, the university had granted him leave to research "broader political problems." My informant said he left to fight for Palestinian independence and that he might be found in the PLO's Amman headquarters.

Abu Omar, a slight, handsome man wearing black rimmed eyeglasses and a dull brown military uniform, greeted me in the office building doorway. He eyed me up and down like a cop who might one day have to pick me out of a police lineup. We shook hands before, on signal, his two gunmen escorted me down a hallway and into a small room with one chair. Otherwise the space was bare concrete. They demanded and received my press card and U.S. passport and left, closing and locking the thick wooden door. I was the prisoner of this dreaded organization in a windowless room, having only my imagination to see the drill of Fedeyeen, training for raids into Israel, in the compound surrounding my cell.

Life in the Mideast amidst the Arab-Israeli conflict over territory had an embarrassing way of turning out like a B-movie melodrama, albeit one written by a moral agnostic, thus having no heroes or villains. I was already familiar with the script.

Two weeks prior to this abrupt imprisonment in Amman, I hired the toughest looking, English-speaking cab driver in Beirut for a trip to the southern slopes of Mount Hermon to follow up an Israeli armored incursion against PLO soldiers—a three-day pocket war with major casualties. Faud, the cabbie, had a Mercedes car and, more important, a cousin in the Lebanese defense ministry who could set me up with the officer responsible for military command of south Lebanon. I needed a permit to travel through their defense lines and into Lebanese territory held by PLO guerrillas.

In crisp green fatigues, the general looked like he had just stepped out of formal military ceremonies at Fort Benning. Faud turned obsequious in his presence, kissing the general's ring. The deal took only a few minutes: an aide drafted the order, the general signed it and then accepted four $25 American Express traveler's checks, courtesy of Hearst Newspapers. The bribe would be duly reported on my expense account. He saluted me smartly and we left.

The first roadblock south of Sidon, a biblical city on the Mediterranean, was a pass. The next at a bridge across the Hasbani River below Mount Hermon was a stop. There were fresh tank tracks, residue of the Israeli pull-back two days before. "No further," a Lebanese lieutenant commanded, despite the $100 (exchanged on Beirut's black money market, $400) defense ministry permit. "Up there is Fatah and we have no control."

At this point, the script would make a skeptic roll his eyes to heaven. But this is life in the Mideast, not the movies, and as the lieutenant commanded me to return to Sidon, a shepherd, clad in a long cloak, and using a staff to tend a flock of five sheep, appeared on the roadway. He had monitored my encounter with the lieutenant and told Faud, in Arabic, he could break the impasse at the Hasbani. He withdrew a ballpoint pen from inside his cloak and wrote orders that I was to be welcomed in Fatah camps on the mountainside. He signed, or rather forged it, "Abu Ammar," the other name for PLO chairman Yasir Arafat. The lieutenant saluted as we drove through his roadblock, destination Kefar Chouba, the occupied Lebanese village from which PLO rocketeers fired Katushkas down on Metulla and Kiryat Shimona, Israeli villages in the upper Hula Valley.

It is the unperceived danger, not the one of which you are aware, that will get you. My fear on the uphill drive over this rough road was of a return of the Israeli Phantoms, bearing 250-pound bombs to complement their .50-caliber machine guns. In the three days before this trip, Phantoms has shot up everything live or moving toward Kefar Chouba. Might they return? Faud barely managed to get around a demolished bridge to cross a small creek. The roadside was littered with wrecked vehicles. Wrecked lives—refugees— were straggling down the narrow road, possessions on their backs, toward camps in Sidon or Beirut, Beirut's Sabra and Shatila being the most notorious. There is no more forlorn sight than a procession of the wretched going from comfort to uncertainty.

There was nowhere to go from Kefar Chouba, a lovely village with a gorgeous view of the fertile plain below and straight fields of fire into the Israeli settlements. We had but an instant to enjoy the beauty. A dozen Fedeyeen rose up from slit trenches, surrounded the Mercedes and snatched Faud and me from our seats, AK-47s aimed from all angles at our midsections. They were wild-eyed from lack of sleep or excessive adrenaline, the glassy-eyed look of combat and insufficient time to recover. They were shouting in Arabic. I was scared to death. "Américaine Phantome! Phantome Américaine!" As the script would have said, they "had my number, all right, and the number was about to be called up." Faud turned white. Somehow, despite dreadful fear, I managed to maintain composure, probably because I did not understand Arabic. What they were shouting, as Faud later translated, was a call for summary execution: "Frenchmen we let live, Americans no! Americans Phantome." My own little death chant. I could discern no dissent.

Before they could shoot I handed a Fedeyeen with a gun in my face the message from "Abu Ammar" (Arafat). There was a pause, a measure of relief. Then he thrust it back into my upraised hand: "Fatah. No Fatah. Saiqi, Saiqi!" My God. The unperceived danger. We had crossed another unmarked border from territory controlled by Al-Fatah to that controlled by As-Saiqi, the Syrian Army controlled faction of the PLO. The death chant resumed. I got ready to meet the Maker.

The chant diminished with the approach of a soldier in clean green fatigues, polished boots, and the gold leaf of an army major. He broke the ranks surrounding me. His manner suggested a man in charge.

"Why have you come here?" the major asked in clear English.

I can't explain it, but somehow, despite a profound fear for my life, I could still talk. I recalled my initial apprehension about destruction from Israeli warplanes.

"You and your troops are brave for coming out of your holes to welcome me and my driver despite all of these Israeli aircraft," I answered before describing my mission as a reporter.

"No," he replied. "You are the brave one." He was looking me square in the eye. A little smile that hinted sympathy curled around the corners of the major's mouth. At that moment I figured I had a chance to survive As-Siaqi. The major ordered an escort to show me the damage done by Phantoms to Kefar Chouba. When completed, he looked me in the eyes again, then ordered my release. The major had spared our lives. Faud and I drove away after two hours' captivity, and never before had release been so sweet.

For the next three days I came down to the street from my room at the Mayflower Hotel on the Hamra in Beirut to pay Faud $200 for his Mercedes and interpretive services. Each morning he showed up drunk. On the fourth morning he came sober. I paid, but he declined a job driving me to Damascus. He did, however, take me to the compound of Camille Chamoun, a former prime minister, leader of a Christian clan central to the government of Lebanon, and a courtly relic of an order fast passing. The heavily guarded compound was south of Beirut on the Mediterranean. We had a lovely supper, attended with quiet grace by Chamoun's English wife and half a dozen servants, a place and manner reminiscent of Mississippi Delta plantation dinners of the late 1930s. He wanted me to tell my government of the potential chaos coming to Beirut, and the prosperous coast, with the influx of PLO and the Lebanese refugees. It was a forecast soon to be realized.

THERE WAS NO IMMEDIATE THREAT inside the room at PLO headquarters on Jebel Hussein, just a locked door and the silence of bare walls. Another reel in the B movie. I sat smoking my pipe, surprisingly calm, perhaps immunized from terror by the trip to Kefar Chouba. With time on my hands, blood in my veins, I wondered what had drawn me back to this tragedy, a war of people with right on both sides, a regional conflict which could—many thought would—ignite international nuclear destruction.

The hangover of fear after the 1967 Six-Day War caused me to avoid reporting our own tragic conflict in Vietnam. I stayed close to lotus land, the Pacific Northwest, writing politics. But two years later and without the hangover, I accepted Hearst's proposal that I return to the Mideast to report both sides of increasingly active warfare. It was not for altruism, a notion that by reporting on the conflict the chance for peace might increase. It was visceral; my body chemistry.

There is nothing so exhilarating as to be shot at and missed. After the routine of conventional reporting, I felt like a recovering drunk in bad need of a drink; in this case adrenaline. Besides, there was a new element in the Mideast story, the emergence of the PLO, a bloody force shooting its way into global politics by raids across the border into Israel and the hijacking of commercial airliners. Who were these terrorists, as they were commonly described?

In essence, the Mideast in 1969 and 1970 featured two wars: one along Israel's borders with Lebanon and Jordan, the PLO's struggle for recognition through terror; the other along the Suez Canal, a fight between dueling Israeli and Egyptian snipers, airmen and artillery, the formally titled (largely forgotten) "War of Attrition." Our government viewed this deadly turmoil between our respective client states as but a hot piece of the Cold War between the U.S. and the U.S.S.R., the potential fuse to a thermonuclear exchange. Accordingly, we held steadfast behind Israel, our outpost in the Middle East.

Senator Henry Jackson, campaigning for reelection in Aberdeen, Washington, in 1970, expressed a prevailing Cold Warrior view that the PLO was a mere puppet of the Kremlin, a misconception I disputed in the privacy of his limousine en route down the freeway to another speech in Elma, Washington. I would never have disputed the senator in news stories of his Aberdeen speech—he was elected, I was not. Privately, I told him that even if by magic the Kremlin disappeared tomorrow, we were left with conflict between

Arabs and Israelis with arms dealers greedy enough to sell them weapons.

"If you knew what I knew," the senator, a ranking member of the Armed Services Committee, retorted, apparently referring to his Pentagon sources. The talk stopped when we sped past Elma doing 120 mph to avoid a reported assassination attempt on Jackson's life. Under state patrol protection, we hid for a while in a motel room just off Interstate 5 in Centralia, Washington. Caution was prudent. Police later arrested a man with a record of mental illness and a gun who had made the threat. They took his gun. The senator refused to accept my Mideast heresy.

Israelis were never so deluded as Jackson and his sources. They knew the Palestinians wanted a homeland territory—if not a return to the territory along the Mediterranean they had surrendered with the creation of Israel in 1948. Israelis may have dabbled in a bit of disinformation, but they understood that the Palestinian determination to have their own flag and passport existed apart from any Kremlin design. The reality of this determination was being written in blood.

The Soviets did have a major naval base in Alexandria and a firm hand on Gamal Abdel Nasser's Egyptian government when I returned to the Mideast in June 1969. Only a handful of Western newsmen were working the Cairo beat, including a Swedish TV crew arrested every day for taking films of the city, then released each evening. Our movements were controlled and accompanied by a tail—full employment for plainclothes cops. The *Egyptian Gazette*, a relic of the British Empire, provided the only English-language news source. A bizarre combination of primitive propaganda and outright fantasy, it featured photos of Nasser greeting official visitors from various African republics and glowing reports of victory in the "War of Attrition." I found one English-language book in the nearly empty Hilton Hotel, a volume devoted to General George Pickett's fatal charge against the Yankees at Gettysburg, scant relief from the tension of Cairo.

The foreign press office, a few blocks from the Hilton, was at the top of a sweeping flight of stairs guarded by two Egyptian soldiers in helmets and battle fatigues manning a .50-caliber machine gun. The press officer was Mr. Kamal Bakr, a Communist, a frog-like functionary whose methods owed much to Franz Kafka. This is a typical exchange between a western reporter and Kamal Bakr:

ME: "Mr. Bakr, I wish approval to visit a friend in Maidi [a Cairo suburb]."

BAKR: "This you cannot do without permission."

ME: "Mr. Kamal Bakr, from what authority may I seek permission to go to Maidi?"

BAKR: "I am that authority."

ME: "Mr. Bakr, may I have permission to visit my friend in Maidi?"

BAKR: "Permission is denied."

Nevertheless, with the help and cover of two German schoolteachers, I slipped my tail, visited Maidi and also the beach outside Alexandria where blond, blue-eyed Russian naval officers and overweight wives took their pleasure with the Mediterranean. So did we. My police tail gave me a dirty look, but not an arrest, when we returned to the steps of the Hilton. An arrest would have exposed his lapse of vigilance.

My guardians, plainclothesmen, along with the rest of Egypt's police, were said to be under the direct control of Soviet advisers. They were so eager for information (or misinformation), cops twice invaded my hotel room and rifled my file of dispatches to New York. One morning I found one of these missing, a story written with much haste to judgment and no prescience whatever. The lead said: "The Palestinians have a major revolution in search of its Mao Tsetung. Until they find such a leader to replace Yassir Arafat, their cause is doomed." It went on to disparage Arafat, a judgment so wrong as to be comical. Thirty years later Arafat remains the leader, one of the most remarkable political figures of the century. But at the time I was angered, not embarrassed, with the loss of my story. In its place in the copy file I placed a note in bold print: EGYPTIAN COP, FUCK YOU! RETURN MY STORY ON ARAFAT." The copy was back in its proper place the next day.

With another slip of the tail and some chance intelligence, I found Egyptian headquarters of the PLO in a shabby walk-up office building at 8 Elfy Street, a grim Cairo backwater. Abul el Abd, or so he gave his name, greeted me, the first American reporter to visit the office of Al-Fatah, the PLO's main fighting arm. He wore dark glasses and spoke perfect English, a bright contrast with his seedy surroundings.

"We intend to liberate our country," he began. "The United Nations has left our people in [refugee] camps like animals. We don't take an interest in the affairs of Arab governments. Regardless of what they do, we will fight until our land is liberated from the Zionists. You had an American patriot, Patrick Henry. He said 'Give me freedom [sic] or give me death.' It is that way with us. We are freedom fighters. We have to revolt. That is the nature of our people."

There at 8 Elfy Street was the bitter fruit of the Palestinian exodus from their homes in what had become Israel; the other side of a tragedy.

A YEAR LATER in Amman, locked in a bare room, fate unknown, I was prisoner of the "freedom fighters" at Fatah's headquarters. I considered my prospects. I was not bound and my host, Abu Omar, gave the instant impression of a man reasonable enough to weigh his choices on the disposition of his guest: terminally dispatch me as a nuisance (no one would ever know), or brief me on PLO objectives and free me to report to the world beyond Jebel Hussein. I thought my chances for survival here were better than those I had faced two weeks previously in Kefar Chouba.

But there was no music to kill time and anxiety, so I smoked and reviewed my notes from the previous weeks and waited. After an hour of isolation, a lock moved and the door to my impromptu cell on Jebel Hussein opened. The two PLO Fedeyeen had returned with my passport and press card to escort me down a hallway and into a spacious office.

Abu Omar rose from a chair behind an oversized desk and introduced himself. "I am John Mikail," he announced with only the hint of a smile and no clear identification of his official rank. Given the size of his office and complement of soldiers, it was obviously substantial. He was at least the spokesman, possibly the boss, of the PLO's foreign office. I felt at ease. He wanted a report on friends in Seattle. "Sol Katz [the University of Washington provost], is he well?" Professor Katz had signed Mikail's leave of absence.

Somewhat brazenly, I noted that Mikail had left an academic sinecure at the university for an uncertain future with a terrorist organization, one which had recently blown up an Israeli school bus killing 15 children. He nodded agreement. "It will be a long struggle. I may die before it is finished." I returned the nod. Mikail stiffened when I asked why Fatah chose to kill Israeli school kids.

"Would you, and others of course, bother to come here if we did not commit such acts?" he asked. No, I admitted. He had made his point, yet he betrayed it with a flash look of distress. For a moment I felt sorry for the man, overwhelmed by the tragedy. John Mikail-Abu Omar did not murder children. History did.

I was freed to leave the PLO compound under the condition that I not reveal the American identity of Abu Omar—a promise which until now, 30 years later, was not breached. Mikail/Omar vanished three years after our meeting when the Syrian Army moved into Lebanon. He had fled to that apparent refuge after Jordan's King Hussein turned his army on the PLO, killing thousands, routing the rest across the mountains to Beirut, Tyre, and Sidon. Mikail was never found, despite efforts by U.S. Secretary of State Kissinger after prompting by Senator Warren Magnuson, who was tipped by me. It was the least I could do.

A long struggle; many casualties. A few evenings after my meeting with John Mikail, the sky brightened on the hill opposite the Amman Intercontinental Hotel, the night air crackled with automatic rifle fire. Business as usual for Amman. No one in the hotel bar gave a moment's attention. I took a morning flight to Beirut the next day, snatching a Jordan *Times* from a newsstand before boarding. Inside, below the fold, the newspaper carried a small item about a firefight outside the U.S. Embassy during which the military attaché, Major Bob Perry, had been shot dead. Perry, a bright, ambitious soldier, proficient in Arabic, had been the U.S. official most informed on the PLO's organization and leadership. He was also my own source for this intelligence.

The story looked fishy, and indeed was subsequently corrected: Perry had been murdered by a burst of Kalashnikov bullets fired by gunmen of a radical PLO faction, the Popular Front for the Liberation of Palestine. His wife and two children witnessed the assassination. Perry, a protégé of Professor Joseph Malone, vice president of the American University in Beirut, had been assigned to the PLO intelligence beat, possibly by Malone himself. He came to know too much. Possibly by chance, I met Malone on arrival at the Beirut Airport and burst out with my feelings of anger, horror, and frustration at the killing of Major Perry. Malone, however, remained calm. He might well have shrugged: another day, another casualty. I admired his professional behavior. It seemed more soldierly than academic.

"Did you find what you were looking for in Amman?" he asked.

"No," I lied, keeping my promise to Mikail.

A few nights later, with a couple of Brit reporters and several Palestinians working for a PLO front organization, Friends of Justice in the Middle East, I got very drunk. Our hostess was Saroya Antonius, heiress to a Palestinian fortune, daughter of the historian George Antonius, and angel to the Friends. An attractive woman of my own age, her wealth and social position gave her great mobility and influence in Beirut society. Her friends were a who's who among the players in Lebanon's murky politics.

Late in the evening, tongues loosened by Saroya's liquor, the Palestinians began to talk about Professor Malone. What they suggested was that his official duties extended beyond his job at the American University. Someone mentioned Bob Perry, our military attaché in Amman. When my head cleared the morning after, Saroya drove me up to her retreat in the mountains above the Mediterranean. Under my casual inquiry, she repeated stories about Malone. That was enough.

Whatever else he may have been, Malone was a son of Seattle, a scholar of some renown—his expertise ranged from studies of the Kurds to the economic origins of the American Revolution— and a friend. He threw a party the night before I left Beirut. I got him aside: "It's time you go," I said. "There is too much talk among the Palestinians. Whether true or not, it's time to get out of this city." He offered no response, not even a thank you for the tip. But later, in the fall of 1970, I got a brief note from Professor Malone under the letterhead, "Chairman, Department of History, Kansas State University." Malone made it safely home yet later volunteered, probably at the risk of his life, to return to the American University in Beirut to succeed its recently assassinated president. He died of natural causes before his offer was accepted. He is my notion of an American patriot.

MY WORK in the summer of 1970 was unfinished. There was another hot conflict to report, the War of Attrition, an appendage of the Cold War waged by Soviet and American client states, using mostly jet aircraft and heavy artillery, producing a steady flow of casualties in 1969 and 1970. The Suez Canal, with Egypt on its west bank, Israel on its other side, was the epicenter of the fight. Almost forgotten by now, the War of Attrition loomed at that time as the potential trigger of a nuclear Armageddon.

It began with Israeli Prime Minister Yitzhak Rabin's strategic air strikes at the Nile Valley, the heart of modern Egypt and its ancient civilization. The United States acquiesced in this escalation of battle beyond the the relative limits of artillery and sniper exchanges across the canal. Washington regarded Soviet warnings against the Nile strikes as a bluff. They were not.

Egyptian President Nasser went to Moscow in January 1970, and returned to Cairo with the commitment of 14,000 Soviet airmen, troops, and technicians, and with these, a complement of their latest surface-to-air missles (SAM-3s) never before deployed outside the Soviet Union. Or so we now know. At the time, this massive addition of Soviet arms was more rumored than ascertained. I aimed to see what was going on in Egypt.

Having said farewell to Joe Malone, Saroya, and other friends in Beirut, I went down the street from my hotel in the Hamra to purchase Egyptian pounds on the black market. Their cost was about one-fourth the official Cairo exchange rate. I stuffed the money into a pocket of my Israeli jeans, then flew off to Cairo via the airport in Nicosia, Cyprus, a standard, but indirect, means of travel between the Arab and Israeli worlds in those years of conflict.

Egypt was still in the clutches of the Soviets, but calmer and less restrictive than I found on my visit a year earlier. Cairo was a target for Israeli Phantoms, but guarded by the SAM-3s and Soviet MIG interceptors. The press office maintained blind censorship—you file copy in Cairo, they dispatch only what they want read in New York—but no police tails. Fearful of inflation, Nasser had the heat on black market money. I declared $100 U.S. to the customs officer at the airport, but not the $400 worth of Egyptian pounds in my pocket.

The Hilton was no longer so empty. There were several American adventure-travelers, a preacher and his flock from Kansas, a lady architect late of Edward Stone's New York firm, traveling alone to see the world. We became friends. The hotel's top floor now housed a flashy casino where I purchased a certificate of entrance, had a beer, and won a few dollars at roulette. I kept the cerificate.

Coming in cold to Cairo, Amman, Beirut, Damascus, or even Tel Aviv, I found the best sources to be Western military attachés, careful professionals. They had information. They also wanted information that might be available only to a working reporter: they give, you give. The Hindi phrase for this is "changee for changee." If asked how a reporter "cultivates" sources, I say they don't. There's nothing to cultivate. Reporter and source come together naturally to give and to receive, each unto the other. I soon learned enough about the lay of the land in Cairo, or who might know what, to call on the British Embassy, a comfortable remnant of the Empire near downtown Cairo. There I hit a journalistic jackpot.

Her Majesty's military attaché, a smartly dressed colonel, provided the lead I was looking for. In exchange for my promise of a detailed report, he told me the purported location of two SAM-3 missile sites near Alexandria. All I had to do was to get there, observe, and return—a minor mission given any luck.

For $100 in American Express traveler's checks, I got a Mercedes and an English-speaking driver, Abraham, for the journey north alongside the Nile to Alexandria. Plainclothes police stopped us once. Abraham showed his papers. Mine weren't requested. Relieved, we moved on to the city created by Alexander the Great, a Macedonian, and populated over the millennia by Egyptians, Phoenicians, Greeks, French, British, and now, Soviets.

The purported missile site in downtown Alexandria looked phoney. A few miles west of the city, on the desert road to El Alamein, at a beach resort and real estate development named El Agami, loomed the real article, a 75-foot mound of freshly dug earth shaped like a shoebox and capped by six surface-to-air missiles. A nearby sign, brightly colored, welcomed visitors to "Honeymoon Beach."

The mound contained the electronic viscera needed to guide the missiles to the attacking Israeli Phantoms. A chainlink fence and dozens of Soviet soldiers guarded the compound, their trucks and giant, red-star marked helicopters all distinctly observed with the aid of my six-power monocular. It was all there, all of it made in Moscow or thereabouts. I had a world scoop.

Abraham stopped once to say his Muslim prayers before we returned to Cairo. I spent the night with my notebook beneath my pillow, and a chair wedged under the knob of the hotel room door. If cops came calling they'd have to bust inside. I finished my deal next day at the British Embassy with its military attaché. His tip was rewarded with a briefing on the missiles, complete with sketches. He was grateful and complimentary, but now I needed to get out of town.

I caught the first jet leaving Cairo and landed in Athens, having bluffed my way through Egyptian customs. My heart sank lower than the Obion River in autumn when the Cairo airport official, checking my papers, looked up to inquire how I had managed to spend two weeks in Egypt on the $100 I declared on arrival? I had done it, of course, on the black market pounds purchased in Beirut. Had I so confessed, I would have headed to the Cairo jailhouse, instead of Athens airport—a criminal matter of currency violation. Easy, I explained, showing the Hilton casino certificate. Good luck at the gambling tables. He smiled, offered congratulations, and let me pass.

Aircraft wheels up and clear of Egyptian customs and censors, I wrote furiously on my Olympia portable, aiming to telex the missile story to New York from the Athens airport. The first cut wouldn't work. I lacked a clean scoop. *Newsweek*, already on the airport newsstand, carried a full-page cover picture of an Egyptian SAM-3 site. It was taken from a satellite and acquired, it would be rumored, through the magazine's excellent relations with the CIA. I rewrote my story, filed to New York, and caught the first flight to Tel Aviv. Two men from *Time* greeted me on the Lod Airport ramp with explicit questions about my visit to the Egyptian missile site. They refused to answer my questions about where they got the tip on my trip to Alexandria. Mossad, the Israeli secret service, is a good bet. "For 35 cents you can read all about it in tomorrow's editions of Hearst Newspapers," I answered. They shrugged and faded from the airport ramp.

To catch the thrill of battle from the Israeli side, I teamed with Christopher Dobson of the *London Daily Mail* and a government press officer to travel in our rented Volkswagen across the Sinai Desert to El Qantara on the Suez Canal. We carried the customary provisions, a case of beer and a five-gallon can of water. The desert by day is very hot and very dry, a threat to survival like Egyptian artillery.

The promise of an army half-track to carry us the last ten miles into Qantara, the range of Egyptian gunners, failed to materialize when we reached the last Israeli Army camp. We decided to push on in the unarmored VW Beetle. Not a living creature or vehicle came into sight as we dashed down the crumbling road, past the British military cemetery where the remains of General Allenby's and T. E. Lawrence's troopers lay buried, and into the shell-shattered city.

The firing started after we got down into the formidable Israeli bunkers, steel reinforced by rails from the old Cairo to Damascus railroad. Fifty-caliber machine guns pointed through slits to Egyptian positions in sight across the canal. The bunkers were surprisingly cool and certainly comfortable when artillery boomed fire from the other side. A little dust, a bit of noise, but no alarm at all inside the fortification. The pop of afterburners, penetrating steel and sand, alerted us to a dogfight between Israeli Phantoms and Egyptian MIGs up above the bunkers. Almost certainly, the MIGs were piloted by Soviet airmen, Egyptian pilots being no match for their adversaries. There were casualties during this shoot-up.

When it ceased a few hours after it began, Chris and I decided to run for it—"it" being the censor in Tel Aviv where we would file copy on the day's firefight at the canal. I had the wheel of the VW, throttle to the floorboard. It bounced like crazy over shell-made potholes. This time there was a sign of life on the highway. An Israeli truck, three soldiers in the cab, rushed past us a few miles out of town. They were going in, probably to resupply ammunition. We waved. They waved back and smiled.

The censor in Tel Aviv gave a funny look and an outlandish comment when Chris and I turned over our copy and showed our credentials.

"What are you doing here? You're reported dead."

"Sorry to disappoint you."

"But you three were the only ones on the road between the town and the military base. A shell hit a vehicle and three were killed."

"Wrong. We passed a two-and-a-half-ton military truck heading into Qantara as we headed out. But please clear the copy before you clear up the casualty report."

He shook his head and proceeded.

I began to think I should never come back to this conflict again. But I would return, still working both sides, looking for signs of a resolution, sometimes, as in 1993, feeling optimistic, usually pessimistic, but never indifferent—a captive to its tragedy, a prisoner of its drama.

Beirut, the Paris of the Mediterranean, in 1977 looked more

like the Berlin of 1945, when I checked into the Mayflower Hotel, an old haunt and favored watering hole for the working press and their friends. Worse than its physical destruction from two years of civil war was the loss of its spirit. The Hotel St. Georges and the Phoenicia Intercontinental were gone. Not even much rubble marked their former presence so fanatical had been the fighting between Lebanese Christians, Sunni and Shiite Muslims, Palestinians shot out of Jordan, and the Syrian intervenors. When Lebanon's fragile, but profitable, political alignment between Christians and Muslims collapsed, war and Palestinians came into the vacuum. Gone also were most of my friends, and those remaining had aged into gray flesh and hair and hollowed eyes. You had to move carefully around Beirut, where assorted thugs and ideologues were kidnapping Westerners for ransom.

I called on Mohsen Slim at his well-guarded compound some distance from the Mayflower and the U.S. Embassy. An elegant, French-educated lawyer, Slim was the leader of the Shiite faction in the Lebanese Parliament. He also had a home in Paris, but he had not quit on Beirut. I wanted Slim to arrange for me a safe passage, meaning PLO escort, into the Palestinian dominated hills of southern Lebanon. I had free-lanced into that territory before, and that was once too often.

And he—surprise!—wanted something from this reporter; the game is essentially the same whether played in Washington, D.C., Cairo, or Olympia. Actually he wanted two things, the first was a visit to his compound by the U.S. ambassador to Lebanon, Richard Parker, one of the best American representatives I have ever encountered in a foreign country. An Arab scholar and a man of common sense, Dick Parker could have laughed me out of his embassy office when I gave him the proposal. He was big-time ransom bait, and no compound in Beirut was that well guarded. Instead he said no.

More than the ambassdor, Slim wanted a courier—that is, me—to contact sources in Jerusalem with word that Lebanese Shiites wished to make common cause with Israelis. They wanted arms with which to fight Palestinians, Syrians, and Sunnis; and in the event—not terribly unlikely—that the Israelis came invading Lebanon, Shiites wished to fight on their side against the other factions.

I did not get an escort into southern Lebanon, and thus didn't go, but I kept my side of his other request, that of the courier to Israel. Why? It was a matter of good faith and curiosity. Not every day does a reporter get to play emissary and, Lord knows, down the line there was probably a story to tell newspaper readers.

I laid this unusual message on the ears of a friend in the Israeli foreign office—a trusted friend. He questioned me and made careful notes, no doubt transmitted to his government, run by the right-wing Likud Party and headed by Menachem Begin. It went for naught. Come the invasion in 1982, the Israelis shunted the Shiites aside and made common cause with the Gemayel (as opposed to the Chamoun) Christian clan of Lebanon. This misadventure was climaxed by the massacre of Palestinian refugees in the Beirut camps of Sabra and Shatila, another show of man's inhumanity and a blot on the Begin government. In spite of all its killing, the PLO survived this war.

Would an Israeli-Shiite alliance, instead of an Israeli-Bashir Gemayel alliance, have altered the 1982 war? The courier doubts it.

THIS REPORTER-COURIER-PRISONER struggled with the return from Mideast turmoil to the calm of civil politics in the Pacific Northwest. I had begun to feel myself like a little brother in the truly disfunctional family of man. There was a practical matter of turning from contacts and news sources in the Mideast to those in Olympia and Washington, D.C. The real trouble, however, was psychological, possibly visceral. I suffered a profound disquiet, if not an emotional depression, shifting from a steady concern over physical security, and its attendant, excessive use of adrenaline, to local venues where there was no such worry; from the problem of filing copy through sometimes hostile censors, to friendly places where filing was as easy as a telephone call to the office.

It would take me weeks to shake the letdown. Brushing with death in the Middle East reordered my values, probably leading to a divorce from my wife, Peggy Lorenz, possibly inspiring a more aggressive approach to my coverage of domestic politics—nobody is shooting, so why not push ahead? For a self-confessed politician lover, I could get awfully rough in the investigation and exposure of officeholders who had conflicts between their public duties and private interests.

I had been advised against marriage by my sophisticated older sister, Catherine. "You are too given to adventure, too restless, too enthralled with your work, wretched as it may seem to some, for domesticity—never mind domestic tranquility. Marriage would not be fair to your wife." She was correct, alas, and much of the time I was gone from home or planning to be gone. Yet I cannot have regrets, given the issue of this marriage—my two magnificent daughters, whom I not only love but like.

Once, when I was in the throes of readjustment, my friend John Haydon, the visionary Seattle Port commissioner, turned on me with a lecture: "Why the hell don't you get out of the way and leave those Arabs and Jews alone to kill each other. Why have you made their killing each other your business?"

Taken aback, I wanted to strike him. Frustrated, I couldn't even mutter a rational response about the conflict's role in the Cold War. And I was helpless to explain how one could become a captive witness to a human tragedy, and, to a lesser extent, remain so to this day—the tragedy being unresolved, blood still flowing.

When will it end? It will end when the sum of Israelis and Palestinians concerned with rational self-interest overwhelms the minority among them blinded and turned fanatic by religious and territorial imperatives; maybe never, given the human condition.

CAMBODIA AND US

"HAVE YOU THE BUDDHA?" asked our guide before we moved across a dry gully in the heavy morning heat and into the no-man's land separating guerrillas of the Khmer People's National Liberation Front (KPNLF) and regulars of the Vietnamese army—the ant and the elephant of Southeast Asia, warring in the scrub forest of northwestern Cambodia.

Despite my initial chuckle, this was not a joke. We were heading into mortal combat against the 8th Regiment of the 5th Vietnamese Division occupying the village of Talei about 13 miles from the Thai border. Our guide, Soeung Sak, an English-speaking intelligence officer, meant did we carry the protection of a good luck charm, the magic to stop bullets.

We did not. We did have our wits, although skeptics might have brought these into question. With Bill Sumner, companion on three mountain climbing expeditions, I had made a deliberate decision to join the jungle guerrillas, and to go with them into combat, to photograph and write about their fight to drive the Vietnamese from their country. This was March 1984, tag end of the rainy season.

Getting to this point of departure for the climax of my mission had been a challenge greater than filing news stories to New York from 18,500 feet on K2. The lure was to give an account of a cause and a war virtually ignored outside Southeast Asia, especially by Americans who played a role in the creation of this political chaos. The chaos was incidental fallout from our war in Vietnam, a kind of global road-kill.

In March, 1969, President Nixon, in secret, launched B-52 bombers against Viet Cong sanctuaries in Cambodia, a neutral in the war. Whatever it did for our military effort in Vietnam, the bombing had an invigorating effect on Communist insurgents, led by Pol Pot, a Stalinist fanatic. Their ranks swelled. So did their arms, sometimes snatched from our own troops, and soon Communists took over the country, scattering our friends in Phnom Penh, reeducating about two million of their countrymen by killing them.

Only invasion and occupation of Cambodia by Vietnam quelled the mass slaughter. It was this occupation, however, against which the non-Communist Cambodian factions joined with Pol Pot's Communists to fight. If there has been a stranger alliance in modern warfare it has yet to be uncovered: officers and men of the KPNLF allied with Pol Pot, the murderer of their kith and kin.

I had only a vague awareness of this sordid piece of international politics when Son Sann, the tall, elegant, Mandarin prime minister of Cambodia under the neutralist ruler Prince Norodom Sihanouk, came to Seattle to address a gathering of refugees, survivors of the Asian holocaust, now settled around Puget Sound. Son Sann invited me to come and observe his fighters in Cambodia. I mulled the offer for a week. It meant getting close again to war, and, worse, war in an environment of extreme heat and poisonous snakes. Growing up around river bottoms, I had cultivated a deadly fear of reptiles, and consequently never met a water moccasin or a rattlesnake that I did not kill. But if successful, the trip also meant first reports on a war otherwise ignored. I weighed risk against opportunity and said yes. So did the *Post-Intelligencer*.

So did Sumner, the physicist, mountaineer, and photographer who had just quit his plans for a winter ascent of Mount McKinley, but retained a yen for dangerous adventure. Given his skill with a camera and calm under duress, Sumner was an ideal choice.

Under auspices of the KPNLF president, Son Sann, who had promised safe passage through one of the world's most fortified borders, we reached Bangkok in mid-March, held a clandestine meeting with four of the organization's representatives, and stalled. The Thai government was tolerating the presence of KPNLF, but only if it stayed semiunderground and away from the Cambodian border, where a six-foot, one-inch white man would stick out like a coal pile on a snowfield. In other words, these furtive gents were saying they could not provide transportation or papers for a border crossing into the KPNLF's military base in Ampil. We would be welcomed there if we could make it on our own. My heart sank as they slipped out of our cheap hotel in Bangkok's flourishing red-light district.

It took nearly two weeks in Bangkok to overcome this lapse in assistance, a major drain on my nerves and the fixed budget granted by the *P-I*. But the alternative, a return to Seattle, mission failed, was out of the question. Through a chance political connection, I got an interview with Arsa Sarasin, the permanent secretary of Thailand's Foreign Office. He was more than sympathetic with my interest in the Cambodian war ("Vietnam's Vietnam") and within a few days papers for the border crossing were expedited and presented. Sarasin wanted to secure American support for the guerrillas. ("You nuts? Can you imagine the reaction at home if we recommended getting involved again militarily in Southeast Asia," said Dave Moran, the spokesman, when I made a courtesy call at our embassy.)

One hurdle down, two more to go. To pass through the Thai Army's tanks and artillery we needed permission from the Defense Ministry and we needed a car and driver to transport us over the border and into Ampil. It took another day of shuffling around among military bureaucrats and more days in suspense before these papers arrived.

My anxiety was exacerbated by the heat, softened by evenings at a bar favored by foreign newsmen, and dinners with local contacts made before leaving Seattle. One of these was an American businessman with Seattle connections, the other a Thai businessman once employed by *Time* magazine as a stringer and by the Office of Strategic Services (OSS, predecessor to the CIA) as a spy. The ex-stringer fed us roast duck and cold beer and told how, late in World War II, he and his American boss recruited for their organization a tall, skinny Vietnamese cook with a stringy goatee. Ho Chi Minh would eventually leave our service to lead Vietnam's successful war against the French and Americans—Western colonialists, in his jargon.

The American contact had a charming guest from Indianapolis, an importer of women's apparel with a car and driver. We spent a day with Ms. Kai Irwin, traveling to a Cambodian refugee camp south of Bangkok. It was the start of what I figured to become a beautiful relationship with car and English-speaking driver, Sittichai. I offered him $100 a day from my dwindling budget for the trip to Ampil. By the time he accepted, all of the papers were in order for a border crossing. I bought a 50-pound bag of rice for sustenance in Cambodia and went to the press bar to celebrate relief from 100 pounds of anxiety. By God, we'd done it! The stall was broken.

Sittichai showed up at our hotel the next morning, but only with regrets. He couldn't make the trip, no matter the sum of money. His nephew, an officer in the Thai Army, had called to advise him that with the dry season nigh, the Vietnamese Army would move on Ampil and other guerrilla bases any day now. "Too risky for me and my car," said Sittichai, who, perhaps to soften my disappointment, offered a trip to outlaw camps, harboring opium growers and antigovernment rebels, across the Burmese border at the bargain rate of $50 a day.

Devastated, I went back to the drawing board, the foreign press bar where an acquaintance, Neal Davis, a correspondent for NBC News, came through like the U.S. Cavalry in a Buck Jones Western. He called a guy with a vintage Chevy and gave him my credentials and price. We met the next day and, following a short haggle, Sounchai agreed to drive us across the border to Ampil and to return us to Bangkok. This deal would stick. Neal, a hard-ass newsman, would not endure. A few years later he was machinegunned to death in a firefight between God knows who or what, near the royal palace.

After the heat and anxiety of Bangkok, I almost looked forward to a war. Its dangers loomed as an anticlimax.

We drove quickly past farmland through the artillery and tanks of the Thai Army and its checkpoints across a deep, red-colored

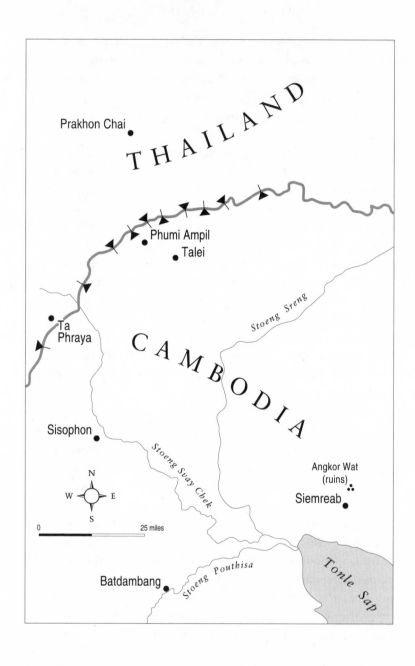

Prakhon Chai

THAILAND

Phumi Ampil
Talei

Stoeng Sreng

Ta Phraya

CAMBODIA

Sisophon

Stoeng Svay Chek

Angkor Wat (ruins)
Siemreab

N
W   E
S

0   25 miles

Batdambang

Stoeng Pouthisa

Tonle Sap

draw in front of the guns and into Cambodia. Sounchai, a stout fellow with a glutton's appetite and a gut to match, was calm and the trip could be likened to a Sunday drive in the country. There was relief from the human and air pollution of Bangkok. We drove a few miles through a scrub forest and then passed under an arched sign that said "Welcome to Ampil." We had arrived. We were arrested.

So much for communications between Bangkok and Ampil. Our hosts hadn't received official word of our visit. But there was too much to observe to be concerned about the questioning that followed. I imagined shades of Edgar Snow, the American journalist, the first to visit the caves of Yenan where Mao Tse-tung was building his armed revolution in China. Ampil's structures were bamboo and thatched, open on all sides to mitigate the jungle heat. There was a large compound for refugees, a middle-sized structure to school refugee children, another designated in Khmer as an officers' school. Two other structures sheltered light industry: textiles and artificial limbs. My heart sank at the sight of crudely made arms and legs. No explanation needed: We'd arrived in the midst of antipersonnel mines and land mines. Unlike Yenan, there was no sign of a small arms factory. Artificial limbs were a more urgent product than rifles.

"So why have you come here," asked Soeung Sak, once under the thatched roof shelter that doubled as the officers' mess. I flashed the papers from Bangkok and the letter from his leader, Son Sann. They weren't convincing. The mess, however, eagerly accepted our 50-pound bag of rice, before Sak gave us a military escort of two armed soldiers to our quarters, a bamboo hut.

It was a most bearable house arrest—four bunks, two for Bill and me, two for our guards. Sak took us to the officers' mess that evening, where I offered a salute to the KPNLF from a quart bottle of Jack Daniel's bourbon. To my astonishment, they preferred a local firewater, rejecting the great nectar of Tennessee stills. Sumner and I seemed to be accepted, and the conversation turned to the guerrillas' needs. As expressed by these soldiers they were protein, guns, and ammunition—in that order. They were hungry. Our meal was rice with funny-looking small meatballs, soaked in a fiery sauce hotter than Tabasco.

Despite our apparent acceptance by the officers, we spent the night under the casual watch of two armed guerrillas. We awoke the next morning to a surrealistic serenade, distant mortar bursts amongst the cries of cuckoo birds. The sound of real cuckoos is about ten decibels higher than their mechanical imitations on Alpine clocks. Word soon arrived over the camp's high frequency radio certifying our credentials and explaining our mission. We were now officially accepted as guests of the KPNLF and observers of their war against Vietnam. Sak called off his dogs.

We spent two days observing and photographing the base camp and its defense and the people of Ampil. Cambodians are especially graceful in movement, exquisite dancers, and, at least on the surface, of gentle disposition. To observe their defenses, we rode on motorbikes behind Sak, our translator guide, and Duong Sakhon, commander of the KPNLF's 216th battalion, to front-line positions several miles south of Ampil. At their insistence, we armed ourselves with Chinese-made AK-47 automatic rifles, defense in case of ambush. The reckless way Sakhon pushed the motorbike made me more wary of a vehicle accident than an ambush.

Ampil's "front line" was a series of perimeter defenses, each a fortified circle about 75 yards in diameter. "The Vietnamese always attack from the rear," explained Sakhon. The troops were young, slight, and lightly armed with AK-47s and an occasional Chinese light machine gun and a small mortar. No matter the quality of the men, this was no defense against tanks or armored personnel carriers, the big tools in a Vietnamese offense. I could better understand Sittichai's reluctance to enter Ampil.

We talked, took pictures and heard more stories about the loss of families to the Khmer Rouge. Before returning to Ampil, Sak presented Sumner and me half a dozen lizards, each about six inches long, rounded up from the forest and tied together with string in writhing bundles. They were fiercely ugly, but physically unthreatening, given their size. The bundles were attached to the handlebars of the motorbikes for our return to the base. "Dinner," explained our guide. And so they would become, turned into tiny meatballs and dosed with Cambodia's version of Tabasco, which dulled the taste buds. Some protein.

We'd seen but a fraction of the total KPNLF force, said to be about 12,000. Ampil, a major base, had arms for only about one-third of its troops. The deputy commander of this force, General Dien Del, lived off by himself in a hut of his own. At least on paper, Del doubled as vice president of the KPNLF. I interviewed him and asked the inevitable question: How can you make common cause with Communists who have murdered most of your relatives? "We'll take care of them after we have driven out the Vietnamese," he said and maybe he believed this to be true. I was not impressed with Dien Del. He was reclusive and when seen from time to time outside his quarters, he appeared to be drunk.

The man in charge of these operations was Colonel Prum Vath, a slender soldier with gray hair who seemed to spend all of his time bent over a table with maps, paper, and pen. He made plans for offensive operations deep in the forest between Ampil and the temples of Angkor Wat, about 65 miles southeast. Their aim was to harass Vietnamese soldiers and cut supply lines to their forward positions at Kandal, Traying, and Talei, villages only a few kilometers in front of the KPNLF's forward defense perimeter.

These classic guerrilla hit-and-run operations almost certainly delayed Vietnam's dry-weather offensive against Ampil, perhaps allowing time for more arms to arrive from China. There was some talk about joining an operation through the forest and its anti-personnel explosives and threat of ambush to strike at Angkor Wat. I was tempted, more for the sight of these extraordinary works than for journalism. I had learned of them years before as a seaman. But the operation would take at least a week, or longer if things did not go well. I got cold feet—too much time, too much danger.

Unlike the strutting General Dien Del, Colonel Prum Vath was a modest man. He did not (or maybe would not) speak English, leaving that task to his aide Khan You, a 22-year-old orphan of Cambodia's instability with a dazzling smile and intelligence to match. Bill and I were much taken with the aide's charm and know-how.

Khan You referred to "my Coro-nal" and seemed more intent than Sak, our official guide, that we stay on this side of harm.

"I was 13 years old in my home in Batdambang (a city south-west of Ampil) when Pol Pot came to power," he said. "Then Pol Pot killed my father and my mother and I went to live in the forest. Now I serve my Coro-nal." As a refugee, he had too much company in 1984. Roughly a quarter million Cambodians lived in camps along the Thai border. Food and shelter came mainly from the United Nations or private agencies, such as the Catholic Relief Organiza-tion. Along with their hatred of the Vietnamese, these refugees were a driving force behind the KPNLF. A very few attained refuge in the United States. Van Sar and Hieam Oung, the former mayor of Phnom Penh, both living in Seattle, were conspicuous examples. They were my principal KPNLF contacts this side of Ampil.

FOR THREE DAYS we lived the life of the beleaguered on a rou-tine of observation and a diet of rice and lizard meatballs. Though the heat was debilitating, I can't recall suffering thirst, probably be-cause we carried purifying pills in order to drink ditch water. Con-tact with the outside came through a small shortwave radio which brought in music from Beijing and news in English from Radio Australia. One morning Beijing broadcast works from Sigmund Romberg, the schmaltz king of light opera. Radio Australia specu-lated about a Vietnamese offensive in Cambodia. Once Sumner re-quested that I turn down the radio volume since it was interfering with the natural sound of the surrounding forest. These were the heavy call of cuckoo birds and occasional bursts of mortar rounds. I obliged.

Now that we'd all become well acquainted, Bill and I accom-panied Sak, the two battalion commanders, Duong Sakhon and Khoun Saroenn, and a gent identified only as a "Thai policeman" back across the border to a lavish meal in Apaya, Thailand. The food was ample, the beer cold, the mood behind Thailand's tanks and artillery quite relaxed. The troop commanders brought along their aides. While we ate they discussed plans for an attack on Talei, the Vietnamese stronghold about 3,000 yards in front of the KPNLF's forward positions. A small-scale military map showed the village and the terrain, a few dips here and there, but not much defilade, depressions or projections in the landscape, to shield one from hostile artillery.

The plan was simple: two squads attack from the right flank, two from the left. A fire base, consisting of one small Chinese mortar and a heavy—about .50-caliber—Soviet machine gun liberated from the Vietnamese, would provide covering fire from a small crease in the landscape.

Care to join us? Sak issued the invitation. The commanders nodded approval. Having come to trust them, I said yes. The attack plan was set for the next morning.

Cuckoo birds woke us to the morning heat, which was not very different from the evening heat. Motorbikes carried us to the KPNLF's most forward position, a circular mound about five feet high, defended for 360 degrees. Hollywood has taught us that pioneers moving West circled their covered wagons in a similar defense when assaulted by Indians. On arrival, Bill and I turned over our AK-47s to the defenders. Lord knows what fate we'd meet if captured during the attack, but if captured bearing arms, it figured to be worse.

On signal from the battalion commanders we moved out. I did have time to notice decorations around the necks of the guerrilla troops, scarves of scarlet or bright amulets, homage to the Buddha; magic. I trusted my safety to Khoun Saroenn, the battalion commander who draped two silver-colored cords around his neck before loading and locking his AK-47. Since he had been in this area before, I figured the commander knew the potential hot spots for antipersonnel mines. I would follow his footsteps for the ensuing three hours, which included three moments of concentrated terror.

Guerrilla warfare—thank you Hollywood—generally brings images of men in blackface, armed with knives, crawling on their bellies toward their target, or, from T. E. Lawrence, a charge of camels in a skirmish line, bearing Arabs in flowing robes, armed with Enfield rifles and scimitars. For contrast, the raid on Talei, Cambodia, April 1, 1984: small dark troopers in camouflage suits bearing disproportionately large automatic rifles, strolling through a no-man's land with the nonchalance of a Tennessee woodsman on a squirrel hunt. This would last for a few kilometers until the forest thickened. So did my sweat.

I walked carefully behind Saroenn, along with the mortar and machine gun, until we reached a modest dip in the red earth where the weapons were emplaced. The position offered a relatively clear field of fire toward Talei. Saroenn used a small hand-held radio to disperse his troops into the void of forest. I noticed a fresh hole near my feet, suggesting the former presence of a land mine. The Cambodians had used this place before, so I was pretty sure that Vietnamese gunners had fixed this position as a target. The clear field of fire was, so to speak, a two-way street.

Saroenn cut a rather dashing figure, although nothing so dazzling as Lawrence of Arabia. He stood upright talking into his radio, calm as a fellow having another productive day at the office. His battle dress was a brown felt hat, crossed bandoliers holding curved AK-47 magazine clips, and a pair of black jogging pants of a sort fashionable men might wear jogging along Alki Beach in Seattle. They had yellow stripes down each side and fancy stitching which said "Le Grand Sport."

I decided with Sak to move before shooting commenced to a small knot of earth, about 150 feet away, which rose slightly higher than the modest depression protecting the fire base. It would afford a small margin of greater shelter from incoming fire, but at great cost to my nerves. There were, in this forest, antipersonnel mines and killer snakes. In order to avoid the former we had to risk the latter, a major decision for a man fearful of snakes.

We felt our way down the depression, using our hands—ever so carefully—to feel for trip wires which would discharge the mines, lifting small twigs and leaves. My mouth turned dry as the Sinai in summer from the heat and tension during this journey. Bill Sumner stayed with the fire base, camera ready. At precisely 10 A.M. the forest exploded.

Automatic rifle fire arched to and from the flanks of Talei. The guerrilla's small mortar popped like a bad tractor engine. The first

Vietnamese mortar round, a big one, at least 82 mm, screamed in to land directly in front of our position. Sak and I clutched the earth. Suddenly I was oblivious to snakebite and antipersonnel mines.

We held for no more than 15 minutes before Saroenn ordered disengagement, first the mortar and the attacking squads and then the heavy machine gun, our cover in case of a counterattack. "Be flexible," Sak suggested, which I took to mean get ready to run like hell. The retreat was rapid, but not a panic.

Having snapped the first photographs of combat in this forgotten war, Sumner retreated with the two soldiers carrying the big Soviet machine gun. I got behind the footsteps of Saroenn. We moved quickly, a few steps ahead of Vietnamese mortars. Twice we dropped flat on our faces, well ahead of the hostile rounds. Then another round came in screaming so close it seemed to suggest "so long world." Saroenn and I fell flat where we walked. I landed in a mud puddle, a remnant of the late wet season, and listened while the shell's whine increased. It was like tuning up the volume on a rock and roll radio station. Having heard similar sounds before, I knew this mortar would come too close.

Seconds passed while I rationalized that the end would be painless. But nothing happened—no explosion, no tearing shrapnel. The Soviets had sold their client a dud, which they had dispatched down on me—nothing personal, of course. Up and running, I had to drop again, this time into a sizable shell hole half filled with water. The mortar bomb dropped well to our rear. We moved on quite briskly to the KPNLF line. I was euphoric about being alive.

That splendid feeling lasted only a few minutes. Safe inside the KPNLF defense where there were guns enough to stall a counterattack, I looked about for Sumner. He wasn't there. He was missing. My God, must I go back through the no-man's land to find my companion? It was terror either way: to go back without him or to go toward Talei to find him. Sak relieved me of the decision. Sumner, he said, was alive, unhurt, but at another guerrilla position. He had returned from the skirmish with the machine gun crew. I felt I had just reached the summit of a difficult mountain.

The pumped up troops acted like schoolboys in a locker room

after the Friday night football game. I saw only one semblance of a casualty, a superficial head wound to Home Bien, a 22-year-old rifleman in the attack squad. A fine day for the Buddha.

From Ampil, I radioed a call for Sounchai and his car for a return to Bangkok. We had done the mission and were unscathed. We had the story and photos. Before leaving, a small ceremony took place with the commanders. Sak had coveted my shoes, a late model from REI with vibram soles and Gore-Tex tops, designed for mountain trails, but ideal for this terrain. They were muddy, but Sak was grateful.

There was also a reproach from Khan You, the colonel's aide: "It was not good of you to go with the soldiers and they should not have allowed you to come." His tone was that of a schoolmaster admonishing a small boy. I felt funny about it; that is, the gap between our brief sojourn into some danger and the fact of his existence in this killing jungle. I thanked him for his concern and imagined that one day Khan You would be a leading figure in a democratic government of Cambodia. Alas, such a government has yet to come.

The offensive commenced two weeks after our departure from Ampil. Initially, our guerrilla friends beat back the Vietnamese armor, killing more than 100 of the attackers, according to press reports from Bangkok—probably, if I may speculate, aided in the defense by Thai artillery. Ultimately, it was no contest: the elephant was too much for the ant, and by the end of the dry season in 1985, Ampil submitted to siege and was lost to the occupiers. The non-Communist Khmer People's National Liberation Front was shattered and never really recovered as a military or political force.

In addition to problems with Vietnamese armor, the KPNLF had a revolt of its military leaders—their identities not reported in the Department of Defense country study from which this information is taken—against Son Sann. The colonels and generals accused their president of being dictatorial.

At the same time as its apparent triumph, Vietnam wearied of the Cambodian occupation, a drain of its manpower and weapons and a strain on relations with its patron, the Soviet Union. Having taken as many casualties in Cambodia as the United States suffered in Vietnam—55,000 dead—Hanoi began to bring home its troops, leaving the government in Phnom Penh to its puppet, Heng Samrin.

There was also movement in the diplomatic jungles of Washington, Moscow, New York, and Beijing where politicians began to negotiate an end to the occupation. The political vacuum would be temporarily filled by a United Nations military force. If Richard Nixon began the blooding of Cambodia, President George Bush was a major force in staunching its flow. The administration's main man in negotiations leading to the entry of the U.N. and free Cambodian elections was Charles Twining. Remarkably upbeat, given his assignment, and skilled, Chuck Twining is one of those quiet Americans who make things work for the better. He is otherwise unsung.

Twining was our de facto ambassador in Phnom Penh when I returned for a visit in 1994. U.N. soldiers had finally made the country relatively safe for visitors and normal life. Pol Pot's Khmer Rouge still maintained an enclave near the southern Thai border, coming out occasionally to shoot up a village and snatch a tourist for killing or ransom. Most violence had ceased and my fellow travelers, my companion, Joan Hansen, and my daughter Margaret, insisted we tour Angkor Wat.

These strange temples are a marvel of man's work on earth, a rival in ideology and enormity to the Egyptian pyramids. The delicate stone carvings and sculptures show the conversion of the Khmer people from Hinduism to Buddhism in the fourteenth century. They also show the march of armies, prelude to violence, and give a hint of the hatred among these Southeast Asian neighbors.

Whenever the subject of Cambodia comes up—and it does from time to time—I'm asked: How could the survivors of Pol Pot's slaughter of his countrymen make common cause with the Khmer Rouge killers?

I wasn't thinking about this when, walking through the ancient temples recovered from the jungle, I asked my guide, "Where have all the indigenous monkeys gone?"

"All eaten," he said. "By the Vietnamese before they left. They are inhuman."

MOUNTAINS

TO ESCAPE the journalism of war and politics, I discovered mountaineering, the safest refuge for the romantic, the best place to sate the quest for beauty and the thrill of life a step away from oblivion. It is not "because it's there" that men and women climb a mountain. The reason is not so complicated. What's "there" is a finite goal and an absence of ambiguity about the mission. The end, a point in space, is clearly defined. You make it or you don't. The effort may demand full use of that partly neglected instrument of modern life, the human body. It is the sport that makes all of the others seem trivial wrote the poet Robert Graves. Mountains and the hills that precede them become lines in space, forms that soar beyond imagination in the Karakoram Range between China and Pakistan, subtle shapes that come up from the evergreen forests beneath the Cascades of the Pacific Northwest. Trying to describe this beauty is as hopeless as trying to describe Beethoven's Fifth Piano Concerto. These are concepts that we understand but cannot fit into words. It is like the beauty of a loved one into which we find escape.

Mountain climbing is remotely kin to the work of the combat infantryman, but it is far more secure, less a hostage to chance. It is a match between man and elements, not a totally predictable pursuit, but one given to more easy calculation. It is possible to assay and weigh risks in mountaineering. Not all of them, of course. There's no certain way to tell if a snow slab will break from a mountainside carrying your life in its ride with gravity downhill. One can, however, make good estimates in mountaineering, not much of a possibility if someone from the other side of a hill is laying mortar fire on the infantryman. Combat is ugly and terrifying. Accordingly, it takes more lives than mountains, including, I suppose, its portion of errant romantics.

I came to mountaineering, however, more driven by curiosity than a romantic search for adventure, or a different professional venue. It seemed a crazy sport, life threatening, energy sapping, and socially unrewarding—unlike the conventional sports of football and baseball. This strange endeavor reminded me of a line from Irvin S. Cobb, the Kentucky humorist, a gent of great appetite and girth: "I shall lift up mine eyes unto the hills—but my carcass, never!" Like Cobb, it had not occurred to me that one could have an appetite for using the body beyond its functions of food and love. Besides, after two years as an infantryman, I'd vowed never to sleep overnight away from home unless in a hotel room, or to walk more than a couple of city blocks without benefit of a taxicab. Yet friends from the University of Washington, otherwise eminently sane and productive, climbed mountains. Why?

Curiosity got the best of good sense when friends from the state legislature in Olympia beckoned me to a few modest climbs in the Cascades. I joined them behind George Senner, a superb mountaineer, an army veteran of the 10th Mountain Division in our Italian campaign of World War II. George was our gentle teacher, giving instructions on how to walk mountain trails using minimum energy; how to use the ice ax to arrest a fall on steep snow or ice; how to rope into a team. We began gently, rising up on short peaks near Snoqualmie Pass, advancing up the lovely pyramid that once was Mount St. Helens before it blew its celebrated top, and Mount Adams, another dormant volcano, until, finally, we climbed Mount Rainier, highest of the Cascade peaks, a 14,410 foot journey from sea level to summit.

On Mount Adams I discovered the beauty: sunset on the soft green hills and valleys below our campsite in the runty hard-core evergreens fighting up toward brown volcanic rock at 7,000 feet. Maybe it was a rediscovery of what I'd forgotten about boyhood camps along creekbanks in West Tennessee hardwood thickets. I felt comfortable and sheltered in woods at night. Later, as a soldier, I had the same easy feeling in night patrol maneuvers. Near the summit of Adams, 12,300 feet, walking behind George Senner, my feet began to feel light, my pace quickened almost to a light jog. Euphoria, that surge of elation near the end of the goal, when the beauty of earth and space, the white and blue colors of mountain and sky, overwhelms the senses. That was the moment I understood the pleasure of mountains, a time when I understood that I was, as they say of other addicts, hooked.

In 1978 Jim Whittaker, the tall, angular Seattle climber famed as the first American to climb Mount Everest, asked me to accompany his expedition to K2 in the Karakoram as its correspondent. For exclusive newspaper rights, Hearst Newspapers would pay a fee, part of the expedition's cost. I jumped at the chance. By that time I'd made more than a dozen climbs of Cascade peaks, steering clear of rock ascents as much as possible. Early on in this sport a 30-foot tumble from a rock face left me cut, fiercely bruised, but alive and keenly aware of the limits beyond which gravity is intolerant. I had missed a handhold; overreached. Rainier is physically demanding, especially if done in our usual two-day push, a prime training ground for handling crevasses, controlling body temperature, and learning the physiological effects of diminished oxygen.

K2, however, was of another dimension. The world's second highest peak (28,250 feet), it had been climbed at great cost by teams from Italy and Japan before Whittaker's 1978 U.S. expedition. Going from Mount Rainier to K2 was akin to jumping from high school to NFL football. The 130-mile approach to its base camp crosses a high altitude desert of extreme heat. It takes two weeks and carries through the infamous Braldu Gorge. At times the trip to base camp can pack almost as much risk as K2 itself. It would be a mountain adventure of extraordinary length, size and difficulty.

Whittaker led an unsuccessful American attempt at K2 in 1975. The expedition foundered at about 25,000 feet in storms and dissension. Now, three years later, he had put together what Willie Unsoeld, the celebrated master of Everest's most difficult West Ridge, called the strongest U.S. climbing team ever assembled. It included the foremost U.S. climbers of the past three decades, John Roskelley, Jim Wickwire, Bill Sumner, Chris Chandler, Lou Reichardt, Rob Schaller, Rick Ridgeway, Terry and Cherie Bech, Craig Anderson, and Skip Edmonds. Jack Doughty, the premier newsman and editor of the *Seattle Post-Intelligencer*, agreed that it was "a go." Hearst would pay a stipend, I'd create a de facto news service and file daily dispatches from the heart of the Karakoram to New York. Neither of us, however, had more than a vague idea of the difficulty in transmitting, via high frequency radio, over the eastern Himalaya, where peaks over 20,000 feet high are as anonymous as Cascade foothills. We had no idea how to get the radio messages from Skardu, provincial capital of Baltistan and the last town with airport and telegraph facilities, to Rawalpindi, first town with a telex connection to New York. But Doughty was a throwback to an earlier era of journalism when a gung-ho editor believed a good reporter could accomplish almost any given assignment. In his time, editors called the shots on what was news. Today they may be forced to take the word of focus groups or opinion polls.

Editor and reporter did have a general idea on how to proceed. From the U.S. Army at Fort Lewis, Washington, we borrowed an ANPRC-74 radio and extra batteries. We counted on United Press International to relay copy from 'Pindi to Hearst News in Manhattan. From the vantage of an editor's desk in Seattle, it looked like a logistical snap, its result giving Hearst newspapers a blow-by-blow account of what would be one of the great adventures in mountaineering, the first American ascent of K2. In fact, it was almost ridiculously difficult.

The expedition was already two weeks under way when I joined a trekking party, bound for K2 base camp, at Kennedy Airport in New York carrying 60 pounds of personal gear, 80 pounds of radio and batteries. Gil Roberts, the trekking leader, laughed at the sight: "How in hell do you think you can get into Pakistan with that high frequency radio?" Roberts, a six-foot two-inch, 280-pound veteran of the 1963 U.S. Everest expedition, was an emergency room physician in San Francisco, a last minute substitute on this trip for Unsoeld, our mutual friend. I figured two bottles of good bourbon would smooth my passage with customs officials in Karachi. The comedy began 36 hours later when I pulled the two bottles from my pack to influence a rather elegantly dressed Pakistani customs officer. He recoiled with such shock I thought I'd dragged out snakes. "No, No—no liquor in Pakistan. Only prohibition." A hard-line army coup had dumped the more liberal president, Bhutto. Pandering to Muslims, the new leaders allowed no booze. Despite this affront, the kindly customs officer not only allowed the radio to pass, he let me keep the bourbon.

I took a massive drink of it after visiting UPI's bureau in Mrs. Davies Hotel (circa 1842) in Rawalpindi, a cantonment of the British Raj adjacent to the modern capital city of Islamabad. The bureau, two small rooms, a portable English typewriter with six keys missing, a teletype of Marconi vintage, looked as old as Mrs. Davies and not much changed since 1842. The bureau chief lived in the smaller of the two rooms with a cot and a hot plate. He dressed in a dhoti, a loincloth, a fashion older than British imperialism. He had no assistants. "I cannot receive your copy," he promptly informed. "We have no radio to receive transmissions. You must make arrangements to get the copy to me on paper. Then I will relay to New York. But I am very busy with the trial." The generals were trying President Bhutto for his life, which they later took in exchange for real or imagined crimes, a major story on the Indian subcontinent. A chap I quickly named Jesse James, an English-Urdu speaking staffer at the U.S. Information office in 'Pindi, agreed, for a nice price, to relay messages telegraphed from Skardu to the UPI bureau, the small man in the dhoti. Fine. That still left a gap of half the subcontinent, the distance from K2 to 'Pindi: How to get messages received in Skardu and then relayed to Jesse James? I despaired. On the other side of the world, poised for great adventure, and apparently finished even before it started.

For one day, I said to hell with it. Gil Roberts and I traveled through the Khyber Pass to the Afghan border, then to an outlaw city called Landi Kotal, where we managed to avoid trouble with hostile natives and where Gil bought a combination ballpoint pen and .25-caliber pistol. One end wrote, the other fired. He said it would be useful in protecting against dope fiends in his operating room. We drank more of the I. W. Harper. It did not begin to take the edge off my desperation.

At the brink of this failure, luck changed. I met the lady at an embassy party, not one of those how-do-you-do, wine and cheese affairs, but an all-out Saturday night drunk. She looked lonely. We talked. She also spoke Urdu, the native tongue in these parts. Would she, for a modest fee, come with us to Skardu, receive my messages from K2, 130 miles away, then relay the same to Jesse James in Rawalpindi? Yes, she would. She sought escape from the confines of Islamabad's diplomatic world—and, perhaps, other adventures. So it was set: I'd radio the lady in Skardu, who would telegraph the copy to Jesse James in 'Pindi, who would give the copy to UPI for transmission to New York. Complicated, of course, but this Rube Goldberg arrangement had a chance to succeed.

Weather cleared a day later and we flew up the valley of the mighty Indus, a river-cradle of human civilization, beneath peaks reaching to 26,000 feet, alighting on the narrow strip at Skardu, a primitive marketplace. Beyond Skardu were the wilds and beauty of the Karakoram. This is where the road and telegraph ended. Gil was pleased with the lady we would leave in Skardu, but for reasons of companionship, not work. "Gil," I cautiously observed. "She's not a bathing beauty." "Yes," the horny giant replied. "But she sure has a sweet ass." Thus "Ms. Sweetass," in practice, if not pulchritude, an absolute marvel, the savvy savior of the world's most hastily wrought, overextended, and remote wire service. The really funny thing about it is that it worked.

The expedition almost did not. It was shaky with dissension when I reached K2 Base Camp (16,000 feet) one month after the team had departed Seattle. I moved with Roberts's trekking party for a week before taking their leave and going up the Baltoro Glacier with a lone porter, Frankenstein, as we called him, a giant Balti who carried the 80 pounds of radio in addition to other gear. I feared, incorrectly as it happened, the expedition would reach K2's summit before the trekking party reached its base camp. Frankenstein was a troublemaker among the 25 Baltis carrying for the trekkers. Thus his early departure was a Godsend to Roberts as well as me. It had not been an easy trip.

Before leaving the trekking party we had been bedeviled by dehydration. The first 50 miles of the journey went through high-altitude, stone-age villages along the Braldu River. Temperatures reached 125 degrees Fahrenheit by each noon. Thirst was almost insatiable. We drank from the Braldu, killing its bacteria with iodine, allowing its silt to settle in our water bottles. Two people from other expeditions already had perished in the Braldu Gorge two weeks before we arrived. The river raged down from K2 and its lesser sisters in a 20-knot current. Rocks tumbled from its nearly sheer sides. The path narrowed to a foot's width, sustained by unstable rocks.

In this passage Mrs. Rosemary Thau, a trekker from New York, got swept into the river when the path collapsed beneath her. In an instant she was carried to the middle of the Braldu, which roared, tossing spray as it ran over or around massive boulders. It happened in one terrifying instant. I had a vision of her funeral, the woman in her coffin; inexplicable, but not inappropriate. I assumed her death. No one could survive the river's battering. Porters watched in terror, shouting "Memsahib," not moving. In the next instant, for reasons a religious person would call a miracle or a scientist would ascribe to the peculiar hydraulics of the river, Thau was carried back by the chop to a point near shore. A large rock protruded from that point. I ran to its top, grabbed the end of my long-shafted ice ax, and swung its pick at the woman's back. What harm, I reasoned. She is already dead. Maybe it will snag. It did, the pick end piercing between her back and the shoulder strap of her pack. I began to pull, resisting the force of her body rushing downstream with the current. At once, the river began to pull me as well as the woman. There was a moment of horror as I started to lose my perch on the rock: If I turn loose, she drowns; if I fail to release the ax, I drown. In the middle of this terminal quandary, pressure on the ice ax eased. I've only a vague memory of standing on the shore with Thau and Tom Anderson, strongest of the trekkers who apparently grabbed the would-be victim while I held on for dearest life. The next half hour is a total blank. I found myself a mile up the trail, where it was safe to stop by the river's edge. I sat near exhaustion, probably caused by having pumped a pint of adrenaline in the rescue. There I found my hands covered with blood from cuts, my boots full of water. Before long Anderson pulled up behind me: "How the hell did this happen?" "Beats me," he answered. "But we saved her." Late that day, reunited at a camp, Thau showed a long, reddish scar down her back where my ice axe scraped flesh. She showed no emotion, either oblivious to her brush with eternity or still in shock. The following December she sent me a Christmas card and a note of thanks.

Whittaker's expedition, one month on the mountain, was not yet near its goal. At Base Camp, I bade Frankenstein farewell and rewarded him with the gift of a spare nylon jacket. My right hand was partly useless from a fall that smashed a small bone in the wrist. Whittaker looked thin and ravaged when we joined for the climb up the Godwin-Austen Glacier to Camp I at 18,500 feet, breath now coming hard at the higher altitude. Roskelley, Ridgeway and Reichardt, and Wickwire were higher on the mountain. The rest were in Camp I, a biologically sanitized place of ice and rock at the foot of K2's northeastern buttress. Save for an occasional flight of Gorax, oversized crows, we were the only forms of life, sustained by tents and freeze-dried food, totally dependent on one another for survival. It was not a happy camp, already divided by "A" and "B" team climbers: those designated for the final push to the top of K2, and those assigned to carry food and fuel for the "A" team's summit effort.

I rigged the radio, running its antenna between rocks, and began bouncing news reports off the ionosphere each morning at a designated time and frequency to Ms. Sweetass in Skardu. It worked quite well, Camp I to Skardu. Of necessity, given radio static, the news dispatches were curt and void of complications. ("Avalanche came down the northeast face. Stopped short of campsite. Wind blast shook tents. No harm to men. Push from camp three to four begins at dawn.") From Skardu to Jesse James and UPI in 'Pindi, transmission was not so good. The Skardu telegraph was faulty. The able Ms. Sweetass adjusted, sending the dispatches back to the

'Pindi via Pakistani Airline pilots when weather allowed their flights. Meantime, she had forgone Gil Roberts for the more available Sheriff of Baltistan, the only law west of Skardu, a splendid relationship that aided this expedition.

Thin air does tricks with body and mind above 16,000 feet. Nothing grows. Flesh does not recreate; it wastes. Tempers quicken. A small slight at sea level can become an affair of honor. After a month above that altitude, the climbers of K2, by sea-level standards, were a tad mad—and not only at each other. And it still wasn't finished. Weather worsening, the outcome was in precarious balance, perhaps tilted toward failure, given the touchy social relations.

New to this high altitude society, I watched as the team fractured like an ice sheet dropped on rock. Old bonds, formed on earlier expeditions, broke between several members on K2. There was talk of taking leave of the expedition, via the glacier on the other side of Windy Gap that came down into China's Sinkiang Province. If there had been certainty on what fate awaited when taken by the People's Liberation Army, it might have happened. My tentmate at Camp I, Dr. Rob Schaller, mediated a pivotal attempt to bring the team back together, a dramatic meeting in which Whittaker apologized for "heavy-handedness" and called for a double assault on K2's summit by both A and B teams. "God willing, we'll make it together," said Jim. The harmony dissolved a day later when the As— Wickwire, Roskelley, Ridgeway, and Reichardt—stole a day's march on the others, thus breaking an understanding negotiated at Camp I. Terry and Cherie Bech stayed high to help the summit assault. The rest would retreat to Camp I or lower.

Acclimatized and fit, I made a side trip with B team members to China, climbing up the Godwin-Austen Glacier 2,000 feet to Windy Gap. A look at the glacier running down into China's forbidden Sinkiang Province cooled any ardor for taking leave of the expedition via that side of the Karakoram. A whimsical radio report next day on the absence of border guards and Chinese flags created nothing but static on the normally reliable ANPRC-74. I changed frequencies. More static. Another attempt in the afternoon radio call to Skardu; same result. Perhaps sunspots were playing havoc with the ionosphere. Again on the second day, the static remained. There was another radio at Base Camp, manned by an imperious Pakistan Army sergeant whose Karakoram command consisted of expedition porters. I climbed down the Godwin-Austen through its ice fall to the Base Camp radio and called Ms. Sweetass. "Never radio about that place again," she said with urgency, implying—accurately as it turned out—that mention of China was taboo and that the broadcasts had been jammed. We dropped that subject and I climbed back to Camp I carrying a load of food and fuel.

We had a strange society on the edge of survival. Even as time and tempers and fair weather ran low, we kept a routine. I shared a tent with Dr. Schaller, who kept radio contact with climbers above us, counseling, soothing feelings. We read. I reread Herman Melville's metaphor for life, *Moby-Dick*, in the shadow of our own, K2. The radio calls to Skardu resumed twice a day, a clumsy means of filing news stories even on the best of days, slow and tedious. But it was welcome contact, mitigating our feelings of isolation in ice, rock, and threadbare air. By day we looked across the crevasse-streaked glacier to Broad Peak and the five Gasherbrums, all at elevations higher than our camp. On clear nights, stars and planets were so numerous they illuminated our campsite. Storms increased as August faded toward fall. Avalanches swept down from K2's flanks on either side of our refuge; howling winds rattled our tents, a nerve-racking noise that we frequently dulled with Dalmane, a sleep inducing drug.

The routine broke abruptly on September 6, a clear day that began downbeat as Schaller talked with Whittaker, who called from his tent at Camp III. Jim talked about withdrawing from the mountain, a resumption of his pessimism about chances for attaining its summit. A week earlier he had radioed of hip-deep snow on the summit approach. He was fearful of losing lives to the storm and in pain from a bad knee. But he did not signal retreat. Instead, he'd wait for one more alley of clear weather that now seemed to come in two-day bursts. September 6 was such a day.

Schaller interrupted his radio talks with Whittaker to search throughout the morning for signs of climbers on the approach below K2's top. At 8 A.M. through his eight-power binoculars he spotted two small dots leeched to the side of a massive gully about 1,500 feet below the mountain summit. Minutes later, when he looked again, the dots had moved. Reichardt and Wickwire! No doubt of it. We watched until early afternoon when silhouettes appeared against the blue sky over K2. "Summit!" somebody shouted. Schaller relayed the word to an elated and vindicated Whittaker. Ridgeway and Roskelley followed their steps to the top on the next day, September 7, hypoxic and hallucinating, at the outer limits of human endurance. Roskelley said later his final steps were accompanied by a band of black musicians playing rock and roll.

They were the first Americans to climb K2, and few would repeat their enormously difficult feat. Three made the final climb without bottled oxygen. Wickwire nearly died as a result of an unintentional bivouac, sans sleeping bag or tent, just below the summit.

The triumph was tempered by the need to come down off the mountain alive despite the climbers' exhaustion and incoming storms. Ridgeway later described the descent as "terrible and dangerous." They were preoccupied with the threat of avalanche, questioning every step. At Camp III they stalled in a snowstorm blowing 40-knot winds. Whittaker, having descended to Camp I, grew concerned about their fate. He implored them to keep moving: "Every day you are up there you are deteriorating. . . . you are mentally and physically affected by lack of oxygen. . . . It's no good lying in your [sleeping] sacks. That's how people die." Schaller and Whittaker, both suffering from painful knees, considered returning to Camp III to shake the climbers out of their tents. Along with myself, one hand still impaired from a broken wrist, they were all of the human remains of this expedition. The others had retreated to the relatively oxygen-rich Base Camp at 16,000 feet, possibly not unaware of the peril facing climbers above them.

"Would it help if I came up?" Whittaker queried by radio. A despairing Wickwire exploded: "You're goddam right! We've worked like hell to get off this mountain. We haven't slept. We feel the expedition is leaving us." It was an intemperate, but not unfair, assessment of the situation. I questioned my ability to climb up the fixed rope to Camp II with a broken wrist, but resolved to make the effort if needed. The four summit climbers, plus their support team, Terry and Cherie Bech, were in desperate shape at Camp III. They couldn't be left. I'd go if Whittaker did so.

We weren't needed. The weather broke its storm pattern. Climbers left their tents in sunshine and made Camp I without help. There was a bittersweet reunion at Base Camp—fracture lines were too deep for anything better. Chris Chandler and Cherie by then had developed a deep love that would abide until his death years later. It happened within sight and sound of Terry Bech, Cherie's husband, in this crucible of a mountain. The rest of the party was torn between approval and disdain. Two months above 16,000 feet had left us shorn of fat, spare of muscle, as skinny and woebegone as survivors of a concentration camp. We climbed down the Baltoro Glacier nipped by cold and snow, at times a comic sight. Terry Bech, standing skin and bones buck naked before a dozen Balti porters, seemed oblivious to their curiosity as he raged against the expedition's leadership. Wickwire, dangerously ill, was evacuated by a Pakistan Army helicopter at the end of the Baltoro, midway in the 130-mile trek back to the civilization of Skardu. There was a celebration at Askole, a stone-age village at 11,000 feet, where there were no wheeled implements to take burdens from human backs, the last place of human habitation. Villagers killed a goat in our honor.

Food and drink were lavish at the U.S. Embassy party in Islamabad, our last time all together—except for the hospitalized Wickwire—for at least two decades. The mood was surprisingly mellow, perhaps subdued by liquor. Whittaker talked about a reunion in five years. It did not happen.

We went from Pakistan on our separate ways, Whittaker to lead an enormously successful Soviet-Chinese-American ascent of Mount Everest, Terry Bech to play the viola in the Dutch National Opera. Cherie left the Netherlands three years later to live with Chris, who perished in their attempt to climb Kanchenjunga a half dozen years after their meeting. K2 had been a triumph of human will and endurance, a failure in human relations. It was, as the climber and social scientist Dick Emerson had predicted, a zero-sum game. There would be intense competition to climb to the top. There would be winners and losers. Some residue of bitterness lingers to this day. So does the triumph.

With the news of success dispatched, Jack Doughty ordered his man on the mountain back in the Seattle office come Monday morning. The trip would take three weeks. His instinct for news was perversely matched by his ignorance of mountain geography. He now laughs about it.

IN STARK CONTRAST with the society of K2, our three-man expedition to the top of Mount McKinley forged even tighter the bonds between Stimson Bullitt, Bill Sumner, and me, at the time the oldest team ever to make the summit of the highest mountain in North America. We did it in 1981 in what the National Park Service called McKinley's worst July weather on record. Storms turned what is usually a two-week effort into an exhausting 28-day struggle. By the end we had spent 14 of those days stormbound inside our tent or snow cave, yet never despairing, bored, or uncongenial. The mountain crucible works in strange ways.

We are an unusual mix of personalities. Bullitt is a lawyer and a writer, author of a classic on American politics, *To Be a Politician*, a reserved individual of enormous intellectual and physical strength. He was 62 years old that summer. Sumner, the veteran of K2 with whom I'd climbed on a 1979 expedition to the Caucasus Mountains, is a nuclear physicist, turned tentmaker and design engineer for REI, the Seattle outdoor goods cooperative. We spent our confinement in conversation. We read the few books allowed ourselves as luxuries, then discussed them at length. While whiskey and good weather lasted, we sat at day's end outside our tents watching the sun on the mountains, much like ordinary folks at home on Main Street sitting on the veranda. McKinley, like K2, is a killer, 20,320 feet high, dangerously easy to underestimate. Because of the mountain's closeness to the Arctic Circle, the Park Service declared it the physiological equivalent of a 22,230-foot peak in the Himalayas near the equator. It is almost always tackled in the summer when there is 24 hours of light and temperatures that range between

112 degrees Fahrenheit at 10,000 feet, then drop at night to 10 below. We recorded same.

Maintaining friendship under such physical constraints was one aspect of this journey. Attaining the peak without getting killed was another matter. Our combined experience in mountains was critical. It leaned us toward caution, which meant more time on the mountain, which meant more fuel and food. We each hauled 125 pounds, initially pulling sleds to 11,000 feet, then ferrying by stages the balance of the gear to 17,000 feet, our high camp. Thus we effectively climbed McKinley 1.5 times. Having no value in turning ice into water or furnishing precious calories, the books were indeed a luxury. We moved by consensus, agreeing at the start that we'd make the summit together or not at all. By planning, there'd be nothing to resemble an A or B team. At 14,000 feet, a plateau at the foot of the mountain's West Buttress, we had a disagreement. Sumner said we'd best camp on the flat, allowing storms to pass around us. Bullitt wanted shelter inside a deep trench dug by a since-departed Swiss team. We fixed tents inside the trench, fired the high-pressure Mountain Safety Research stoves to make water (the most essential ingredient for McKinley since its severe cold dehydrates the body as quick as the superheated Sinai), drank the last of our 150-proof rum, and settled into bags for a long sleep. A storm came, rattling our tents despite the shelter. I awoke a few hours later in a beautiful quiet. Lovely, I thought. Then I felt pressure from my side of the tent and looked up. "My God, Stim—we're two-thirds buried!" The next two hours were furious with digging. The storm dropped snow as fast as one of us could shovel it clear of the tents, which we finally removed and staked on the flat surface of the snow.

Sumner had been correct. Wet with sweat, beards dripping icicles, we struggled in a 40-knot wind to secure the tents. Finished, we crawled inside and waited, in some suspense. Would we become buried again, or blown away? It worked. Wind carried snow around and past our camp, leaving our two tents intact and uncovered. That day 10 feet of snow fell around us on the plateau. The trench where we initially camped no longer existed. Neither, it appeared, did Peter, a strange Austrian trying a solo climb of McKinley. By sheer chance, a hired guide taking a party of climbers up the mountain remembered the trench where the Austrian sought shelter, and when the storm abated we dug for an hour, four of us, to reach the air pocket where the Austrian awoke and asked why all the fuss. When he learned, he left the mountain with 25 others who were either depleted of supplies or determination by the fiercest storm any of us had ever witnessed.

That left Bullitt, Sumner, and me and a strong team of young Colorado climbers still aiming for the summit. We had made one carry of supplies to the ridge line of the West Buttress before this deluge of snow. After a week of storms at 14,000 feet, we started up again, this time on snowshoes, advancing for three hours before the mountain closed shut in another storm. It lasted only a day. We came awake to a brilliant sunshine and promptly agreed to try again, despite the obvious danger of avalanche from the torrents of new-fallen snow. Sumner and I took turns breaking trail on snowshoes up the 45-degree slope, mentally tiptoeing for fear of avalanche. I kept my spirits by singing, à la Roy Acuff, the "Snowshoe Cannonball." No one complained, perhaps from lack of strength. Up we trudged, the Coloradans following in our hard-to-come-by steps. Even with snowshoes, the point man sank in up to his hips in the new snow. But it did not avalanche. We reached the 16,000-foot ridge, where I dropped, exhausted. I aimed to camp and rest.

"We can't," said my companions, noting the lenticular cloud that came from a blue sky to shroud the top of Mount McKinley, the certain telltale of another incoming storm. "We'll get blown off this ridge if we camp here. We've got to keep moving to 17,000 feet," said Bullitt. Sumner agreed. The ridge site, five feet wide, rose up from 45-degree slopes on either side. Somehow, I summoned strength to keep inching up over rock and ice of the West Buttress to what in minutes became another storm. My goggles iced the instant I put them on to cover my eyes from the freezing wind. They were useless. Limited vision had to be endured along with fatigue. It was indeed terrible, yet beautiful, moving around a narrow rock ledge hovering over 2,000 feet of open space, observing white streaks of snow that laced a pure black rock outcropping. At the top of the buttress we fell in silence to our routines: Bullitt and Sumner pitched the tent, I fired the MSR stove for hot liquids. Warmed a bit and inside shelter, Bullitt said, "I feel tired, cold, and old." I barely had the energy to nod agreement.

We took 19 hours to attain the summit. Another storm and deep snow forced us to take a route over the steep rock, ice, and hard snow of the West Rib, to avoid the near certainty of avalanche through the less exposed Denali Pass. No point roping together. One man's fall from the West Rib would kill us all, given its angle and obdurate surface. Bullitt led through its steeps, at one point spread like a large dark spider as his arms and legs searched the mountain's face for rock ledges that would allow our passage. The sight was more awesome to an observer than frightening, the sum of man against his goal, his life at a fine point of balance with oblivion. Stimson found the way, and the weather held good. The summit was exquisite in an Arctic twilight that illuminated all the great mountains of Alaska's Denali Range. The temperature, 38 degrees below zero, was freezing my toes. Sumner gallantly allowed me to remove my boots and warm my toes on his belly as we lay at the top of North America. He winced when I took them away, the frozen extremities having snatched the hairs off his stomach.

We went slowly back to our ice cave at 17,000 feet, moving with care down Denali Pass in early morning when snow was most firm, lest it avalanche. It did so a few hours after we had passed safely. Three days later we were clear of the mountain that had taken 28 days to climb, my toes burning from frostbite, my ego warmed by the dubious acclaim of having been part of the oldest team ever to climb the mountain. We savor the friendship to this day and go together, occasionally, on less strenuous trips to the hills. I lift up my eyes to the mountains and my heart follows. There is no better place for the incurable romantic.

HICKMAN

"Life must be a seeking for there is nothing to be found"—Anon.

THE MISSISSIPPI RIVER, a willful thing of nature, comes down about 25 miles from its junction with the Ohio below Cairo at Byrd's Point before it ignores the forgotten towns of Columbus and Hickman, Kentucky, on its passage to the Gulf of Mexico. The river made those places on the bluffs of southwestern Kentucky, a few miles north of the Tennessee line, just as the railroads, and later highways, broke them and left them nearly abandoned relics of steamboat America.

Columbus, "the Gibraltar of the Confederacy" in 1861, is recognized from the rolling Kentucky landscape by a few houses built close together, a tertiary highway junction, and a nondescript convenience store with a Sinclair gas pump. Hickman, about nine miles south, still stands as constructed in the mid-nineteenth century, except that it is mostly vacant, easy to visualize as the victim of a late twentieth-century invention, the neutron bomb.

"A pretty town perched on a handsome hill," the riverboat pilot Mark Twain wrote of Hickman in his memoir *Life on the Mississippi*. A frequent visitor, Twain stayed at the LaClede Hotel, whose entrance was framed like a horseshoe—good luck for guests? These included, as the Chamber of Commerce boasts, celebrities: President William Howard Taft, Charles Lindbergh, and George "Machine Gun" Kelly. Lindbergh's airplane was stuck in a nearby

Mississippi mud flat. Kelly, a gangster on the fly, was a pal of the local police chief, no stickler for law enforcement propriety.

All of this I learned recently when, to borrow from the Prophet Isaiah, I decided to report neither war nor politics any more, but instead go back and look at where I had come from and review my heritage, aiming to sort fact from myth, and to reflect on my profession. This was nearly half a century after I left.

Unlike Columbus, there remain in Hickman alongside the bluffs above its two main streets, handsome old houses—near mansions—some of these occupied by descendants of the settlers of the 1840s and well kept. Rich from the produce of the adjacent land, tobacco being the most lucrative crop in the town's early days, and from commerce on the docks, cotton, corn, and molasses from West Tennessee and Kentucky, the settlers built well and high to avoid the infrequent but devastating intrusions of the Mississippi into the town's commercial district, even to the lobby of the LaClede.

An early memory from the great flood of 1937 was the sight of the refugees from the river bottoms, young ones shoeless and unwashed, housed in National Guard army tents, probably a step up in comfort from their riverside shanties. Will Alexander Percy, the poet-writer from Greenville, Mississippi, downriver, described such river folk as Anglo-Saxon white trash, lazy, dull-witted, and of a lower class than the black serfs on his plantation. I only saw them as people with the same faces of fright and despair as I would come to see in refugees in the Middle East and Southeast Asia. A local newspaper ran a picture of a fellow rowing his small boat through the horseshoe into the lobby of the LaClede. Some luck. The river had reached over Hickman's seawall, a willful beast. It gave and it took.

For a long while, almost from the purchase of the fertile territory of western Kentucky and Tennessee in 1818 from the Chickasaw Indians, the river was a most generous giver—to the whole nation as well as Columbus and Hickman. The national government paid $300,000 for this black earth, I'd argue the richest land west of the Volga and north of the Mississippi Delta. The sale was negotiated by Tennessee's Andrew Jackson, hero of the Creek War and the War of 1812, and Kentucky's Isaac Shelby, whose victory and the subsequent massacre of British loyalists at Kings Mountain in 1780 sent Cornwallis running for Yorktown and surrender. Considering the military skills of Jackson and Shelby, "the Purchase" as it came to be called, was surely driven as much by the threat of arms as by the federal treasury. It's now forgotten, even by those whose ancestors came to inhabit and farm.

Settlers rushed into this new American frontier, most of them over the Appalachians through Tennessee and Kentucky, others up the river from New Orleans or down the Ohio. Chief among the latter were the Byrds of Virginia, who stopped at the Mississippi junction, settled, and claimed the enriched lands to the south in Missouri and Kentucky—land still farmed by their descendants. This migration was marked, tragically as it would happen, by slaves brought along to work the land for produce that would come to Hickman by wagon, and later, rail, for shipment via steamboat to the more populous Northeast. Thus Hickman thrived. By the 1840s the town attracted immigrants different in religion, manner, and culture from the Scotch-Irish Protestants from Virginia and the Carolinas who settled the farms and small towns just as few miles east of Hickman. Fulton and Union City are conspicuous examples of such towns.

Joseph Amberg came from Germany, perhaps to escape religious prejudice. His younger brother Moses arrived a few years later. Joseph wed Jane Stephens, a frontier woman. Neither brother nor their offspring ever practiced Judaism. They, literally, wed the frontier. So did William Bondurant, originally from a family of Huguenots from Lyon, France, and also my great-grandfather, Joseph Jesse Tamms of Staffordshire, England, who married Harriet Ferrill of the American frontier on June 27, 1849. All prospered as farmers, craftsmen, or merchants, especially the Ambergs, farmer-merchants. Anton Steagalee came from Baden to help build the town, and his brother opened a bar probably selling spirits distilled by Laughlin Daihl of Ireland. Hickman's 1870 census showed a population of 1,272 of which 121 were foreign born. The same record lists no foreign-born residents of Cayce, a railroad town close by but inland, nor is it likely foreigners would live among the starchy Protestants of Union City, with its churches for every sect from foot-washing Baptist to high Episcopalian. Behind this invisible yet perceptible boundary, they stayed close together in Hickman, alongside the mighty river, the way back to their old homeland as they might have thought of it.

What I have related thus far about these old places is formal knowledge gained long after my Southern Presbyterian youth spent ten miles down the road in Union City. What I knew of these folk as a lad came from the occasional Sunday excursion to view the river and the battlefield at Columbus—spectacles in the preelectronic era—and to visit the Amberg family. It also came, word of mouth, from my grandmother, a devout Christian by then an old woman, but one with a clear memory and vivid speech. Although ignorant at that time of the census facts just related, I gathered something distinctive about Hickman, a slight difference in accent, something almost peculiar and exotic; an attractive place. There were old mansions, nearly swathed in our overabundant vegetation, to contrast with its bare and decaying commercial buildings. It had a ghostly feeling and a Roman Catholic Church.

Victoria Tamms, my grandmother, was born about 1855 on her father's farm at the eastern edge of a prosperous Hickman. Although deeply religious, she abjured the special dogmas of a particular sect. I suppose she reckoned Jesus to have subscribed to neither Sanctified Baptist nor Cumberland Presbyterian. She delighted my childhood with her recollections of the Civil War as it came down the Mississippi upon Columbus and Hickman.

Here I digress again.

"The War," as it would forever be known in these parts, came down from Cairo on Yankee gunboats commanded by Brig. Gen. Ulysses S. Grant. In September 1861, Confederate Gen. Leonidas Polk breached the neutrality of Kentucky by fortifying the bluffs at Columbus. His cannon and troops were welcomed to this slave-holding section of the state and they would have appeared capable of controlling the river south to New Orleans, given his supply line via rail south to Mobile. No one, least of all Halleck, the Union commander in St. Louis, reckoned on Grant's skill and audacity.

"Control the Ohio and Mississippi and you control the nation," allowed Grant's subordinate, William T. Sherman. Grant wanted the Mississippi and began his campaign down the river against the Southern Gibraltar. He attacked Confederates at Columbus and across the river at a hamlet called Belmont. There was a fierce battle and, for Grant, a narrow escape with his forces back up the river to Cairo. Historians have called the result indecisive. Grant claimed otherwise, saying it gave the initial proof of his leadership—if the proof, as it turned out, was only to himself—and provided a test of fire for his rookie troops.

Grandmother remembered, recalling the pop of muskets, roar of cannon, and the flash of gunpowder at night and soon afterwards the coming of the bluecoats to occupy Hickman. She was about six years old at that time. Grant stole Columbus's strategic value to the Confederacy by flanking it through an invasion of Tennessee by way of the Cumberland and Tennessee rivers 60 miles east. Having snatched it from the South, the Yankee commander then used Hickman and Columbus, terminus of the Mobile and Ohio Railroad, as his main route of supply from Northern farms and factories.

Grant's troops moved south from Hickman with spoils of war, including the cattle and horses from Grandmother's farm. Time and again she would tell of the loss of Buttercup, a bay colt beloved by herself and her sister Lizzie. The Yankee captain saddled the colt, gave polite thanks, and rode away with his troops. Grandmother recalled the officer as "civil."

For a Southern woman of this period to speak of Yankee troops without rancor, indeed describing one of them as "civil," is most exceptional and must have reflected an absence of fear despite the long rifles wielded by bluecoat pickets stationed around Hickman and Columbus.

With his forces aiming for Nashville and Vicksburg, Grant abandoned Columbus and Hickman to the ravages of guerrillas, brigands said to sympathize with the South, but in fact the bane of southwestern Kentucky for the rest of the war. To civilians they were worse than Yankees. They robbed and murdered without sentiment or regard for the competing North-South loyalties. Grandmother frequently told of the day a band came by horseback to her farm home, with a barrel of oysters stolen from the Hickman dock. They were led by the notorious Tom Hook:

My father, an Englishman not fully accustomed to the ways of this land, hid in the cellar. My mother came to the porch. Fortunately, she was recognized by Tom Hook, who removed his hat and commanded his men to "cease firing weapons and quit cursing—you are in the presence of Harriet Tamms, a Christian lady." Tom Hook requested mother to prepare a meal of the oysters. Mother said of course, provided the men wash their hands and faces and conduct themselves as gentlemen, for which they were but lightly equipped. At mother's command, Tom Hook gave a brief prayer of thanks, although not acknowledging to the Lord the source of their feast. It was a fine meal. When finished they rode away never to come again. One band—whether it was Tom Hook's or another I do not know—demanded money from cousin Will Bondurant and when he refused they hung him to a tree in his farmyard. He died, Lord rest his soul, a fine Christian man but with a weakness for money.

Apart from its foreign-born population, and its plague of guerrillas, there was another significant difference about this part of Kentucky. While it supported the Confederacy, unlike West Tennessee and the rest of the South, it was not unanimous in this sentiment. Records in the Fulton County Courthouse at the top of the bluff at Hickman reveal that while 5,500 sons of southwestern Kentucky fought for the South, 550 went to battle for the Union. The result was a residue of bitterness unique to the late Confederacy when war was done. Grandmother told of this, and there is partial verification of her story in those records. These show that "Andy Bondurant was a member of Company 'A', 12th Kentucky cavalry (Confeder-

ate). His brother Thomas fought for the Union Army." Grandmother remembered them well.

Andy would not bear his brother's defection from the South to
the Yankee army and one day, not too long after they'd come back,
Andy announced before his father, mother, and brother, that he was
not forgiving and that he intended to kill Thomas for his disloyalty.
In charity he said he would give his brother a five minute head start
before giving chase. Thomas got up and ran and after five minutes,
measured by his watch, Andy went in pursuit, a pistol in his right
hand. He ran his brother down to a cotton warehouse along the river,
then ran him around the warehouse until Thomas dropped from exhaustion and pled his brother for mercy. The plea, unanswered, Andy
shot Thomas to death with his cavalry pistol.

Grandmother passed no judgment on either brother. Nor did
she wail and curse when the news came about my brother Arthur, an
exceptional athlete and promising musician turned pilot of a B-24
bomber. He did not return from the disastrous mission against the
Nazi oil refineries in Ploesti, Romania, in the summer of 1943. He
was 22 years old. I have never overcome the sadness of his loss or
forgiven the waste of his gifts. I cannot share my grandmother's conviction of "God's will."

There remains no further record of the fratricide on the Hickman docks, which is forgotten, save in a few memories fired by the
recollections of an old woman.

For a young lad in an adjacent, but different, county there
were these tales of the war as well as the sight of the river itself to
attract one to Hickman. Our kin, the Bondurants and Hubbards,
had faded away through migration or marriage. The Ambergs,
themselves an attraction, remained. One of their grandsons married
Charlotte Hubbard, a distant relative, a favorite of my mother and
my grandmother.

Handsome and well structured, like the old Amberg house itself, Charlotte Amberg seemed to me the essence of the town—well
mannered, well to do, and comfortable with the decline of the local

economy despite its connection to the family drygoods business. Years before, Mark Twain had warned that the coming of the railroad, the cause of Hickman's boom in the 1850s, might ultimately work against the riverport. And so it did when the Ohio River was bridged for railroads after the war. The Hickman docks, like the guns of Columbus, became superfluous. Trains ran directly from Memphis, Nashville, Mobile, and New Orleans to St. Louis and Chicago, and from there to points east and west. The steamboat, although not yet obsolete, was no longer the engine tying the nation together by supplying a national economy. Mark Twain couldn't visualize the concrete streams of highway ten miles east further isolating Hickman, eventually even dooming the NC&St.L and the GM&O. At the end of the twentieth century, General Sherman might say "control the interstates and you control the nation." Such is the change.

Yet the Ambergs continued to prosper, not so much as merchants but as farmers of the black earth behind the dying town. The social life of these agrarian communities, Hickman, Union City, and Fulton never diminished. The Christmas dances at the Fulton Country Club—they were never elevated to the status of "balls"—flourished with ladies and girls in fine dresses, the men and boys in tuxedos with ample flasks of excellent corn whiskey from nearby stills.

At one of these dances, late in Prohibition, my older brother William met and fell, as they would say, head over heels in love with Leonore Amberg, a beautiful and vivacious young woman. Subsequently, he went off to college in the North, the first of our family to do so since the 1850s, carrying the torch for Leonore with him up the Illinois Central to Chicago. Soon he proposed marriage. To his sadness Leonore said "no." An outgoing man with good looks and considerable charm, in time he would become a successful businessman and parent in another part of the country. Yet from our conversations it seemed he never completely got over the romance and rejection of Leonore Amberg. Is it always thus with first love?

Leonore did marry. He was a physician from nearby Fulton, a drinking buddy of my older brother. But it did not last long and ended in divorce, and thereafter—this is according to the version passed on by my older sister—the beautiful and headstrong Amberg daughter took her own life. The implication of this version is that Leonore was even more forlorn then our brother.

I had no reason to question this tale of romantic tragedy because of my own suspicion of something ever so slightly amiss about the Hickman people, and certainly because of the intensity of my own first experience with love. From the start I seemed to ascribe to Alta the exotic qualities my older sister attributed to Leonore Amberg; that is, intelligence, curiosity, wit, and beauty—and an air of mystery. But if to me Leonore was a legendary figure of a much earlier generation, a woman whom in fact I never met, Alta was with me in person for an impressionable decade after our eleventh birthday, and she was, in fact, beautiful, intelligent, the life of every party, and the dream of every young son of the gentry of our country with normal hormones and a flask of whiskey. For those not of the gentry, sons of small farmers or sons of the town's menial workers, she was out of their class, simply too much for which one of these could aspire. My social position, close to genteel poverty, was on the fringe. Like Hickman, but unlike the Ambergs, my family had seen better times. We met again but twice before she died, wasted from too much liquor and the premature death of her oldest son in a car wreck. I went on to another part of the country and the life of a journalist.

GIVEN THE CHANGE in its pace during the past three decades, the coming of the computer and the Internet, some might argue with Ben Hecht's observation that journalism is akin to telling time by the minute hand on a clock, and history is equivalent to telling time by the hour hand. It's faster now than at midcentury, sure as the Interstate is quicker than the steamboat.

From the first job with International News Service, I was given to the second hand; fast work, faster shifts of subject matter. No time for reflection. The tools were typewriter and teletype. Only rarely did I suffer boredom, and those times came in the dead morning hours of an overnight shift on a wire-service desk. Away from the desk as a reporter there was always something, a topic or an object, arousing curiosity and warranting a report. Almost always curiosity was primed by a feeling of the need to right a wrong, or rectify an anomaly in the social system—say, a crooked politician or a powerful lobby overwhelming an underfunded opposition on behalf of a pernicious special interest. Sometimes simple curiosity was enough to initiate inquiry, as in "What the hell is going on here?"

"No other profession, even that of arms, produces as fine a version of the selfless hero as journalism does," wrote Ben Hecht of Chicago and, later, Hollywood. "Unlike the profession of arms, journalism does not coerce and discipline its own into selflessness. The journalist's dedication to his craft is based on his own nature, the one he brings to it as a duck brings its webbed feet to a pond." That nature, I would add, is a mixture of curiosity, economic necessity, skepticism, and ideals; skepticism, not cynicism. The latter, overblown by cheap fiction, comes only with a loss of ideals, or despair with particular conditions. Time to quit, and most do so.

Hecht wrote this description about the time my own profession changed from arms to journalism. I took to the latter like a duck to water at a time when the profession was changing from Hecht's *Front Page* of picture chasers, such as himself, Roy Benzinger, and T. Aloysius Tribaum of the *Chicago Evening American*, to reporters with actual college degrees who wrote analyses of the news.

My generation—the post-*Front Page* generation—came in conditioned by military service and the Great Depression as well as by land grant colleges. Socially, for nearly all of us, it was a big step up from small farms or factory towns—environments as different from the great American suburbs as baseball is from astrophysics. A peer from the *Washington Post*, a graduate of Princeton, asked me why so many Southerners wind up in journalism. "Did you ever try to plow," I answered. I could have taken the answer one step further. Most Southerners were raised on the prose and poetry of the King James version of the Holy Bible. Its rhythms conditioned the way we think, and consequently write, and maybe our morals.

If railroads and interstates changed the economy of Columbus and Hickman, television and the American Newspaper Guild permanently altered the course of our journalism. The Guild (union) brought us living wages, money for retirement, and a medical plan that would come to include treatment for alcoholism, a malady for a profession which once thought of work as the curse of the drinking press. The 1990s reporter can not only think of himself as middle class. He can live like one. In 1957, as president of the Southwest Wire Service Guild, I pressed for a resolution calling for a $200 per week minimum wage. My salary then: $72 per week. The resolution passed by three votes, newsmen of that era being unaccustomed to conceiving wages of such grandeur.

If not "coerced and disciplined" into the duty of journalism, we were most severely coerced and disciplined by editors into its fundamental strictures, the blocking and tackling of the profession: fairness and accuracy. Lapses were ultimately punished by loss of job, a professional equivalent of the death penalty. A new generation seems less concerned and less pressured on these strictures by their supervisors.

This is more than a personal impression. A recent Gallup Poll of 600 veteran journalists made for the Nieman Foundation showed a supermajority believed the standards of fairness and accuracy had sharply declined. Going down with the old standards are the ranks of newspapers and so, I judge, the ranks of reporters and editors who turn to work from a sense of duty instead of a soft way to make a living, the pen being less arduous than the plow.

The quality of a daily press, with a few notable exceptions, has followed television down the road through opinion polls and focus groups to entertainment, running hard to keep up with twice as many pages given to sports, food, and soft gossip as given to hard news. I'm waiting for the morning when I open my newspaper to the Food Pages for the headline "Seven Fun Ways to Boil Water." It will surely come, a how-to-do-it story with no danger of libel or even an angry reader—everything but, alas, sex.

The gap between daily newspapers and supermarket tabloids has narrowed as a consequence, and there is almost no gap at all between TV "news" ("if it bleeds, it leads") and the hot-selling tabs. Political scandal is almost certain to deal with sex—no greater example in the history of our nation than the television and newspaper attention given to salacious details about Monica Lewinsky and President Clinton. The sex news came every day in our living rooms and front doors. No need to purchase the *Globe* or *Inquirer*. Common sense and common decency finally recoiled against the overkill.

Lewinsky's story marks a major change in the course of the wayward press. An unstated rule of our profession was that a politician's private life was his own business, not ours, unless it came to influence public matters. No longer. If anyone cares, there is the dubious rationalization that errant sex—that is, any sex outside a marriage—reflects the politician's character. But sex not only sells, it costs less than investigating a crooked pol or rigged legislature. These require talent, time, guts, and, most likely, legal expenses. Why bother? The answer, of course, is for the good of the community or the righting of a wrong. A minority view holds that it might sell more newspapers and reverse their slide into oblivion. But that view is old-fashioned, as outdated as this forgotten river town.

ON THE LAST DAY we were together in this remote country, I took Alta to Hickman. We went to a show at the Gem Theatre, a tearjerker about a dying woman played by the actress Margaret Sullavan. Then we walked along the riverbank and talked. When I went back to look, the Gem still stood, dilapidated, vacant as the eyes of a Skid Road derelict, not likely to have had a customer in the forty-five years since Alta and I departed the river town and each other.

A local historian in Hickman took me to a barbecue lunch and corrected one part of our family legend. After her divorce, Leonore Amberg came back to live in her family home on the bluff, enjoyed herself as the town's leading hostess, and died of natural causes. The confusion arose from her sister, who did herself in by strolling one day into the Mississippi just beyond the seawall, and sinking to her death.

Now the river has changed, shifting course some distance to the west of the seawall, the latter a useless relic. My host blamed the diversion on an unintended effect from a canal dug near Hickman by the Corps of Engineers. My own feeling is that, given gravity, the river has a will of its own, and like life itself, is inexplicable. It keeps moving south, ignorant of the change and relics it leaves behind. Not unlike American journalism, which has veered from its old course because of the gravity of entertainment.

A FEW WORDS
ABOUT SOURCES

MOST OF THIS MEMOIR comes straight from a well-used memory bank. Where the bank has been overdrawn or reluctant to be forthcoming, I've relied on files of the *Seattle Post-Intelligencer* kept at the Joel Pritchard (Washington State) Library in Olympia. Stories I filed decades ago came to life again on the library's microfilm; this was acute in the case of Governor George Romney, whose remarkable run for the GOP presidential nomination in 1968 I had covered and flat forgotten.

I had not forgotten the extraordinary fight over Camille Gravel's credentials as Louisiana's Democratic National Committeeman in 1958, a microcosm of the South's showdown over racial integration, but significant details were lost or scrambled. Thanks to a former wire-service competitor, Ed Tunstall, I had access to the files of the *New Orleans Time-Picayune* and got the record straight. While in New Orleans, I interviewed two of the principals, Gravel and his attorney Edmund Reggie. They were as gracious with their time as I was proud of what they did in the days of apartheid.

LBJ and Vietnam by George Herring (University of Texas Press, 1994) and *The Unmaking of a President* by Herbert Schandler (Princeton University Press, 1977) filled gaps in my understanding of that pivotal year, 1968. So did working on my own book, *Warren G. Magnuson and the Shaping of Twentieth-Century America* (University of Washington Press, 1997).

Willie Rainach is quoted in *Earl K. Long* by Michael Kurtz and Morgan Peoples (Louisiana State University Press, 1990). The "Nixon Doctrine" on Vietnam appeared in *Foreign Affairs* magazine in October 1967, a prelude to Richard Nixon's presidential primary campaign in New Hampshire. It read like Dean Rusk.

The most useful undiscovered work on the Mideast conflict is *The Politics of Miscalculation in the Middle East* by Richard B. Parker (Indiana University Press, 1993). Parker is a distinguished Arabist and American diplomat, and, at least in this instance, so saying is not a contradictory description. His study of the War of Attrition, 1968–73, may be unique.

A Fantastic Journey: The Life and Literature of Lafcadio Hearn by Paul Murray (Japan Library, 1993) provided a glimpse into an unusual career which preceded my own inside the crumbling walls of the late *New Orleans Item*.

On the Trail of the Assassins by Jim Garrison (Time-Warner Books, 1988) raised questions about Kennedy's assassination, some of which haven't been answered even yet.

The quote by Martin Luther, page 120, is taken from *Hitler's Willing Executioners* by Daniel Goldhagen (Vintage Books, New York, 1997). Teddy White's appreciation of Senator Estes Kefauver is from a private conversation between me and four other Nieman Fellows in the Harvard University Faculty Club, March 1963.

Sideshow: Kissinger, Nixon and the Destruction of Cambodia by William Shawcross (Fontana Paperbacks, Great Britain, 1979), a British journalist, does not tell the whole story of the fall of the Khmers, but it does give a detailed indictment of the role played in that tragedy by the Nixon Administration. Would that readers pay as much attention to more recent books on the involvement of the Reagan Administration in Central America.

U. S. Grant, says my scholarly friend Stimson Bullitt, was our greatest general and our worst president. Grant is also the author of an American masterpiece, *The Personal Memoirs of U. S. Grant* (Literary Classics of the United States, New York, 1990). He wrote cool, lucid, straightforward English, and few have done it better.

By contrast, *Bedford Forrest and His Critter Company* by

Andrew J. Lytle (J. S. Sanders and Co., Nashville, 1931) is a work of idolatry in a murky writing style. An offense to the politically correct of the late twentieth century, this account of the ex-slave saleman's West Tennessee campaign may be the best ever recorded. One would probably find this volume in the libraries of Heinz Guderian, Erwin Rommel, and George Patton, as well as in those of unreconstructed Southerners.

The Fulton County (Kentucky) courthouse in Hickman yielded land deed registrations and the county's 1870 census. An article by Donald Livingston (1985), "Fulton Countians in the Civil War," may be read in the Hickman City library. The names and numbers reinforced my grandmother's memory of those times and people.

The George Gallup Poll of newsmen, indicating a precipitous decline in the quality of our media, was carried in the *Nieman Reports*, a quarterly, in Fall 1995.

INDEX

Library of Congress Cataloging-in-Publication Data

Scates, Shelby
War and politics by other means : a journalist's memoir / Shelby Scates.
p.   cm.
Includes bibliographical references and index.
ISBN 0-295-98009-5 (alk. paper)
1. Scates, Shelby. 2. Journalists—United States—Biography. I. Title.

PN4874.S3 A3 2000
070.92—dc21
[B]   00-033788